RELIGION AND AMERICAN CULTURE

GEORGE M. MARSDEN

The Divinity School
Duke University

HARCOURT BRACE JOVANOVICH, PUBLISHERS
San Diego   New York   Chicago   Austin   Washington, D.C.
London   Sydney   Tokyo   Toronto

BR
115
,C8
H27
1990

ISBN: 0-15-576583-3

Library of Congress Catalog Card Number: 89-84694

Printed in the United States of America

PREFACE

To the extent that Americans have a collective memory of their past, religion plays an astonishingly small role. This national forgetfulness concerning religion is reflected in the way we have written our histories. In public school textbooks religion is almost absent except in reference to the Puritans and some other early colonists.[1] College textbooks are only slightly better. Most of them acknowledge substantial religious influences in the era through the Civil War; but they then let religion fade from their portraits of the modern era. Yet there is evidence that in the late twentieth century most Americans are remarkably religious. For instance, in the 1980s more-or-less traditional Christianity reemerged as a considerable force in American political and cultural life; yet the nation's history books had poorly prepared the educated to anticipate or to understand such developments.

The present volume is a response to this gap in our national self-understanding. It is written first to supplement college textbooks that typically neglect the role of religion in shaping America. My hope, however, is to offer an interpretative account of religion and culture that will be of wider interest than the usual text would be. My goal is not simply to "cover" everything religious in American history. Rather, this book is designed for students in American history courses, students of American religious history, and for general readers interested in exploring the intriguing issues of how American religion fits into American civilization. So I see the present work as an interpretive and narrative essay that seeks to illumine the role of religion in American culture. Rather than focus on religious institutions and religious practices, I chose to deal with the broader theme of the relationship of the religious to the secular in American history.

Because it is since the Civil War that the role of religion in United States history is most often neglected, I have weighted this work somewhat in that direction. I provide an overview of the Puritans and the seventeenth century, but I say increasingly more about later religious dimensions of the culture, those dimensions that are more likely to be neglected in standard histories.

• • •

ACKNOWLEDGMENTS

I want especially to express my gratitude to the Pew Charitable Trusts whose generous grant for the study of "The Religious and the Secular in Modern America" provided me with time to work on this book. I am particularly grateful to Martin P. Trimble for his support of this project. I am also grateful to the Divinity School of Duke University and to Dean Dennis Campbell for release from some duties while I worked on this project.

I also owe substantial debts to those who read the first draft and provided valuable commentaries on it. These include Diana Butler, Tony Jenkins, Paul Kemeny, Evelyn Kirkley, Brad Longfield, Bruce Mullin, Jeff Trexler, and Grant Wacker. I am especially grateful to Paul Kemeny who, in addition to making extensive comments on the manuscript, served as research assistant in preparing the notes and checking many details. Tony Jenkins also did some work on checking details. I also thank Russell Congleton for his work on the index.

In a work of this sort one is dependent on many colleagues in the field who have provided research and insights that are appropriated into a larger synthesis. I have attempted to acknowledge any direct dependency; but since one's understanding grows over the years and is shaped by a community of scholars, there are contributions whose sources are not easy to identify but for which I wish to express my gratitude.

I also wish to thank the staff of Harcourt Brace Jovanovich for their assistance in bringing this study into its present form—in particular the contributions of Drake Bush, acquisitions editor; Sarah Randall, production manager; Paulette Russo, art editor; Gina Sample, designer; Brett Smith, production editor; and David Watt, manuscript editor. David's excellent editing and thoughtful suggestions were a most positive contribution, and Paulette worked diligently to provide appropriate illustrations for the text.

My deepest gratitude is to my wife Lucie and to our children Greg and Brynne, who provided an atmosphere of love and mutual support that is invaluable in sustaining a project of this sort.

. . .

CONTENTS

$\mathscr{I}$NTRODUCTION

*In the United States the sovereign authority is religious, and consequently
hypocrisy must be common; but there is no country in the world
where the Christian religion retains a greater influence
over the souls of men than in America.*

Alexis de Tocqueville, *Democracy in America* (1835)

$\mathscr{T}$he United States is both remarkably religious and remarkably secular. Observers from Alexis de Tocqueville in
the 1830s to George Gallup, Jr. in recent years have agreed
on this point. Today's pollsters consistently find levels of professed
religious faith that could make one question the common belief that
Americans are less religious now than a century ago. Not only do
ninety-five percent of Americans polled say they believe in God, but
over seventy percent say they would not vote for a presidential candidate who did not believe in God, "even if [they] really liked him
. . . and shared his political views." Seven out of ten also say Jesus
is the divine Son of God, and the same number believe in life after
death. At least a third say they have been "born again," almost half
say that "the Bible is God's Word and all it says is true," and six out
of seven say that the Ten Commandments are relevant today. Fifty-
seven percent say religion is "very important" in their lives. Yet one
only has to turn the television dial on a typical evening to confirm
that most Americans are not tuning their thoughts to things above.
The fact that less than half of those who said the Ten Commandments should apply for today could not name four of them makes one
wonder how deep the religious belief goes.[1]

This book is built around the questions raised by such paradoxes.
Particularly, two parallel questions will be addressed: What does

• • •

American religion tell us about American culture? And what does American culture tell us about American religion? For instance, in what ways have American religions shaped American morality, value systems, beliefs about priorities, and views about themselves, other humans, families, and the nation? At the same time, to what extent has the American experience transformed traditional religious beliefs?

Religious History for Historians

Despite the intriguing mix of the strongly religious and the strongly secular in American life, which might be a central clue to understanding American culture, most historians have dwelt almost solely upon the secular.

This stance reflects the state of modern academia. For the past century the dominant interpretations of human behavior have emphasized nonreligious factors. Moreover, many theories, especially those of the first half of the twentieth century, predicted that traditional religion, like primitive medicine and the horse-drawn plow, would inevitably disappear as modern culture and education advanced. Hence, the standards for much of the study of humanity were shaped around the assumption that religion would not have to be taken seriously in order to understand the modern world.

In the United States and other nations of the late twentieth century, this assumption has been proven false. Academics, however, are often slow to abandon their interpretative traditions.

Religion as an Organizing Principle

Even aside from the question of how influential religion is in a society, a good case can be made for giving religion a more central role in historical interpretations simply in the interests of gaining a more balanced account of human behavior. Other academic disciplines (economics, sociology, psychology, biology, and the like) that look at human behavior tend to view it through the lens of their own disciplines. Economists see economics as primary, sociologists measure social forces, psychologists evaluate the psychological, biologists see humans as living organisms, and so forth. Historians, however, are supposed to look at the interrelationships among the forces that shape human behavior. They have to weigh the relative importance of the economic, social, psychological, biological, physical, political, aesthetic, ethical, technological, and many more. How do these all fit

• • •

together? To answer that question, historians need a unifying principle. Usually they find this by reverting to one dimension of human behavior, such as the political, the economic, or social status, that they see as central.

It might be more fruitful, however, to seek a unifying principle in how the historical participants themselves understood their experience. In other words, what would be their own explanations for what they did and why? What were the worldviews that organized their lives? What set of moral principles did they try to follow when deciding what to do next?[2] Biography almost inevitably asks such questions, which makes it one of the most enjoyable types of history.

We must recognize, of course, that expressed beliefs—which one supposes are one's central commitments—are not always as central as one may think. Certainly they are not often as central as people claim. Other factors, such as economy, social status, psychological state, and so forth, are often the truly dominant ones. These must all be identified and taken into account when explaining history. They are part of a person's functional worldview, which may be somewhat different from a person's professed worldview.

• • •

Worldviews are also shaped by underlying and sometimes unconsciously assumed cultural values. Anthropologist Clifford Geertz defines culture as "an historically transmitted pattern of meaning embodied in symbols . . ."[3] The symbols that define a culture are not only words, but all sorts of artifacts and structures that reflect shared meanings and values. The historically transmitted meanings of a culture also include the underlying assumptions, taken-for-granted wisdom, and ways of looking at things that almost everyone at a particular time and place share.[4]

Formal religion will often play a major role in shaping both the articulated worldviews of individuals and the assumed patterns of shared meanings and values that make a culture possible. Even in cases where formal religion is not a major shaping force, worldviews and underlying patterns of meaning may have religious-like qualities. They may define a people's highest commitments, whether to the nation, to a party, to a humanitarian cause, to art, to business, to success, to the pursuit of pleasures, or simply to self.

In summary, one finds organizing principles for understanding human behavior in moral visions, in worldviews, and in underlying patterns of cultural meaning. And in religion, either traditional religion or other highest commitments, one can often discover the organizing principles that tie an outlook together.

Two Meanings of Religion

The term religion can be used in two senses. Much confusion can be saved if these two meanings are kept clear. Unless otherwise explained, our primary meaning refers to organized religions, involving some faith in the transcendent, usually a deity or deities. However, the term religion may be used in a broader sense, as we have just done, to refer to a person's highest commitments, such as to nation, party, humanity, wealth, family, self, and so forth. Although these latter are not formally organized, for some people they *function* as their true religions.

What This Book Is About

The central problem this book examines is how the United States has always been simultaneously a very religious and very secular nation. The ways in which that paradox manifests itself have changed over the centuries. These changes are related to three other major

• • •

themes. (1) The roles of competing religions and their moral visions in struggles between insiders, who aspire both to dominate and to provide moral leadership for the culture, and outsiders, who wish to live free from that domination and follow their own moral vision. (2) Closely related to this is the transition, especially since the Civil War, from an era when Protestant Christianity was at the center of American public life to the present, when it is on the periphery. No one religious group can any longer claim dominance in shaping an American moral consensus. (3) Finally, there is a remarkable expansion in this technological culture of areas that religion does not address, yet there is a simultaneous proliferation of new religions and vigorous renewal of old ones.

Protestants on Center Stage

The story of American religion, if it is to hang together as a narrative, must focus on the role played by certain groups of mainstream Protestants who were for a long time the insiders with disproportional influence in shaping American culture. Outsider groups, including many smaller groups of Protestants, Roman Catholics, Jews, secularists, and others, until recently had to contend with the culturally dominant Protestants. These ongoing interactions give the story of American religious history much of its continuity.

It should be explained that keeping the culturally dominant Protestants on stage much of the time does not necessarily imply a positive evaluation of them. Depending on one's point of view, one may find the dominance of such white Anglo-Saxon male Protestants reprehensible, laudable, or paradoxical. Descriptively, however, there is no escaping their significance.

The United States is not simply one culture, just as it is not based on one religion. Rather, it is an amalgamation of many subcultures. At the same time, however, almost all of these subcultures do eventually take on common American traits, so that in some sense there is also one common American culture. Some groups have had, for better or for worse, far more influence than others in shaping this common culture, although eventually almost all contribute to it. The story of the interactions of the dominant insider religion with the nondominant outsider religions helps provide some insight into how the one and the many of America are related.

• • •

The Religious and the Secular

The other themes examined in this book are related to the central, paradoxically curious mix of the religious and the secular that has long characterized American civilization.

We need, therefore, to clarify what we mean by "secular." We shall use the term in its simplest sense, to refer to that which is not controlled by formal or organized religion. Secularization means simply the removal of control by formal, organized religion from some areas of life.

During the past century, secularization has spread dramatically in some areas of American life. The huge enterprises of high-tech business, government, and the military allow little room for real religious control. Moreover, today's opinion-forming centers of the culture—public education, most of higher education, and the major media—are vastly more secular than a century ago. The absence of traditional religious dominance over such areas may have vast implications for shaping the shared values of the future American culture.

On the other hand, it appears that considerably higher percentages of Americans regularly attend places of worship than they did in the colonial era—a time that is often thought to have been especially religious. Colonial society was a mix of the secular and the religious also; but the lines between the secular and the religious were drawn in different ways. Public life, such as government, education, and the media were much more often tied formally to religion than they are today. However, partly because religion was an official aspect of public life, private resistance to it may have been more widespread than today. Today, many public spheres are much more secular; but, perhaps even in reaction, more private religion and distinctive religious groups flourish.

So the story of religion in American culture is not that of a simple move from the religious to the secular. Rather, it is the story of the repositioning of the religious and the secular in an emerging modern society. This repositioning may have momentous implications for the culture as a whole. Yet religious communities may flourish better than ever.

Whatever the outcome, the story of religion in American culture is intriguing, and reveals much about American life that is often ignored.

• • •

PROLOGUE

The Almost-Chosen Nation

In the beauty of the lilies Christ was born across the sea,
With a glory in his bosom that transfigures you and me:
As he died to make men holy, let us die to make men free,
While God is marching on.

Julia Ward Howe, "The Battle Hymn of the Republic" (1861)

We regard our success in the war as due to divine mercy, and our government
and people have recognized the hand of God in the formal and humble
celebration of his goodness. We have no fear in regard to the future. If the
war continues for years, we believe God's grace is sufficient for us.

"An Address to Christians throughout the World," from a convention of
Confederate ministers assembled at Richmond, Virginia, April 1863.[1]

---

f we are to believe the rhetoric, each side fought the Civil
War for Christian civilization. Clergy and politicians in each
region assured their people that God approved their cause. The
rhetoric among Protestants in the North routinely equated the success
of the Union with the dawning of a new age, or the millennial (a
symbolic thousand-year) reign of Christ. "The Battle Hymn of the
Republic" was popular because it applied the widely known biblical
symbols to the Union cause. For those who took such imagery seriously (and many did), this millennium would be the crowning era in
the progress of humanity. Jesus would reign "where'er the sun," as
the popular missionary hymn put it.

· · ·

The coming reign of the triumphant Christ would first of all be spiritual; but it would also transform civilization. The Holy Spirit would remarkably change the hearts, or fundamental dispositions, of people throughout the nation and the world. This worldwide awakening, or spread of Christianity, would bring spiritual progress to fulfill all the dreams of humanity. The coming age would see the end of wars, slavery, oppression, and vices such as prostitution and drunkenness. It would bring momentous advances in science, technology, human learning, and the realization of democracy with its promise of liberty and justice for all. For the United States to fulfill its destiny as a leader in this mission, it would have to eliminate outrages such as slavery to prove that a nation dedicated to liberty and justice could endure.[2]

In the South the rhetoric was typically less grandiose but probably more often taken seriously by the white ruling class. There, almost everyone was Protestant; at least few were anything else. White Southerners' ideals for a Christian civilization had been similar to Northerners' through the revolutionary era. The presence of slavery, however, and then, especially after 1830, defensiveness toward abolitionists had chilled most white Southern enthusiasm for a mutual heritage celebrating progress and change.

Most mid-nineteenth century white Southerners emphasized instead the traditional belief that the deity ordained humans to live in a socially ordered world. This had long been the dominant social view throughout the Western, or European, world. Just as God created hierarchies in nature, with some creatures clearly more skilled and powerful than others, so he created orders in society. In every society some classes had wealth and power and others were less wealthy and called to do the menial tasks. Social health, they argued, depended on not disrupting such God-ordained orders. The Bible, they claimed, said as much.

At the same time, however, the Southerners were themselves enough products of Thomas Jefferson's revolutionary America to preserve a firm attachment to a form of American individualism. God had ordained individual liberties, guaranteeing equality before the law, personal and economic liberties, and freedom from undue governmental regulation. As most Americans, they believed such liberties applied fully only to males; but unlike Northerners, they applied none of these principles to blacks. So, compared with Northern leaders,

· · ·

Sunday Mass at a Civil War camp.

they spoke less of universal liberties and emphasized more that the orders of society, whether patriarchical family or paternalistic slavery, were ordained by God.

The Civil War, then, can be understood at one important level as a conflict between two moral and religious visions of society. Ultimately, the conflicting dimensions of these outlooks were rooted in and focused on the differing attitudes toward slavery, which drove a wedge between peoples with a largely common heritage. These differing attitudes toward slavery were reinforced by social and economic factors that made it easier for the dominant classes in the North to follow further what they professed concerning human rights than most white Southerners. White Southerners' social and economic circumstances forced them to emphasize the parts of their heritage that stressed the importance of good order. These competing moral visions, though having multiple roots in various traditions of political thought (such as classical, enlightenment, or British), as well as in distinctly Christian teachings, were widely regarded on each side as having absolute

• • •

divine sanction. People are more willing to die for a cause if they believe that God is on their side. One result of this was the bitter irony that Lincoln commented on in his second inaugural speech: "Both read the same Bible, and pray to the same God; and each invokes his aid against the other."

We can see, then, that at a pivotal moment in American history, religion was central to the self-definition of the nation and the self-understanding of many of its citizens. This was not true simply of the white Protestant elites who dominated both Federal and Confederate policy. It was even more true of cultural outsiders who had little access to power. Certainly it was true of most slaves who understood their prospects for freedom as a "day of jubilee," the dawning of the age of the reign of Christ. For immigrants, most notably the many Catholics who had recently arrived, their religion was also central to their identity, as well as to their outsider status. Similarly, those less prestigious Protestant groups who appealed especially to the less prosperous and the less educated, were often the most intensely religious. For members of new sects, like the Seventh-Day Adventists, or of new religions, such as the Mormons, religion was almost everything.

Today, although we can still see religions providing a major part of the identities of many Americans, we can also see other vast reaches of the culture that religion seems not to touch at all. The story of the nature and extent of this secularization will provide a central theme for this book. But this transition was not a simple transformation from a religious or "Christian" culture to a secular one. Even at its most religious the United States was in many ways a very secular place. During the Civil War era, for instance, even though religious participation had increased markedly since colonial times, smaller percentages of Americans attended religious services than do today. The frontiers were renowned for their sparse religious influences. And the burgeoning American commerce, arguably the heart of the nation, often seemed to have little to do with religion. Nonetheless, the places where religion was influential were often strikingly different from what we see today.

In order to appreciate the remarkable transformations in the role of religion in the United States since the Civil War, we must first examine the extent to which religion, especially Protestant Christianity, shaped American civilization from the first settlements through the mid-nineteenth century.

. . .

CHAPTER ONE

Christendom and American Origins

---

*Thus was human nature chained fast for ages in a cruel, shameful,
and deplorable servitude to him [the Pope], and his subordinate tyrants,
who it was foretold, would exalt himself above all that was called God,
and that was worshipped.
From the time of the Reformation to the first settlement of America,
knowledge gradually spread in Europe, but especially in England;
and in proportion as that increased and spread among the
people, ecclesiastical and civil tyranny . . .
seem to have lost their strength and weight.*

John Adams, "A Dissertation on the Canon and the Civil Law" (1765)

---

o understand the role of religion in American history it is essential to recognize the immense importance of the ideal of "Christian civilization." The Europeans who settled the Americas throughout the colonial era simply took for granted that they represented Christendom. This was as much a part of their identity as being Spanish or French or English.

Christendom, however, was bitterly divided. The Eastern Orthodox church and the Western church under Rome had separated early in the Middle Ages so that Eastern Orthodoxy was a distant reality to most western Europeans. Central to the Westerners, though, was the split in the Church of Rome brought about by the Protestant Reformation. The Reformation, triggered by Martin Luther in 1517, shattered European unity and dominated Western politics for the next century. This coincided almost exactly with New World explorations and early settlements. The Protestant reforms, though motivated primarily by deep disagreements over religious issues, had immense political implications. Europeans in the sixteenth century, as they had through the Middle Ages, assumed that a country's ruler would determine not only its religion but would eliminate heresies and false worship. "One state, one religion" was the rule.

The Cold War

The success of the Reformation depended not only on persuading the population about Protestant doctrines; it hinged as much or more on converting rulers to the cause. The result was that existent political divisions and monarchical rivalries in Europe were vastly deepened by fierce ideological-religious struggles for political control of the ruling houses. The closest counterpart in recent times would be the lengthy cold war between Marxists and anti-Marxists through much of the twentieth century. Sixteenth-century Europe was similarly divided between two contending ideologies vying both for the hearts of people and political control.

The largest group of early Protestants were Lutherans, followers of Martin Luther (1483–1546) whose churches became state churches in many German provinces and in Scandinavia.

By the second generation of the Reformation, the most aggressive major Protestant group pushing for political-religious revolutions were the Calvinists. Calvinists were followers of theologian John Calvin (1509–1564), who had established a model for Christian rule in the

• • •

independent city of Geneva, Switzerland. Since Calvinists had a disproportional influence in shaping the future culture of the United States, we should pay attention to their teachings.

Calvin attempted to build a thoroughgoing Reformation theology based on the Protestant principle of "the Bible alone" as religious authority. This principle challenged the institutional authority of the Catholic church. Catholics believed that God had ordained the institutional church, ruled on earth by the Pope, to interpret biblical revelation and especially to provide the sacramental means through which people could receive the grace of God necessary for their eternal salvation. Protestants claimed the church had become a corrupt human institution. It needed to be reformed, they asserted, by testing its claims against the Bible alone.

Calvinists attempted to carry as far as possible the principle that one should rely entirely upon God and not on humanity in religious matters. God, they emphasized, was the absolute sovereign ruler of all creation. Nothing happened outside his ultimate control. Humans, accordingly, could do nothing to promote their salvation. They were corrupted, sinful beings whose only hope was the grace of God. Through the sacrificial death of Christ, God graciously provided salvation from the sins of those whom he would save. The Bible alone and the sovereignty of God were thus the two organizing principles of Calvinist Christianity.

During the 1500s Protestants battled Catholics for control of a number of European countries, with Calvinists often taking the lead in pressing for further expansion.

Catholics fought back ardently, especially under the influence of the new Jesuit order. The Jesuits were instrumental in countering the Reformation, sending out missionaries, and securing centers of Catholic influence. The New World had strategic importance to the Catholic powers, especially to the Spanish, who dominated European advances in South and Central America throughout the 1500s. Catholic missions were prominent in bringing these territories into Christendom's orbit.

The English Reformation

The English eventually began to settle the eastern coast of what became the United States; but the permanent settlements, starting in Jamestown in 1607, were a small beginning in a hemisphere already

• • •

long dominated by Catholic power. About the same time, France, which after a bloody Protestant-Catholic civil war in the late 1500s had remained Catholic, was beginning to settle to the north in Canada. Soon, French Jesuit missionaries such as Father Jacques Marquette (1637–1675) had penetrated into the Mississippi valley, into the areas that are now Michigan, Illinois, Wisconsin, and Iowa (where we still have place names such as Eau Claire, Des Plaines, and Des Moines).

The English, who after 1607 were establishing a beachhead on the eastern coast of North America, had a peculiar role in the ongoing Protestant-Catholic struggles. England had more-or-less backed into the Reformation. In the early years of Luther's revolt they had been in the Catholic camp. But by the late 1520s Henry VIII (1491–1547) wanted to change wives, and when the Pope refused to grant a divorce, Henry decided to change churches. In 1534 he severed the English church from the Pope in Rome and declared himself the sovereign over English church affairs. This opened the door for Protestantism in England. The issue was far from settled, however.

Henry's first wife, Catherine of Aragon (1485–1536), was Spanish and Catholic. When their daughter Mary (1516–1558) became queen of England in 1553, she reinstituted Catholicism, putting to death many Protestant leaders. Others escaped to the continent; some went to Geneva, where John Calvin presided. When Mary died in 1558, Elizabeth (1533–1603), Henry's Protestant daughter by his second marriage, acceded to the throne and England went back to the Protestant fold. Elizabeth forged a compromise for the Church of England, retaining the episcopal form of government (leadership by bishops) and much of traditional Catholic ritual, but instituting Protestant doctrine. This "Elizabethan compromise," although putting England solidly on the Protestant side, did not please all Protestants, especially some of the exiles returning from Calvin's Geneva who wanted to press the Protestant principle of "the Bible alone" as the guide for the church. The church, they contended, should have only practices explicitly commanded in Scripture. Hence, the episcopal hierarchy, lavish ecclesiastical adornments, and the formal rituals of Anglican worship should go. This Calvinist party within the Church of England, who wanted to further purify it, became known as Puritans.

Protestant England under Elizabeth emerged as a leading naval power and successfully challenged the dominance of Catholic Spain.

• • •

British Protestants saw God's hand in the defeat of the Spanish Armada.

The turning point was the defeat of the Spanish Armada by the English fleet in 1588, an event which, for centuries after, English-speaking Protestants viewed as evidence of God's providential intervention on their side. The defeat of the Spanish Armada gave England sufficient security on the seas to begin North American settlements.

The Religious and the Secular

Despite the prominence of religion in these national conflicts, it is difficult to tell how deeply religious motives figured for those who settled the colonies. In the rhetoric of early Virginia, for instance, the first settlers boldly proclaimed themselves, as John Rolfe (of Pocahontas fame) put it, "a peculiar people, marked and chosen by the finger of God, to possess it, for undoubtedly he is with us."[1] In reality, the Virginia colony in its earliest decades was more like a company town, like an outpost today in the distant reaches of Alaska. The founders strictly maintained the religious formalities of the day, including laws requiring church attendance. But the England from which the settlers came was itself a mix of the religious and the secular. This, after all,

• • •

was the age of William Shakespeare, whose plays reflected the sophisticated, Renaissance, this-worldly humanism of the day. The corresponding contrasts between formal religiosity and practical this-worldly materialism in much less sophisticated Virginia foreshadowed a pattern found throughout American history.

The Puritan Heritage

At the same time, British-American colonies were soon influenced by some very intense Protestantism, especially through the Puritan movement. When Elizabeth I died in 1603 she was succeeded by a cousin, King James VI of Scotland, who as king of England (1603–1625) was known as James I. James's Stuart family in Scotland had been forced, reluctantly, to accept a Calvinist Presbyterian church. James and his Stuart successors, who ruled England for most of the 1600s, accordingly disliked English Puritans intensely. The feelings were mutual. A small group of more extreme Puritans felt they must leave the Church of England and hence England itself. Eventually they founded the Plymouth Colony in 1620, famed largely for its early struggles and the first Thanksgiving. When James's son, Charles I (1600–1649), came to the throne in 1625, the tension in England became so severe even for moderate Puritans that a substantial number of them were willing to brave the high seas and the wilderness to found an alternative society, based on Puritan principles. This society, the Massachusetts Bay Colony, would be, as governor John Winthrop put it in 1630, "a city upon a hill," a model Christian state that all the world could imitate.

The Puritans in the Massachusetts Bay Colony were convinced that they had been commissioned by God to play a major role in world history. Their rule for life was the fundamental Protestant principle that the Bible alone should be their supreme guide. For a model society, they looked to the Old Testament, which described God's governance of Israel. Surely, they reasoned, these God-given principles should apply to nations today.

Central to the Old Testament view of the nation was the covenant. By far the most crucial factor determining the success or failure of a nation was its relationship to God. The covenant defined this relationship simply as a contract whose terms were the law of God. If a nation kept the law of God, it would be blessed. If it broke God's

• • •

law, it would be punished. Morality, based on biblical law, was the key to success.

The seventeenth-century Puritans were by far the most articulate and best educated of North America's early settlers and so had an immense and disproportional influence on the later American culture. Their New England heirs were often the educators in the new nation and so succeeded in presenting the Puritan tradition as the national heritage. This was not entirely misleading. The Puritans were rigorous Protestants in overwhelmingly Protestant British North America, stating views that fit the outlook of many other colonial Americans. So when the new nation was formed, Americans readily accepted covenant talk about being blessed by God or in danger of God's judgments. Americans liked to think of themselves as having a special mission. They readily spoke, almost like the Puritans had, of the United States as a new Israel chosen by God to play a leading role in a new era of the world's redemption.

Puritan traditions thus helped shape Americans' collective self-understanding. For instance, Americans are prone to claim that the perennial national prosperity has been the result of their virtue. The feast day of national thanksgiving is a vestige of this covenantal tradition. The counterpart, national fast days of repentance, have been less popular, though occasionally presidents have proclaimed such days even in the twentieth century. When things seem to go wrong, a long-standing national tradition has been to claim the nation faces calamities because the people have lost the supposed virtue of their grandparents. This form of national lament has been called the jeremiad, named for Old Testament prophet Jeremiah's laments about Israel turning from God and morality. The jeremiad first appeared in Puritan preaching by the 1670s, as soon as there was a third generation.[2]

Perhaps most importantly, the central belief in national virtue has helped shape the nation's view of its mission. When the new nation was founded, Americans saw themselves as a beacon to the world demonstrating the virtues of a republic. The sense of being a chosen nation, a new Israel, heightened nineteenth-century Americans' sense of mission, or "manifest destiny," to become a transcontinental power. Vast tracts of land were taken from native Americans and from Mexico, partly on the grounds of the United States' supposed moral su-

• • •

periority. In the twentieth century, when America became a world power, the chosen nation ideal was an important rationale in American foreign policy.

Defining the nation's uniqueness in terms of its virtues has involved many ironies. But the alternative, defining a nation's mission without reference to morality, seems clearly worse. And the emphasis on moral responsibility in the American tradition has helped create an important sense of civic responsibility among the citizenry, clearly an important ingredient in a successful republic. Most people have to play by the rules.[3] Moreover, such moral emphases have fostered countless reform efforts at home and humanitarian concerns both at home and abroad. The irony is that such a sense of the importance of virtue, which the Puritan heritage helped provide, can lead to an arrogant moral superiority that transgresses the very rights of others that the moral system claims to protect.[4]

Christians as Outsiders

Not all of the Protestants who settled the American colonies were happy with the close fusion of church and society assumed by the Anglican establishment (state church) in the South or in the Puritans' vision of themselves as a new Israel. Throughout Christian history some of the faithful have believed that it is not the role of the church to run society; rather, they see society as simply "the world," the domain of Satan, and believe the church should be a separate community. This outsider version of Christianity prevailed for centuries in the ancient church before Christians had any prospects of power in the Roman Empire. After the emperor Constantine was converted to Christianity in 312, the vision of a Christian society predominated. The older ideal—of Christians literally giving up the world—survived, however, especially in monastic movements.

At the time of the Reformation, the outsider version of Christianity appeared among Protestants in the radical Anabaptist movement. Anabaptists insisted that Christians must form "gathered" churches made up of believers only. To symbolize the separation of the believer from the world, they required baptism by immersion for adult converts, even those who were baptized as infants in the Catholic church. The name "Anabaptist" means to baptize again. Many Ana-

· · ·

baptists expressed their separation from the world by forming their own communities. They believed firmly in the separation of church and state, and most Anabaptist sects were pacifist. The best known Anabaptist groups to settle in America were the Mennonites and Amish.

The Baptists were more influential in later American society. Early Baptists appearing in England just after 1600 were a degree less radical than the Anabaptists (though considerably more radical than most of their Baptist heirs today.) Growing from the Puritan movement, but influenced by Anabaptists, Baptists carried the Puritan emphasis on conversion a step further, to insist that baptism of adults symbolized spiritual separation from the world. Interested above all in the spiritual purity of the church, early Baptists believed in separation from the state Church of England, rather than working for reform from within as most Puritans did. For the Baptists, the separation was a spiritual concern primarily of individuals. Unlike most Anabaptists, they did not insist on withdrawing into separate communities, or on pacifism.

In early seventeenth-century England the Baptist movement—as a church outside of the Church of England—was illegal. Not surprisingly, Baptists were from the outset champions of religious liberty and the rights of individual conscience.

In Puritan Massachusetts one of the first clergymen, Roger Williams (1603?–1683), soon adopted radical views much like the Baptists. Williams, who became Baptist for a brief time, challenged the Puritan notion that their society represented a new Israel. For instance, he argued, Puritans had no right to take land from the Indians as though they were ancient Israelites taking over the Promised Land. All political arrangements, Williams thought, were corrupt. So Christians should not claim that they were building Christian societies. Only the separated church, said the dissident Puritan, could be Christian. The church must be a purely spiritual entity, not corrupted by aspirations to run the state, or by the need to depend on it for support.

Williams thus championed the separation of church and state, but not for the same reason that later Enlightenment thinkers, such as Jefferson, did. Jefferson was concerned that the church would corrupt the state; Williams feared that the state would corrupt the church.

• • •

Spiritual Sources of Equality

Because they were radical, Williams and the early Baptists anticipated a number of principles that in the next century were popularized in secular as well as religious terms. Separation of church and state, and the civil rights of individual conscience, are the best known. Just as important were the twin emphases on the role of individuals and equality within the church. For Baptists the individual was the basic unit of the church. This was reflected in the emphasis on conversion experience as the test of church membership. The church was not primarily a hierarchical institution, but a gathering of spiritual individuals. Baptists and most American Puritans had a congregational system of church government, giving the male members of the local church the supreme governing authority. Such churches were thus more egalitarian than most of the institutions of the era.

Moreover, the doctrine of conversion was a radically levelling doctrine. Anyone, even the poorest person in society, could become the spiritual equal of anyone else, and the spiritual superior of those unconverted who held power and prestige in the world. Such definitions of men and women in terms of individual spiritual qualities instead of solely by group status planted seeds for later demands for social equality.

More Radicalism: The English Civil War

In England such exotic views suddenly gained a sizeable following with the outbreak of the Civil War in 1642. More than any other event in English history during the colonial era, the war is central to understanding the role of religion in the later American experience. Indeed, the war is crucial to understanding American culture generally.

While some leading Puritans left for the colonies in the 1630s, others remained in England to contend with Charles I and the hostile archbishop of the Anglican Church, William Laud (1573–1645). Civil war broke out with the Puritans, Parliament, and the Scottish Presbyterians (who were Calvinists much like the Puritans) on one side, and the king, most of the nobility, and anti-Puritan Anglicans on the other. The revolutionary parliamentary party won, executed Archbishop Laud, and called the Westminster Assembly of Divines which drew up a Confession of Faith for what was at first to be an estab-

• • •

lished Presbyterian Church as the one church of the nation. The war, however, released more radical sentiments. Oliver Cromwell (1599–1658), a Puritan general with much popular support, rose to power, had King Charles I executed in 1649, declared England a "commonwealth" or republic, and allowed religious toleration of dissenters. Cromwell became the virtual dictator of the Commonwealth until his death, and the Puritan rule came to an end with the "restoration" of the monarchy in 1660, when Charles II (1630–1685), son of the executed king, came to power. Puritans and other dissenting groups were then repressed.

During the Cromwell era, however, there was a great release of popular religious enthusiasm in England. The closest analogy to modern times would be the spiritual experimentation and the social radicalism of the 1960s. In England, once the power of aristocratic Anglicanism was removed, all sorts of popular religious movements flourished, going beyond Puritanism and even beyond the more radical Baptists.

The Quakers

For American history the most significant of these groups were the Society of Friends, popularly called "Quakers." Of all the seventeenth-century religious groups, the Quakers illustrate best that principles of equality and liberty, so important to modernity, first took a spiritual form.

The Quakers went beyond the potentially equalizing doctrine of conversion and beyond most of the Christian tradition by emphasizing that all persons had an innate "Inward Light" of the Holy Spirit. Quakers saw themselves as leaders of a new age of the Spirit that would be socially revolutionary. Their social revolution, however, was to be effected by purely spiritual means. Quakers were pacifist and insisted on a strict puritan lifestyle, including simplicity as opposed to materialism. Like some later revolutionaries, they rejected any social deference to nobility and insisted on addressing everyone as "brother" or "sister."

In this new age women were the spiritual equals of men. Quakers accordingly instituted the revolutionary practice of allowing women to preach. In the colonies Anne Hutchinson (1591–1643) anticipated some Quaker teachings. Hutchinson, who challenged the authority of the clergy by teaching in her home, was exiled from Puritan Massachu-

• • •

The trial of Anne Hutchinson.

setts in 1637 for claiming a direct voice from God's spirit, a doctrine that challenged Puritan reliance on the Bible alone. In exile, she died at the hands of Indians in 1643, but her close friend Mary Dyer (?–1660) returned to England and became a Quaker. Dyer than came back to Massachusetts and after repeated warnings, punishments, and exiles was executed in 1660. Contrary to some once-popular mythology, religious liberty was not a principle, other than for themselves, in which American Puritans yet had an interest.

In William Penn's "Holy Experiment," the colony of Pennsylvania founded in 1681, the Quakers, dedicated as they were to spiritual

• • •

freedom for all, eventually found a refuge where they could practice their principles. For a radical movement that had appealed mostly to poor outsiders, the access to political power and eventually to wealth was something of an anomaly. Such worldly success created some tensions within the movement. Nonetheless, by the mid-1700s Quaker spiritual values helped create a society in Pennsylvania that anticipated many of the ideals of modern secular politics and of later America. Being one of the first places in the Western world to have no established church, the Pennsylvania colony was genuinely open to religious, and hence ethnic, tolerance.[5]

Most striking in the Quaker anticipation of later ideals that spread to more secular communities was their opposition to slavery. Almost no one else in the early eighteenth century, except presumably the slaves themselves, recognized slavery as a moral issue. As early as 1657, George Fox (1624–1691), the founder of the Society of Friends, was condemning slavery and pointing out that blacks were as fully human as whites. Such ideas spread slowly. In 1711 Pennsylvania banned the importation of slaves. In the eighteenth century, led by John Woolman (1720–1772), who saw the desire for wealth and security as the source of most human oppression, Quakers took the lead in arousing moral outrage at the enslavement of one race by another.

The Eighteenth Century

In eighteenth-century British colonies such radicalism was the exception. Most Americans had more conventional religious heritages; for the majority, religion was probably a largely formal affair. Many were Anglican, especially in the South where the Church of England was firmly established as the state church. New England was still overwhelmingly Puritan and the most intensely religious region of the colonies. Congregational churches were established by law, though the Congregational heirs to the Puritans now had to tolerate Anglicans and a few others.

The middle colonies were a religious mix. Dutch Reformed (Reformed is the word used for Presbyterians from Europe) were prominent in New York, while Maryland was still home to most of the few Catholics in the colonies. In Pennsylvania the tolerant Quaker policies opened the doors for German immigration, including mostly Lutherans, but also such sects as the Mennonites. The most influential new religious group in the middle colonies was the Presbyterians,

• • •

strict Calvinists who were mostly Scots and Scotch-Irish (Scots whose forebears had earlier moved to Northern Ireland.)

In the early decades of the eighteenth century the British colonies in North America were distant from each other and far from unified culturally. During that century, however, the American nation took shape and a discernible American culture appeared. Undoubtedly, the events surrounding the American Revolution were the major factors in shaping this new identity. Preceding the Revolution, however, was another intercolonial set of events, far less remembered, which anticipated many of the American traits since associated with the Revolution.

The Great Awakening

The Great Awakening, like the American Revolution, was a series of events. The first sparks were revivals in the 1720s among the Dutch Reformed in New Jersey, in the 1730s among Presbyterians in the middle colonies, and in Jonathan Edwards's Congregationalist church in western Massachusetts. These, however, turned into a "great and general" conflagration with the spectacular preaching tour in 1739 and 1740 of George Whitefield (1714–1770), a young British Calvinist. Whitefield's triumphant journey up and down the East Coast, preaching to large gatherings wherever he went, was one of the first truly intercolonial events. Whitefield was the first "media star" in American history. His medium was the pulpit; and he had immense skill with the spoken word. His tour anticipated a pattern in American culture: lacking long-established traditions and rituals, Americans have been susceptible to waves of popular enthusiasm for "stars." This pattern had its beginnings in revivalism and remains a prominent dimension of American cultural and religious life.

The American Great Awakening was part of a broader "pietist" revival throughout the Protestant world, beginning in Germany in the late 1600s. Pietist groups, such as the German Moravians, came to the new world to settle and evangelize. In England the Methodist movement organized in the late 1730s by John Wesley (1703–1791)— at the time a close friend of Whitefield—was in the beginning a party for pietist renewal within the Church of England (Wesley never admitted his group was an independent denomination; but it was in effect independent by the time of his death). Pietists attempted to renew churches by emphasizing the individual's personal relationship

• • •

Evangelist George Whitefield, America's first "star."

with God, a devotional life, a strict discipline of moral piety, and vigorous evangelizing about the necessity of being converted, or "born again," in Christ. These emphases (today usually known as "evangelical") found fertile soil in eighteenth-century America. Puritanism, with its emphasis on individual conversions, helped pave the way. The more separatistic seventeenth-century Baptists, who grew out of Puritanism, also anticipated some pietist emphases, but were few and scattered in the colonies. The Awakening now brought some more moderate versions of such emphases to the colonies on a large scale.

These "new light" revivals were revolutionary in that most of them challenged established authority by appealing directly to the people. In most of British North America preaching had been reserved for a highly educated elite, expert in Hebrew, Greek, and Latin. The authority to preach was especially important since, except for a

• • •

few newspapers, preaching was virtually the only form of public communication.

Travelling or "itinerant" preachers such as Whitefield upset this
pattern of social authority. The traveller could challenge local authority in the name of God and then move on. Moreover, Whitefield used
a more popular style of preaching, dropping the elaborate expositions
and arguments of elite clergy. Whitefield and his imitators frankly
appealed to the emotions of their listeners, a practice shocking in an
"enlightened" age when rationality was so highly valued both within
and outside the churches. More alarmingly, Whitefield and his successors suggested that so many church people were unconverted because the clergy were unconverted: the blind were leading the blind.
Such challenges to the authority of established clergy often brought
divisions in American churches between "new lights" and antirevi-
valist "old lights." [6]

Jonathan Edwards

Deeply involved in this debate was Jonathan Edwards (1703–1758).
Spending almost his whole life in small towns near the Massachusetts
frontier, Edwards was both a leading preacher of the Awakening and
an incisive analyst of the current religious questions.

Edwards was deeply faithful to New England Calvinism, but
understood better than his contemporaries the threats it would face
in the modern era. Calvinism, the point of departure for dominant
American theology for the first two centuries of settlement, was built
around the sovereignty of God. Humans were inherently sinful or
depraved and could do nothing to save themselves. God's grace in
Christ was their only hope.

Edwards identified the threats to this God-centered outlook as
coming from two directions. First, it could come from religious liberals who adopted eighteenth-century enlightened views denying humans' total depravity and trusting more in human rational abilities and
natural moral sense. On the other hand, complete trust in God could
be undermined by the Awakening itself. To an extent the liberal champions of reasonable Christianity were right. It was possible, at least,
that sensational preachers could simply excite people's passions and
so simulate religious conversions, which really would be human-
generated rather than acts of God's grace.

Edwards defended God-centeredness against these two threats

• • •

(which anticipated many of the trends in American Christianity for the next two and one-half centuries) by describing God's creative relationship to his creation as always dynamic. The essence of God was love, which meant that he was always communicating or giving of himself to his creatures in creation. Edwards saw created nature, in almost a mystical way, as the language of God through which one could hear, see, and sense the love of God. If anyone truly saw this love and beauty of God, she or he would be overwhelmed by and drawn into it, as one might be drawn to the beauty of another person or to a great work of art. Being drawn to such beauty would be fully voluntary in one sense; but would in another sense be an involuntary response to overwhelming beauty and love.

Humans, however, were so preoccupied with themselves that their eyes were closed to the love and beauty of God that surrounded them. Only if they were awakened by God's Holy Spirit to see his love fully revealed in the sacrificial love of Christ would they turn from love of self to love of God and all his creation. This experience, said Edwards, was like receiving a "sixth sense," a spiritual sense to see God's love.

So in answer to the religious liberals of the day, Edwards maintained that God must always be the active agent in turning humans from their selfish ways to true religion and true virtue. He also argued—in answer to the liberal criticisms of the Awakening's excesses—that any true religious awakening essentially involved strong human affections, ultimately the overwhelming sense of love of God. At the same time, Edwards defended the centrality of affections so carefully within traditional Calvinist theology that he excluded sheer sensational emotionalism that failed to meet strict biblically-based tests of validity.

The Continuing Awakening

Though few other Americans appreciated and fully comprehended the subtleties of Edwards' thought, Calvinism remained the dominant theology of the new lights and they generally followed Edwards by evoking emotion through preaching traditional doctrine, rather than through extravagant sensationalism.

While the Awakening was strong among Congregationalists in New England and Presbyterians in the middle colonies, its most lasting direct impact was in the spectacular burgeoning of Baptists. Many of

• • •

the ardent new light converts, emphasizing the importance of a dramatic conversion experience, believed that only adult baptism was valid. Moreover, this Baptist doctrine appealed especially to non-elites. Emphasizing spiritual qualities as more important to church leadership than education, Baptists encouraged lay people to preach. This radical departure from most Protestant traditions helped the movement to spread quickly, as Baptist missionaries, often with little training, were crisscrossing the colonies, preaching their more egalitarian message. Such emphases appealed to the less educated in the colonies, who were, of course, the majority. By the end of the century Baptists had become the largest religious group in the country.

The thunder of the Awakening thus continued to reverberate throughout the colonies long after Whitefield's famous tour. In the South, particularly, this ongoing religious enthusiasm effected a remarkable cultural transformation. Prior to the Awakening the religious life of the South was largely monopolized by an established Anglican church, the official state church, supported by taxes. The established church was part of a pattern in which it was assumed that, as in England, the culture would be controlled by a gentry who enjoyed God-given social authority. The Awakening marked the beginning of a process which eventually gave Southern culture an entirely new stamp. First, in the 1750s Presbyterian revivalists in the backcountry inspired new religious enthusiasm. The Presbyterians were soon followed and surpassed by the Baptists. These non-Anglicans, or Dissenters as they were known, were largely the ordinary people rather than the gentry.

No dimension of this revolution was more momentous in the long run than its impact on the slaves. Up to this time the African slaves had only begun to be evangelized and had not shown great interest in Christianity. Now, after the mid-1700s they found a form of Christianity more congenial to their African religious heritages which they could appropriate as their own. Evangelical Christianity offered them a new standard of values that asserted the superiority of the spiritual over the merely temporal, and promised that the last should be made first. Baptist worship was informal, allowing for individual expression, and often was open to both blacks and whites. Almost immediately blacks were contributing to new styles of worship that influenced both whites and blacks. Soon, blacks were developing their own semi-independent religious culture, based especially on Baptist and Methodist models, including some of their own preachers.[7]

• • •

The awakenings were important for women also. Throughout the eighteenth century, women constituted the majority of church members in the colonies. Their growing religious interests helped pave the way for the pietist revivals. Though the legal status of colonial women was severely limited and in formal church activities they were expected to play only a secondary role, the value system of the revivals proclaimed the worth of the spiritual individual that transcended social or ecclesiastical status. Especially in conversion-oriented Christianity that judged people by their spiritual and moral standing, women could find spiritual and moral equality to men, and even superiority to unconverted men. Women, whose overwhelming domestic vocations were arduous, whose lives were often at risk in childbirth, and who suffered the most intense agonies from high death rates among children, often found in these values a basis for self-fulfillment.[8]

RELIGION AND THE AMERICAN REVOLUTION

Dissent: An American Tradition

The overturning of social values implicit in the Awakening contained a potential for social change. In the American Revolution, which followed on the heels of the Awakening, the impact of the new cultural style was especially evident. While the Awakening surely did not cause the Revolution, it did anticipate many of its attitudes, especially the assertion of the rights of individuals from almost any rank in society to challenge established authority.

Perhaps more important was a direct link between the Revolution and an older tradition of Protestant dissent which the Awakening helped reinforce. This tradition went back to Oliver Cromwell's Puritan Commonwealth in the 1650s. The American colonies were populated largely with people—especially New England Congregationalists and Scotch-Irish Presbyterians—who thought of themselves as heirs to that heritage. They were dissenters rather than part of the powerful Anglican establishment. The Awakening, without itself involving any direct political program, intensified the dissenting traditions in America and increased their numbers. When the Revolution came, Con-

• • •

gregationalists, Presbyterians, and Baptists were almost invariably on its side.[9]

One dimension of early America that is often overlooked is its almost tribal ethnoreligious diversities. Politically, the most significant tribe was the Scotch-Irish. Beginning in the Elizabethan age, these Scots migrated to Ulster or Northern Ireland. As Scots they disliked the English and as Presbyterians they despised the Anglican establishment. In the eighteenth century they moved in large numbers to the colonies, constituting about one-fourth of the population of Pennsylvania, and to the inland regions of the South. In Pennsylvania, they developed a strong animosity to the ruling Quakers, who were English and whose pacifist principles the gun-toting Scotch-Irish thought cowardly. Eventually they brought to an end the Quaker rule.[10] Their even stronger hostility toward Anglican English, who controlled the imperial government, was an important ingredient in the Revolution. The British sometimes referred to the American army as "Presbyterian."

As is often the case, religion was a significant factor but not an isolated variable in political events. Rather, the resurgence of dissenting religious heritages in the eighteenth-century American awakenings reinforced other ethnic and regional loyalties that contributed to revolution.

A Secular Society

While the role of religion is often neglected in accounts of the shaping of the nation, it should not be exaggerated either. As is always true, at least in modern Western societies, a great deal that went on in eighteenth-century America had little to do with traditional organized religion directly. Although most white Americans thought themselves part of Protestant Christendom, their society was Christian largely in a formal sense. Many people, especially new lights, were intensely religious. Many more were religious only occasionally or ignored religious services entirely. People also trusted in minor folk magic that had little to do with their traditional Christian connections.[11]

In some areas of eighteenth-century life, such as war and commerce, traditional religion seemed hardly to play any perceptible role. The society was violent, cruelly oppressive of other races, and given to many vices attractive to human nature. Alcohol provided a chief entertainment. Indeed, one would have found much of eighteenth-

• • •

century America thoroughly profane. Such tendencies would appear more often in areas, such as the South before the awakenings and in frontier areas, where traditional religious organizations were not strong.

The overall trends in Western civilization seemed to favor the expansion of areas of life that religion would not touch. Eighteenth-century England and her colonies were both considerably more secular in the mid-eighteenth century than in the mid-seventeenth. One senses this from the novels of the day, such as Henry Fielding's *Tom Jones*, which recounts the ribald exploits of a profligate young man. Or, as was observed about Anglican clergy of the day, they were expected to handle their religion, like their liquor, as gentlemen.[12]

A combination of forces favored such developments. Perhaps most important were the technological and scientific revolutions. Although these had not yet revolutionized everyday life, they were terrifically exciting to eighteenth-century educated people with their promise that many new areas of life could be mastered by the application of practical scientific reason. It seemed to them that they were the midst of a vast human breakthrough not simply in better understanding their physical environment, but also in applying the same rational principles to mastering most other problems. So they thought they ought to be able to discover universally valid scientific principles for questions of morality, politics, and (for some) even for religion itself.

The Scientific Age

Basic to this set of attitudes, broadly known as the Enlightenment, was the belief that humanity no longer had to depend on tradition for its surest authority. Until that time, almost everyone in Western civilization assumed that the older a belief was, the more likely it was to be true. Now in the eighteenth century enlightened thinkers were claiming that there was no need to depend on the past. The human race could solve its problems if it started over following the scientific method, beginning with no prior assumptions or superstitions inherited from tradition.

Such views became widespread among both educated and uneducated eighteenth-century Americans by the end of the century. The American Revolution came just at the time when the vogue of such ideas was at its height and so the popular definitions of the new nation were undeniably shaped by these ideas. Leading American revolutionaries, such as Thomas Jefferson or Benjamin Franklin, en-

• • •

dorsed these views in their purest form. Both were practical philosophers; each was responsible for a long list of inventions. Practical scientific reason, they assumed, was the key to solving many of humanity's long-standing problems, whether they concerned how to make life more comfortable or how to build a better society. Such an outlook—that most of the important questions of life have a technical solution—has had an immeasurable impact on shaping American society.

Jefferson and Franklin as well as many of the other sophisticated revolutionaries were Deists. Although they abandoned those parts of Christian heritage that they thought were not based on reason, they retained faith in a creator deity, since they believed it was unreasonable to think that the wonderful machine of the universe appeared without a designer. They also believed in a created moral order, reflecting the wisdom of the supreme being, and necessary for the practical ordering of society.

We might suppose that the nation Jefferson, Franklin, and their Deist friends helped create would become a very secular place, accelerating the forces in the society away from the impact of traditional Christianity. The relationship of American culture to such secular trends, however, has always been far more complicated than that, filled with paradoxes and contradictions. We can get some sense of this deep mix of the Christian and the secular if we look at the central event in shaping American society, the American Revolution itself.

A Moral Age

We can start with the Declaration of Independence. Why were Americans willing to fight and die to separate themselves from what in retrospect looks like a rather mild British rule? Although there were many practical reasons, these would have seemed hardly sufficient if the Revolution had not been regarded as a *moral* issue of some cosmic significance. Jefferson—when drafting the Declaration of Independence—stated in Enlightenment language these moral factors on which most Americans could agree.

While there were many sources for Jefferson's thought, the most direct parallel is to the views of John Locke (1632–1704).[13] Locke was an early English Enlightenment figure who attempted to do for politics and morality what his contemporary Isaac Newton did for physics. He tried to discover universal moral laws based on reason

• • •

alone. When Jefferson proclaimed in the Declaration that rights to life and liberty were beyond doubt, or "self-evident," he was summarizing views of Locke that had become commonplace in eighteenth-century political thought.

Jefferson also followed Locke in building a theory of revolution on these foundations. If the government constantly violates fundamental moral laws, for instance, by arbitrarily taking away its people's life, liberty, or property (taxation without representation), then the supposed governors become, literally, outlaws. So it is the people's right and duty to alter or abolish that government and to set up a proper government that honors the moral law.

Locke and the Puritans

From the standpoint of American religious history, the striking aspect of this familiar Lockean-Jeffersonian formula is its similarity to the Puritan view of the covenant. In each, the nation and its rulers are bound together by a contract, the terms of which are divinely ordained moral law. If the governors break the contract by systematically breaking the laws, then the contract is dissolved. Yet while the Puritans emphasized that one's certainty about the moral law came from the Bible (though it might be confirmed by reason), Locke and Jefferson grounded their certainty on human reason alone (though they agreed that the Bible said the same thing). All parties agreed that the Bible and reason concurred on fundamental moral principles. For instance, the biblical commandment, "Thou shalt not steal," and the self-evident "right to property" were two ways of stating the same truth.

This similarity of the two views was not accidental. The Puritans who stayed in England in the 1600s were the first modern revolutionaries. In 1649, after winning a civil war in England, they executed King Charles I as an outlaw. As we have already seen, many of the modern principles for redefining human relationships were anticipated in the religious radicalism of mid-seventeenth century England.

John Locke lived during the very next generation. The British crown was restored to the throne in 1660; but in 1688 there was another revolution, the "bloodless revolution." King James II (1633–1701) was a Catholic. Protestant political leaders, fearing tyranny, invited the Protestant ruler of Holland, William of Orange (1650–1702), and his wife Mary (1662–1694), of the English royal house, to be

• • •

their monarchs. Seeing his cause as lost, James II fled without a fight. Locke developed his political views and his justification of revolution in this context. Though his most influential arguments for revolution were based on self-evident principles of reason, rather than on Scripture, the influence of the Puritan model was substantial.

Science and Christianity Agree

This connection illustrates the important point that most eighteenth-century Americans perceived no conflict between scientific or rational "Enlightenment" ways of looking at things and their Christian heritage. The strengths of their Christian commitments, of course, varied widely and for many, perhaps for most, their Christian heritage had only a vague impact on their beliefs. Nonetheless, even when Christian commitments were strong, as for many of the heirs to the Puritans in New England, Christian and scientific Enlightenment beliefs were almost always seen, not as contradictory, but as complementary. This was especially true for those Americans who supported the Revolution and hence had the most to do with shaping the characteristic outlook of the new nation.

A Land of Dissenters

The connections, however, were still more formidable. British North America was, as we have seen, largely a land of dissenters; that is, the colonies contained sizeable populations loyal to churches, such as the Congregationalist, Presbyterian, or Baptist, outside of ("dissenters" from) the Church of England. The Congregational establishment in New England had a long and bitter history of antagonism with the Anglican church. In the middle colonies and the southern backcountry there were large numbers of Scotch-Irish immigrants who had similar histories of antagonism to Anglicanism. The new light movement swelled the numbers of dissenters just prior to the Revolution.

What is significant about the strength of dissent in America is that the most important eighteenth-century political tradition, almost universally appropriated by American revolutionaries, came from English dissenters of the earlier eighteenth century. This tradition of thought, developed first in the 1720s, has been variously known as the "Real Whig" or "Commonwealth" tradition. The commonwealth referred back to the days of Puritan rule in England in the 1660s. The eigh-

• • •

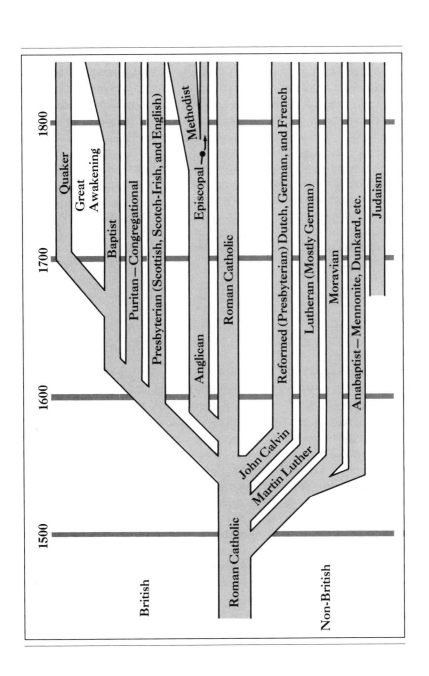

teenth-century "Commonwealth men" were heirs to this heritage in that they belonged to "nonconformist" or "dissenter" denominations.

It is very important for understanding American culture and the role of religion in it to recognize the political implications in England of having an established church. Reflecting the very old practices of "Christendom," the Church of England was practically a department of the state and political power was tied to church membership. In the eighteenth century other denominations were tolerated; but the memory of the Puritan takeover was recent enough that Anglicans were not ready to give up their political and social control. Throughout the eighteenth century in England, if one were to hold public office or attend the major universities, Oxford and Cambridge, one had to belong to the Church of England.

The Course of Empires

For the dissenters, such discrimination sharpened their awareness of political tyranny. By the 1720s they were producing a body of political thought that linked political and ecclesiastical tyranny with the accumulation of executive power around the monarch. Citing the precedents of ancient Athens and Rome, they pointed out that republican governments tend to be subverted if the republic acquires an empire. Then massive colonial administration brings accumulation of power around an executive. Soon corruption sets in. There is buying and selling of offices and privileges. This is what they saw happening to England. Its "mixed government" of monarchy and parliament was losing its balance of powers in the direction of growing executive power and growing arbitrary privilege. The privileged Church of England was on the side of this executive power. Though in theology the dissenters were not as strict as their Puritan forebears, they shared with the Puritans the belief that high-handed monarchical power is always supported by ecclesiastical privilege. So the Commonwealth men championed both the inalienable rights of humanity to life, liberty, and property, in the tradition of John Locke, and the inalienable rights of conscience in the traditions of English religious dissent.

One could hardly overstate the importance of this Commonwealth heritage in shaping American revolutionary political thought.[15] Most Americans were dissenters and even many of those who were Anglicans, such as the Virginia gentry, were outsiders to the political privilege surrounding the crown. Most of those who held local political or

• • •

social power in America stood only to lose if the full-fledged English system were exported to the colonies. So, when England after 1763 began to take an interest in reorganizing her newly expanded North American empire, many colonists grew alarmed. They stated their alarm in the terms of Commonwealth or Real Whig heritage. This dissenting tradition became the base for the "republican" outlook that long dominated American political thought.

An American Bishop

The most striking evidence of the religious dissenting factor in colonial alarms about the Anglicization of the colonies was what one historian characterized as "the Great Fear," or the fear of an Anglican bishop.[16] Anglicans in America operated at a considerable inconvenience by having no resident bishop, since the church held that direct laying on of hands by a bishop was essential to ordination of clergy. But the same republican Americans, including many Anglicans, who opposed the new taxes for the empire were dead set against such an otherwise sensible proposal for an American bishop. They saw it as a major step toward imposing on the colonies the entire English hierarchical model for governing society.

Catholicism and Monarchy

Such fears were compounded by the militant anti-Catholic sentiments of many American revolutionaries. Ironically, movements that champion freedom do not extend it to those whom they consider their mortal enemies. The Catholic population, mostly in the middle colonies, was small and—though often discriminated against—generally tolerated. They were not the problem. Some Catholics, such as the influential Carroll family in Maryland, supported the Revolution and even hoped to make the American Catholic church more republican. The problem was that the English colonies were still Protestant enclaves in a largely Catholic hemisphere, so the cold war mentality lingered. This was especially true in New England. A number of times during the eighteenth century, amid much religious fanfare, New Englanders mobilized for military action against French Catholic Canada. In 1763, at the conclusion of the French and Indian Wars, they rejoiced that Canada was finally in British and Protestant hands. Soon, however, they were chagrined that in the Quebec Act of 1774 the British administration of Canada allowed for continued tax support for

• • •

An attempt to land an Anglican bishop in America.

the Catholic church and allowed for the continued spread of Catholicism in the trans-Appalachian west (now upper midwest).[17]

Most of the American revolutionaries took for granted a "Real Whig" or republican view of history that grew out of the British religious and political experience. They associated tyranny with the Middle Ages and the marriage of ecclesiastical and royal power. "Thus,"

• • •

as John Adams put it, "was human nature chained fast for ages in a cruel, shameful, and deplorable servitude to [the Pope] and his subordinate tyrants."[18] Protestantism was thus seen as crucial to the rise of freedom. According to the Whig view, Protestantism opened the door for reason or common sense to challenge superstition and privilege. Once again we can see that dissenting Protestant views and Enlightenment views would blend far more than they would disagree. Both saw superstition as the problem and common sense reason as the solution. Both regarded Catholicism (and some Anglicanism that resembled Catholicism) as defending monarchy and the authoritarianism of the Middle Ages, while dissenting Protestantism was on the side of liberty.

A Republic of Virtue

These revolutionary traditions also agreed in seeing virtue as essential to the American republican enterprise. This point was central also in Greek and Roman classical thought. Classical models, as we can still see in the neoclassical "colonial" architecture, were immensely important to those who were shaping the new republic. In the republican blend of dissenting Protestant, classical, and enlightened thoughts, all authorities agreed with the fundamental moral maxim, "Power corrupts." Americans, who were far from the centers of power, saw themselves as relatively virtuous.

As we have seen, it is this definition of their cause as a matter of virtue, as evidenced in the Declaration of 1776, that could rally Americans to risk dying for independence. This lens through which the revolutionaries viewed their cause accounts for what, from the British point of view, must have looked like a colossal misperception. Even from our modern perspective, we have difficulty understanding how the British rule was quite as tyrannical as the Declaration describes. The British Empire, despite some administrative faults, was one of the relatively more enlightened regimes in world history. It seems a far cry from the tyranny of ancient Roman rule and not even in the ballpark with our more advanced twentieth-century tyrannies, such as those of Hitler, Stalin, or Idi Amin. The British, quite sensibly, were attempting to reorganize their empire and have the colonists help pay for it. How could so many Americans see this as an extreme case of despotism that called for revolution?

This puzzling question can be answered if we understand that the

· · ·

Americans viewed these events through the lens of their Whig blend of dissenting Protestant, classical, and Enlightenment ideologies. In that view there was a history of repeated tyrannies associated with Catholicism, Catholic-leaning Anglicanism, monarchy, and the corrupting development of empires. Protestantism, republicanism, common sense reason, and freedom were reputedly locked in a centuries-long struggle against repressive forces. The American revolutionaries thought they had to save their heritage before they were overwhelmed by these forces of tyranny.[19]

The New Order for the Ages

Given this perception of the larger historical issues at stake in the Revolution, it is not surprising that American preachers often raised the cause of liberty to sacred status. The minions of the Anti-Christ, said Samuel West of Dartmouth, Massachusetts, in an annual election sermon before the legislature in 1776, "Better be understood as political rather than ecclesiastical tyrants." Turning to the book of Revelation, West suggested that the "horrible wild beast" ascending from the bottomless pit could refer to the British army. So West announced, "We must beat our plowshares into swords, and our pruning hooks into spears."[20]

To understand such rhetoric coming from the nation's most respected public speakers, we must know something of the cosmic view of history which the dissenting clergy typically tied to their republican sentiments.

During the Great Awakening, some of the new light preachers successfully popularized the notion that the earth was near the dawn of a new era. The Bible, which was widely regarded as an absolute authority on all subjects, spoke of a "millennial" age, or thousand-year reign of Christ. By the mid-1700s the most common interpretation of this prophecy by American revivalists was that it symbolically foretold the culminating era in history when the Spirit of Christ, or the Holy Spirit, would reign on earth. The Awakening itself was seen as the chief evidence of the beginning of this age, which would witness massive conversions to the Gospel.

Inevitably such prophecies took on political connotations. In order for the millennium to come, according to Scripture, Christ must defeat the Anti-Christ. In Protestant thought, the Anti-Christ traditionally referred to the Pope. So, reasoned the American dissenters, any

· · ·

political defeat of Catholic countries was a step toward the dawning of the millennium. The French and Indian Wars of 1756 and 1763 fit this model exactly. For instance, the famed Presbyterian evangelist, Samuel Davies, described the British efforts against France as "the commencement of this grand decisive conflict between the Lamb and the beast." A British victory, he proclaimed, would help bring "a new heaven and a new earth." [21]

When the victory of 1763 brought not a grand new age, but the reorganization of the British Empire, it took some rhetorical gymnastics for the Dissenter preachers to put Protestant England into the columns of the Pope. Their Puritan-Whig traditions, the fears of a bishop, and the Quebec Act of 1774 continuing the Catholic establishment in Canada, however, all contributed to this reading of the conflict. Simply by virtue of lining up on the side of tyranny against the colonists, reasoned the pious revolutionaries, England had signalled its betrayal of the *true* cause of Protestant civilization. So we find the Reverend Alexander MacWhorter, chaplain to Washington's troops at Valley Forge, describing the enemy as "Papist Highland barbarians," even though most of them were actually fellow Presbyterians. [22]

Important as it was to have the respected clergy of America's popular religions providing the Revolution with such cosmic historical significance, we should not push this dimension of the origin of American identity too far. As we have seen, the revolutionaries welcomed the Catholics who would join their cause, and the new nation would be committed to legal tolerance of Catholics. Moreover, when the very survival of the nation was at stake during the Revolution, few raised any objections to the convenient alliance with Catholic France, which made independence possible. During wars, of course, people find themselves with strange bedfellows. We might recall the alliance of the United States with Stalin's Soviet Union during World War II. As soon as each war was over, the longer-standing cold war attitudes reemerged.

A Paradoxical Heritage

The Dissenter rhetoric allowed the dominant white Anglo-Saxon Protestant group in America to do what they always have done since the Puritans—view their civilizing efforts as a divine mission.

Americans today tend to talk about this propensity as either wholly

• • •

good or wholly bad. On the positive side, this sense of national calling certainly has contributed to the vitality and success of American civilization. It has also provided a moral idealism and sense of civic and national responsibility. The American nation, when it was founded, became a beacon for liberty and order in an age when the combination was rare. Peoples of every race and nationality have rallied under the beacon of these moral ideals, finding in them realistic articulations of the best in their own traditions. Much of whatever one regards as successful in America must be attributed to such ideals.

There is a negative side, however, that is just as undeniable. Critics point out that the very virtues of this American tradition often become its vices. High moral idealism and a sense of divine calling to spread the ideals of liberty and justice, as one conceives them, can easily lead to injustice. This is particularly true of those who combine these ideals with power. Once in power, champions of liberty and order often use the rhetoric of liberty to impose an order that favors themselves. Groups out of favor can be exempted from the liberties. In the case of the new nation, the most outrageous example of this inequity was the failure of white Protestants to apply the moral ideals of the Revolution to the slaves. Moreover, moral idealism, just because of the important virtues it self-evidently stands for, can lead to an overestimation of the nation's rights toward other peoples. In the new nation liberty and justice were seldom applied toward relations with Indians. Moreover, the United States developed a questionable sense of "manifest destiny" to spread its ideals from coast to coast and eventually around the world. Sometimes lofty moral ideals were true motivating forces in American foreign policy; but they were often used in the self-interest of the powerful and the ambitious.[23]

On balance, and compared to most of the alternatives, the American experiment has been attractive to many people, in part because of its traditions of high moral ideals of liberty and justice. Expressions of high ideals, however, make groups particularly vulnerable to criticisms for failure to apply such ideals equally to all.

Civil Religion

America's religious heritage also contributed to a sort of deification of the national enterprise. In recent years, this tendency, first seen during the American Revolution, has been tagged "civil religion." Civil religion is the attributing of a sacred character to the nation

· · ·

itself. Throughout history rulers had claimed divine sanction either by saying that they themselves were divine (as Roman emperors did) or that they were chosen by the God or gods of the nation. Typically, national loyalty was focused on loyalty to the person of the monarch. In eighteenth-century France, for instance, the kings claimed to rule by divine right and the person of the king was considered a sacred object.

The Puritans in America and England challenged such claims in important ways. In America, as we have seen, the early Puritans claimed divine sanction for their enterprise by seeing themselves as a new Israel. God would bless the colonies only if they were explicitly Christian and obeyed God's law. In England at the time of the Revolution of 1649 this Puritan principle was most succinctly labeled by the Presbyterian revolutionary Samuel Rutherford: *lex rex*, "the law is king." From the Puritan-Presbyterian outlook loyalty was directed not toward the person of the rule, but toward a set of principles. In eighteenth-century England questions of loyalty to principle or person were still hotly contested. In America, however, the loyalty to principle triumphed. Thomas Paine (1737–1809) put it best in his immensely popular pamphlet of 1776, "Common Sense": "in America, *the law is king.*" The spirit of 1649 still lived.

But now the Americans had a problem. How could they claim religious sanction for their nation? Thomas Paine, for instance, was a notorious infidel. After the Revolution he authored scathing attacks on Christianity. With leading citizens such as Paine or Jefferson, clearly the nation could not officially claim a Christian sanction.

Americans resolved this problem by three primary means, all aspects of civil religion. First, Deist leaders of the Jefferson sort argued that the natural laws on which American rights were founded demonstrably originated with the Creator. Thus, as stated in the Declaration of Independence, whether Christian or not, Americans could appeal to the Creator who stood above all sects. Hence, official references to "God" in American life, as "In God we trust," or "so help me God" could have this vague meaning.

Second, American civil and political leaders informally continued to speak of the nation as though it were a Christian nation, or at least a biblical nation. Both politicians and clergy continually referred to America as the new Israel, and Americans as a chosen people, a covenanted people. Even presidential inaugural addresses throughout the

• • •

twentieth century have applied the rhetoric, first enunciated by Puritan governor John Winthrop in 1630, of America as a "city on a hill."

Finally, the United States was the first modern nation systematically to shift public veneration of the government from veneration of persons to veneration of the nation and its principles. Soon the United States developed a set of rituals and symbols that bore striking resemblances to traditional Christian rites and symbols, but in which the nation itself was the object of worship. The flag (like the cross in Catholic churches) was a sacred object. Elaborate rules developed as to when and how it could be handled. Pledges to the flag arguably played the role of crossing oneself in a church. One pledged to a creed. The nation developed holidays (holy days) and its own brand of saints. George Washington, for instance, soon took on mythical qualities. National architecture and shrines provided centers for pilgrimages and worship. Some recently have even pointed out that three of the most popular shrines in Washington D.C.—those to Washington, Lincoln, and Kennedy—have designs that would be appropriate symbols for each of the three members of the Christian Trinity (the transcendent obelisk for the father, the personal presence of the martyred champion of national reconciliation and charity, and the eternal flame, for the spirit of service to country.)[24]

Such specific analogies should not be pushed too far; but the crucial practical test of a functional religion is ultimacy. Here the nation, the model of the modern nation states, qualifies. The United States, like all modern nations, demands unswerving allegiance from its citizens. It is to the nation that one is expected to make the supreme sacrifice. So in American wars, national loyalty has always been demanded above church loyalty. Presbyterians killed Presbyterians during the Revolution, Anglicans killed Anglicans. In the Civil War Baptists killed countless Baptists, Methodists countless Methodists, Catholics and Jews killed fellow Catholics and Jews. And so forth. So, too, in every war.

The major exceptions, of course, were pacifists, such as Quakers, Mennonites, Amish, and Moravians. Loyalty to Christ's principles of love, they maintained, must stand before loyalty to nation. Pacifists often suffered for this radical stance. Pennsylvania Mennonites and Quakers, for instance, sometimes had their property confiscated by patriots for failing to pay taxes for the war.[25] Other citizens felt they

• • •

neglected their civic responsibilities and aided the enemy by refusing to fight in a good cause.

Except for the pacifists, almost all American religious groups saw their national loyalties not in conflict with their traditional religion but simply as an extension of their religion. Throughout the nation's history Americans overwhelmingly have insisted that loyalty to God and nation go hand in hand.

A Secular Constitution

Recognition of the roles played by Dissenter Protestantism and civil religion should balance the more familiar accounts of the secular origins of the American republic. Enlightenment and classical categories did dominate the political discourse of the new nation, but Christians did not see these as conflicting with Christian principles. Truth was one principle they held. God was author of both Scripture and nature. So, they were convinced, they had nothing to fear from practical principles derived from scientific reasoning. True principles of governments, they reasoned, were as universal as the laws of physics.

Dissenter Protestantism and Enlightenment thought combined to guarantee separation of church and state in the new national government. This alliance, which emerged before the Revolution in the fears of an Anglican bishop, led to the momentous effort to disestablish the deeply-entrenched Anglican church in Virginia after the war. Thomas Jefferson saw his role in the passage of the Virginia "Act for Establishing Freedom of Religion" in 1785 as one of the three great accomplishments in his life, along with authoring the Declaration of Independence, and founding the University of Virginia. Crucial to the success of this effort was the vigorous support of Virginia Baptists and other Dissenters.

The Virginia law was a precedent for the U.S. Constitution, authored in part by James Madison (1751–1836), Jefferson's right-hand man in the Virginia disestablishment. On the other hand, the connection can not be pressed too far since the Constitution is very different from the Virginia law. It neither establishes nor disestablishes religion. In fact, this is precisely how the policy was stated when the First Amendment was added. "Congress shall make no law respecting an establishment of religion, or prohibiting the free exercise thereof." Established Congregational churches, supported by taxes, remained

• • •

in New England into the early nineteenth century. Traditional religious practices were not touched. The government and the army had Protestant chaplains, legislative sessions were still opened with prayer, and Protestant theology was standard fare in most state-supported schools.

In fact, the best explanation of the Constitution's stance on religion is very simple. The Constitution stays away almost entirely from the subject of religion. The only thing it says is that "no religious test shall ever be required" for public office. As historian John F. Wilson explains, the framers of the Constitution were political realists. They knew that getting the new document ratified was going to be a very close call. In the religiously divided tribal United States, nothing could kill the proposal quicker than to take a stand on religion. So the framers said as little as possible about the subject, not even invoking any pious language.[26]

The assumption at the time certainly was that religion, and especially Christianity, should be able to flourish in the republic, without interference from the state. Though the federal government was not going to take any new steps to promote religion, neither was it systematically setting up "a wall of separation" between church and state as Jefferson later claimed it was. Jefferson may (or may not) have been right as to what the Constitution *should* have done; but in fact it did not interfere with Christianity as a dominant and privileged force in the culture. As William Lee Miller puts it: "So Christianity, the great muddy Mississippi of Western Civilization, was able almost uniquely in the American setting to flow unvexed to the sea of modern democratic life."[27]

CHAPTER TWO

The Age of Democratic Revivals

*It was pretty ornery preaching—all about brotherly love, and such-like
tiresomeness; but everybody said it was a good sermon, and they all talked it
over going home, and had such a powerful lot to say about faith and good
works and free grace and preforeordestination, and I don't know what all,
that it did seem to me to be one of the roughest Sundays I had run across yet.*

Mark Twain, *The Adventures of Huckleberry Finn* (1884)

*L*yman Beecher (1775–1863), a leading Congregational evangelist and one of Connecticut's champions of antidisestablishmentarianism, later said that the ending (in 1818) of state tax support for Congregationalism was *"the best thing that ever happened to the state of Connecticut."* It threw the formerly Puritan churches "on their own resources and on God" and increased their influence "by voluntary efforts, societies, missions, and revivals."[1]

Most observers have agreed with Beecher that, despite forces from the Enlightenment, Revolution, and denominational rivalries that might have undermined Christianity's cultural impact, the churches actually gained influence during the succeeding era. Although church membership statistics for the era are somewhat unreliable, reported membership percentages doubled between 1800 and 1860. Far more people apparently attended churches than met the rigorous criteria of most Protestant churches for full membership. We can probably get a fair picture by noting that in 1860 there was church seating of 26 million for a population of 31 million.[2] These figures suggest that if you had visited the United States on a Sunday in this era probably half the people would have been in church.

Cultural impact is more difficult to measure. Alexis de Tocqueville remarked in the 1830s that "I do not know whether all Americans have a sincere faith in their religion—for who can search the human heart?—but I am certain that they hold it to be indispensable to the maintenance of republican institutions." Other foreign visitors said much the same.[3]

The great dynamo generating this remarkable American religious vigor was continuing revival. The period from about 1795 to 1865 was marked by recurrent outbursts of revivals throughout the states. In 1801 there were spectacular new camp meeting revivals among both whites and blacks, especially on the Kentucky frontier. At the other end of the sociological spectrum that same year, Timothy Dwight, president of Congregationalist Yale College, spurred a campus revival that helped inspire a whole generation of Connecticut Yankees to spread the gospel into the new settlements of the West (now Midwest) and throughout the world. Meanwhile, the Methodist movement, which had become an independent denomination, was growing at a spectacular rate among the common people, surpassing even the Baptists in numbers by 1820. At the same time countless local revivalists sprang

. . .

up, often with highly popularized and democratic versions of the Gospel. Several new denominations were formed, filled with grand expectations of ushering in a new age of the spirit. During the 1820s and 1830s Charles G. Finney brought many of these trends together in immensely popular revivals that made him a major national star. By the 1840s and 1850s impressive percentages of slaves had turned to Christianity, which became the overwhelmingly dominant religion of their culture. While women were usually the majority in these revivals, in 1857–58 there were urban revivals among businessmen in the North, drawing them to noontime prayer meetings in numbers unlike anything anyone had seen. During the Civil War, notable revivals were reported in both the Union and Confederate army camps.

Just the overview of these remarkable developments lends plausibility to the estimate of the renowned historian Perry Miller that "the dominant theme in America from 1800 to 1860 is the invincible persistence of the revival technique."[4] The revival fire, said Miller, "sometimes smoldering, now blazing into flame, never quite extinguished (even in Boston) until the Civil War had been fought, was the central mode of this culture's search for cultural identity."[5] William McLoughlin goes even further to say, "The story of American Evangelicalism is the story of America itself in the years 1800–1900, for it was Evangelical religion which made Americans the most religious people in the world . . ."[6] Though other forces must be acknowledged as well, evangelical Christianity was unusually significant in shaping nineteenth-century American cultural values.

This way of characterizing American culture in the national era may seem odd, given the prevailing image of a dominant secular outlook introduced with the American Revolution. Indeed, the cultural impact of the Revolution has been aptly depicted as driving religion off center stage. As Edmund S. Morgan has written, "In 1740 America's leading intellectuals were clergymen and thought about theology; in 1790 they were statesmen and thought about politics."[7] As the new century opened, the American republic seemed to be set on a secular course. In 1801 Thomas Jefferson, an avowed Deist and a champion of the secular state, became president. His vice president was Aaron Burr. Burr was a grandson of Jonathan Edwards; but like many young men who came of age in the revolutionary generation, he rejected the Christian faith. The violence, ambition, and intrigue

• • •

that were parts of enlightened American culture were conspicuous when in 1804 Vice President Burr killed the Federalists' most brilliant leader, Alexander Hamilton, in a duel.

The United States, however, had a paradoxical society in which strong religious impulses survived side-by-side with the secularism of political life. The dual heritage can be illustrated by noting that another of Edwards' grandsons was Timothy Dwight, the president of Yale who helped spark the nineteenth-century revivals, beginning the same year that Jefferson and Burr were sworn into office.

If we assume a longer perspective that includes the ongoing revivals, we can see that the development of American culture involved a major religious dimension that paralleled and qualified the better known secular political, social, and economic developments. With this perspective we can see the era of the American Revolution as, in a sense, an interruption of a longer trend of awakening that started in the 1720s and continued through the Civil War, and in fact longer. The Second Great Awakening, as the nineteenth-century revivals have been called, was surely not the only thing shaping American culture in this era, but it was one of them.

Today the cultural impact of the revivals is largely forgotten when looking at the dominant northern culture of the United States because other spectacular developments have since changed the dominant culture's character, and history is written by the winners. Nonetheless, some dimensions of the nineteenth-century outlook have been preserved among nondominant groups and when historians look at them they still give prominence to the religious factor. The two major cultures in which the revival style has survived, although in differing ways, is in black communities and in the Bible belt of the South. Though these cultures have changed in many ways since the mid-nineteenth century, they have also held on to much. It is illuminating to remember that in the mid-nineteenth century the dominant white culture in the North differed little religiously from these communities.[8] Virtually the whole United States was a Bible belt.

America's Revivalist: Charles G. Finney

We can get some idea of the cultural impact of these revivals if we look briefly at the career and character of Charles G. Finney (1792–1875), the most famous revivalist of his day. Finney was not quite to the Second Great Awakening what Whitefield was to the first. By the

• • •

nineteenth century there were too many competing sects for one person to be central to the whole movement. Finney, nonetheless, was popular because he embodied so many typical traits of the American evangelical spirit.

Finney had been a school teacher and then a lawyer in New York state. In 1821 he experienced a dramatic religious conversion. He closed his law office and dedicated himself to evangelism. By the mid-1820s his revival campaigns in western New York had made him a national sensation. Western New York, being rapidly settled largely by New Englanders with intense religious backgrounds, was perfect tinder for revival fires. It was becoming, in religious terms, comparable to what southern California became in the twentieth century—new settlements open to religious experiment. Several of the era's more exotic religious movements, including Mormonism, Adventism, Shakerism, Spiritualism, and the Oneida community had western New York bases. These grew in the context of almost constant evangelical revivals sweeping the new territories. Eventually, after decades of such intensity generated especially by Finney and his followers, the area became known as the "burnt-over district."

Finney's revival tactics, or "new measures," which first brought him dramatic success in the 1820s, raised sharp controversy. Frontier revivals at turn-of-the-century camp meetings already involved some controversial methods and results. The camp meetings were originally interdenominational affairs, at which large numbers of frontier people gathered for days or weeks of revival preaching. These "protracted meetings" generated some spectacular physical responses when people experienced dramatic changes of heart. These spiritual "exercises" at the camp meetings included sometimes involuntary physical responses such as the jerks, dancing, falling, running, shouting, and barking. These ecstatic phenomena were at the time somewhat peripheral to most American religion, and died out even in the camp meetings, which were taken over largely by the more disciplined Methodists. Finney now brought milder versions of the frontier revival methods to the more settled areas of the Northeast.

The biggest similarity between Finney's work and the camp meetings was that Finney did systematically what the meetings had happened upon—building up and sustaining spiritual intensity. His meetings were protracted, being held in one town or city for a week or more. While he did not look for or get ecstatic exercises, Finney

· · ·

Charles G. Finney made a science of producing revival intensity.

did bring about many life-changing conversions. He used methods such as "the anxious bench," on which those actively seeking conversion could sit as special objects of preaching and prayer. He carefully prepared his campaigns and did not hesitate to name names and specific sins that could bring people to their knees. He urged people

• • •

to testify to each other about their spiritual experiences, and in a revolutionary step, specifically encouraged women to do so.

Evangelicalism and American Culture

By the mid-nineteenth century evangelical religion was a major force shaping dominant American values. Rather than conflict with democratic and republican ideals inherited from the revolutionary era, evangelicalism coalesced with such values, reflected them, and reinforced them. Hence, we can see illustrated in the work of Finney and other evangelicals that the traits of evangelicalism were also becoming traits of the greater American culture.

The Free Individual

First, he and the many lesser-known evangelists of the day were promoting the American emphasis on the free individual. Conversion was becoming more and more a question of individual choice. This was revolutionary because it took place in the context of a Protestant culture that had generally taught the opposite. Most of American Protestant evangelicalism through the eighteenth century had been Calvinist. Calvinists emphasized the sovereignty of God and the sinfulness and resultant disabilities of humans. Salvation, they taught, must be attributed solely to an act of God, with no element of human control.

With new views of human nature developing in the eighteenth century, however, challenges to the Calvinist view grew. Especially important were the formulations of John Wesley (1703–1790), the English founder of Methodism. Wesley developed ways of affirming the sovereignty of God's grace but allowed more room to assure potential converts that their choice for God was also decisive. Immediately after the Revolution, Methodism took firm root in the American soil and, aided by efficient centralized organization, grew so rapidly that by 1820 it was America's largest denomination.

Finney's work brought an essentially Methodist outlook into the old Calvinist denominations of the Northeast. During his career, Finney was affiliated with either the Presbyterian or the Congregational churches, which at the time of the Revolution were America's two largest denominations and still disproportionately influential on the middle-class culture. Like the Methodists, Finney talked about the ability of sinners to make a choice for Christ. Also, following Meth-

• • •

odist examples, he emphasized a strict moral discipline and even that Christians could reach a state of moral "perfection," or freedom from voluntary sinning. Debates over such theological issues preoccupied many of the best minds of the day and dominated much of American intellectual and academic life.[9]

At a more practical level, debates over revivalism and its characteristic theologies involved a continuation of the challenge to the authority of elites begun in the Great Awakening. In the early days of the American republic the predominant assumption was that in both politics and religion the educated elite would govern. Increasingly, however, such assumptions gave way to more democratic tendencies. Popular Methodist and Baptist growth was the first major manifestation of these trends. Preachers increasingly claimed that formal training and formal worship were inhibitions to the Gospel and that the common person with Bible in hand was a more reliable guide to authentic Christianity. They succeeded with an informal, popular vernacular style of preaching accompanied by another nineteenth-century development, the rise of the gospel hymn.[10]

In these respects, as in his tempering of Calvinist theology, Charles Finney was a bridge between the older Calvinist elite culture and the newer democratic styles of the popular Methodists and Baptists. Finney himself was not anti-intellectual. He viewed his approach to sinners as primarily logical, like a lawyer pleading a case. After some spectacularly successful urban revivals in cities such as Rochester and New York, in 1835 Finney accepted a position as professor of theology at the newly founded Oberlin College. He continued revival tours, but also published some formidable books on theology and the theory of revival.

This was an age of oratory and the spoken word was crucial to the revival. Nonetheless, the standards of oratory were still set by a culture dominated by print as a primary form of communication. Hence, logical arguments were still considered essential to effective communication. Just as crowds would flock to hear Abraham Lincoln debate Senator Stephen A. Douglas before the Civil War, so they would turn out to hear Methodists, Baptists, and the like debate their differing theologies. Popularized techniques that appealed more to emotions were taking their place in American religion; but in most cases they were taking a place along side of continuing respect for intellect.

• • •

Camp meetings were a familiar part of popular culture.

Education

Most American religious groups either inherited a tradition of education (as Finney and others with a Calvinist heritage did) or came to believe that education was important to lasting influence. Indeed, by building schools and colleges, evangelicals ensured a major influence in shaping shared cultural values. In an era when the state did relatively little for education, evangelicals were to a large extent the educators of America.

Traditionally in Western culture, education had been a domain of the churches and in pre-Civil War America that tradition was only beginning to change. In higher education religious dominance was conspicuous. By far the majority of college presidents were clergymen. This was true even in state schools. State colleges typically required Protestant chapel attendance, taught the Bible and Protestant

• • •

doctrine, and sometimes required church attendance of their students. "A state university in this country should be religious," declared the president of the University of Michigan in 1863 in a typical statement of the era. "It should be Christian without being sectarian."[11]

Most American colleges were founded and operated by denominations. In towns and villages throughout the nation religious groups would band together to provide colleges. The great majority of these were also evangelical. New Englanders, particularly, with a strong heritage of education, were especially prominent in spreading Christian principle through their colleges.

Evangelical—and often New England—dominance was commonplace at lower levels of education as well. Religious training was assumed to be part of good education and both private and public schools routinely taught Protestant doctrine (often to the chagrin of Catholics and others). The standard American elementary textbook until around 1830 was *The New England Primer*. This work exalted Protestant martyrs and taught Calvinist theology; most famously, "in Adam's fall, we sinned all," to illustrate the letter A. When the grade school texts that dominated American education in the latter half of the century, *McGuffey's Eclectic Readers*, were first published in 1836–37, they also taught a strongly theistic, Calvinistic, and biblically oriented worldview emphasizing that this life is only a preparation for the more important life after death.[12]

Science and Technique

Evangelicals in the early Republic did not see the learning of the day, especially science, in conflict with Christianity. Rather, as products of the peculiar American alliance of enlightenment and dissenting Protestantism, they regarded science as the best of their allies. They thought, in fact, that natural science should be the foundation on which to build irrefutable proofs of the truth of Christianity. Just as if one found a watch on a deserted beach, one would have to infer a skilled watchmaker, so in the face of scientific discoveries of the laws of nature, one should infer a wise creator. *McGuffey's Readers* contained a story in which George Washington discovered cabbage plants growing in a pattern that spelled his name. When little George correctly guesses that his father planted them that way, his father teaches him the lesson that everywhere in the "beautiful, orderly, purposeful world," we see evidence that "there must have been a designer."[13]

• • •

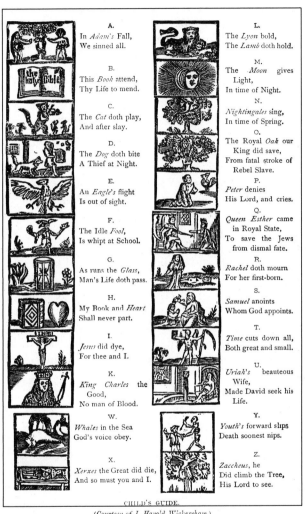

A.
In *Adam's* Fall,
We sinned all.

B.
This *Book* attend,
Thy Life to mend.

C.
The *Cat* doth play,
And after slay.

D.
The *Dog* doth bite
A Thief at Night.

E.
An *Eagle's* flight
Is out of sight.

F.
The Idle *Fool*,
Is whipt at School.

G.
As runs the *Glass*,
Man's Life doth pass.

H.
My Book and *Heart*
Shall never part.

I.
Jesus did dye,
For thee and I.

K.
King Charles the
Good,
No man of Blood.

W.
Whales in the Sea
God's voice obey.

X.
Xerxes the Great did die,
And so must you and I.

L.
The *Lyon* bold,
The *Lamb* doth hold.

M.
The *Moon* gives
Light,
In time of Night.

N.
Nightingales sing,
In time of Spring.

O.
The Royal *Oak* our
King did save,
From fatal stroke of
Rebel Slave.

P.
Peter denies
His Lord, and cries.

Q.
Queen Esther came
in Royal State,
To save the Jews
from dismal fate.

R.
Rachel doth mourn
For her first-born.

S.
Samuel anoints
Whom God appoints.

T.
Time cuts down all,
Both great and small.

U.
Uriah's beauteous
Wife,
Made David seek his
Life.

Y.
Youth's forward slips
Death soonest nips.

Z.
Zaccheus, he
Did climb the Tree,
His Lord to see.

CHILD'S GUIDE.

The New England Primer *taught Protestant doctrine.*

· · ·

Evangelical educators typically went one step further, to argue that *"the theology of natural science* is in perfect harmony with *the theology of the Bible."* [14] This affinity of nature and the Bible was particularly strong in the moral order. What Enlightenment common sense told us were self-evident principles of morality conformed to Scripture. "So complete is the coincidence," argued Francis Wayland, the Baptist author of the most popular college texts of the day, "as to afford irrefragable proof that the Bible contains the moral laws of the universe; and hence, that the Author of the universe—that is of natural religion—is also the Author of the Scriptures." [15]

Charles Finney was typical of the evangelical educators in combining concern for eternal souls with respect for science. Finney was especially interested in the practical applications of science to revivals. Whereas earlier Calvinists insisted that revivals were simply the work of God, Finney introduced planning techniques to make revivals succeed. Producing a revival, said Finney, was just as scientific as producing a crop of grain. God did it, but he used means that we can predict and control.

Charles Finney was, in fact, one of the progenitors of modern advertising technique. Rather than concentrate on just the message, he analyzed the audience and the conditions under which people were likely to respond. His pioneering work paved the way for later twentieth-century radio and TV evangelists to master mass communication techniques.

Primitivism

American respect for science often went hand in hand with a trait among revivalists that might at first seem wholly unrelated: the desire to go back to the practices of the New Testament churches. This principle, called primitivism, paralleled the scientific method. In both, one starts by freeing oneself of traditions and prejudices, thus getting back to the facts, either the facts of nature or the facts of the Bible.

An excellent example of primitivism was Alexander Campbell (1788–1866), founder of one of the most successful new denominations, the Disciples of Christ. Campbell appealed to popular audiences in the western regions of the country; but his writings were filled with appeals to logic, natural law, and the "common sense" principles of a Christian version of Enlightenment philosophy. One of the early colleges of the Disciples was in fact named for Francis

• • •

Bacon, the seventeenth-century progenitor of the scientific method. Bacon was such a popular figure among evangelicals generally, that one historian has described their typical stance as the "beatification of Bacon."[16]

Campbell's appeals to Baconian science fit not only with the spirit of the times, but also with the revolutionary approach to Christianity for which he became famous. The church would rely on the facts of New Testament Christianity alone and so follow only primitive Christian practices. So, for instance, it would include the New Testament ceremony of foot-washing, but not allow musical instruments, which are not mentioned as part of New Testament worship. This extended the Puritan principle of "the Bible alone" as the authority for the church. But this principle was now reinforced by the popular Enlightenment conception of true scientific reason. Just as Enlightenment science believed that if the proper methods were followed all rational persons would agree with the laws thus discovered, so Campbell believed that a new fellowship, built on the Bible and scientific reason, would eventually draw all true Christians to it, and hence end the divisions of Christendom.

Back to the Bible and the New Order for the Ages

This "back to the Bible" theme, which became one of the most pervasively popular slogans throughout much of American Protestantism, fit perfectly with the Enlightenment scientific method of starting over. The nation itself was perceived of as an experiment to establish a *novus ordo seclorum* (new order for the ages), as the slogan on the one-dollar bill puts it. So many popular churches and sects likewise saw themselves as a new Christian order for the ages. They believed their renewed group would then become the basis for the renewal of civilization.

Such appeals were democratic, since they challenged existing authorities, based on traditions. The Bible was crucial in such challenges, since the reformer could always appeal to the accepted Protestant principle that the Bible was the only supreme authority, standing above all traditions. The common person who stood by the plain, common sense meaning of the Bible could confidently disregard the authority of educated clergy or prestigious churches.

Such popular appeals were effective since almost all American Protestants agreed in principle that the true church and the true civ-

• • •

ilization would have to be based on the Bible. One could hardly overestimate the degree to which American Protestants thought of the United States as a Bible civilization.[17] The Bible was widely revered as an authority on all subjects, including history and the sciences as well as theology and ethics. Throughout the nineteenth century American school children read lessons from *McGuffey's Readers* with titles such as "The Bible the Best of Classics" and "My Mother's Bible."[18]

Americans often defined themselves in biblical terms and imagery. They followed New England Puritan precedents in this regard, still speaking of themselves as a New Israel and a covenanted people. The covenantal concept—that the success and prosperity of the nation was the result of blessings from God and hence dependent on national morality—was an important practical belief, influential in every political movement for moral reform. Moreover, biblical cadences influenced rhetorical usage; the speeches of Abraham Lincoln are a prominent example. The Bible provided much of their literature, and their knowledge of history was confined largely to biblical history.

The idea of a new order for the ages based on the Bible had dramatic implications for the future. The Bible, regarded as equally reliable for prophecy and history, spoke of a "millennial" age, or a thousand-year reign of Christ, as the culmination of human history on earth. Many Christians through the ages, and some American Protestants in the nineteenth century, took the millennium to mean a literal one thousand year reign following Jesus' return to earth. The dominant nineteenth-century American Protestant view, however, was what is called a "postmillennial" view; that is, that Jesus would not return until *after* the millennium.[19] According to this view, the predicted millennium would be a golden age, the reign of the *spirit* of Christ, or the Holy Spirit. This would be the last great age in world history marked by great awakenings, the evangelization of the world through missions, and the turning of the nations to Christ.

Missions

Nineteenth-century American Protestants typically thought this new age was beginning and that they, together with their British brothers and sisters, were its vanguard. Forgetting by then most of their anti-British prejudices of the Revolutionary era, American Protestants typically identified themselves with the worldwide advances of the

• • •

essentially Protestant Victorian empire. They saw their cause as part of a trans-Atlantic effort in which English-speaking people would lead the advance of Protestantism throughout the world.

Concretely, this meant the organization of concerted foreign missionary efforts, a practice that was not well developed among most Protestants prior to the nineteenth century. The spread of evangelical doctrine, with its emphasis on conversions to save souls, inspired efforts to preach the Gospel in non-Christian lands. The American Board of Commissioners for Foreign Missions (ABCFM), an interdenominational agency dominated by New England Congregationalists, was founded in 1810 and became the leading foreign mission agency of the era. The ABCFM was particularly successful in its mission to the islands of Hawaii. Altogether, about 2,000 Americans served abroad in missionary efforts from 1810–1870, laying the base for a vast expansion of missionary efforts by the early twentieth century.[20]

Depending on one's perspective, such mission consciousness can be seen as simply a dimension of Anglo imperialism or a way of tempering the economic and military aspects of imperialism with genuine spiritual and moral concerns. Or both. In any case, such millennial zeal made the nineteenth century the "great century" of missions, far exceeding the total foreign missionary efforts of any earlier era.[21]

Reform

Millennial imagery had important implications for Americans at home as well. Americans regarded themselves, and were widely regarded, as "a city on the hill" for the advancement of civilization. They combined classic republicanism, Protestant dominance, and religious freedom into a belief that American civilization would be in the forefront of an outpouring of the Holy Spirit that would usher in the last millennial golden age of world civilization.

Such an age would combine spiritual, social, and political advances. Not only would individual hearts be changed in revivals, but so would the nation, as biblical principles were voluntarily applied to all aspects of life. Vices would be eliminated, and slavery, wars, and oppressions would cease. Evangelicals accordingly formed a host of societies to combat what they saw as the leading vices of their era, such as duelling, prostitution, alcohol, and Sabbath-breaking. These, together with home and foreign missionary societies, Bible societies, Sunday school societies, tract societies, and education societies, formed

• • •

*A 1846 temperance tract. The evangelical empire tried to
reform a violent society in part by prohibiting alcohol.*

what has been called an "evangelical united front." Most of these
societies had British counterparts and fostered a transatlantic dimension in the movement. In the United States the combined budgets of
this evangelical empire rivalled those of the federal government.
Evangelical institutions were thus providing some of the nation's leading
forces for cultural change.

We can return to Charles Finney as an illustration. Not only was
he the leading revivalist of his day, but he was also in the forefront

• • •

of American social reform. He and other evangelists with whom he worked closely were leaders in the often unpopular causes of the abolition of slavery and greater equality for women. Oberlin College in Ohio, Finney's base after 1835, was the Americas' first coeducational college. Moreover, it was notorious as a hotbed of abolitionist sentiment and a center for the underground railroad.

Divisions within the Evangelical Camp

The existence of slavery suggests that making the United States into a Bible-based nation which would usher in the millennial age was much easier to preach than to put into practice. For one thing, evangelicals were divided into competing denominations. By the mid-nineteenth century, the Methodists and the Baptists were the largest religious groups, followed by the Presbyterians and the Congregationalists. These accounted for 83 percent of American Protestants and claimed populations that accounted for over half of Americans.[22] Underneath their doctrinal rivalries, there was also a tradition of some cooperation and, in principle, considerable unity of purpose.

In practice, however, these groups were divided more sharply by social realities. Class differences separated staid traditionalists who placed more value on higher education from popular informal groups. Even deeper divisions were ethnic. America was a land of immigrants, and religious affiliations were usually the strongest elements in providing an immigrant group with a distinct identity. So many Lutherans, for instance, tended to remain aloof from other Protestants, not simply because of a slightly different theological heritage, but also because of German versus Anglo traditions.

By the mid-nineteenth century, however, the deepest religious divisions among the dominant evangelicals had become sectional. In 1844 the largest national denomination, the Methodist church, divided in the North and South over the slavery issue. The next year they were followed by the Baptists. Presbyterians had already divided more-or-less sectionally over a complicated set of issues, including abolitionism. These schisms in the nation's most influential denominations were widely perceived as foreshadowing an inevitable division in the nation itself. Evangelical Christianity, rather than being a bonding force for the union, was becoming a source of disunity and bitterness. Abolitionists argued vehemently that, based on the Bible, the spirit of Christianity forbids the enslavement of one race by another. Slav-

• • •

ery's defenders in the South argued just as vehemently that the Bible itself did not condemn slavery, but took it for granted. Each side hurled charges of heresy and hypocrisy at the other. By giving the issues cosmic significance, religion thus helped heat up the sectional rivalries and increased the likelihood of secession and war.

The American Paradox

The institution of black slavery itself illustrates poignantly a central paradox in the character of American culture. At a time when the United States was known for both its Christianity and its concerns for human rights, not only was slavery practiced, but in some respects it was more severe and inhumane than the slavery of less modern epochs. For one thing, modern American slavery involved the enslavement of one race by another. It was built on the premise that it was permissible to do to blacks what would have been considered a violation of sacred human rights if done to whites. Moreover, black slaves in America were treated in some respects as though they were not humans. This was particularly conspicuous in the legal definitions of slavery. American slave codes treated slaves as though they were simply property. Before the law they were treated like farm animals or furniture. Not only could they be bought and sold, but their servitude was permanent and transmitted from generation to generation. Being defined as property, they had no rights of family, and so children could be separated from parents, husbands from wives, and "sold down the river."

These laws might not have been so astounding if they were typical of slavery in all times and places. The fact was, however, that the American system was unusual. Throughout history, the status of slaves was often a temporary condition. Moreover, even in Latin America, slaves typically had a better legal status. For instance, the Roman Catholic church recognized them as persons who had rights of marriage and family. In practice, Latin American slave conditions were often more severe than those of their North American counterparts. Moreover, the harshness of North American slavery was sometimes tempered by kindness and charity at the personal level. But legally, the arrangements in Protestant America were strikingly more harsh.

A number of factors contributed to such harsh codes. Racism, reinforced by wide cultural differences between transplanted Europeans and imported Africans, was certainly a major force. The firm

• • •

*Harriet Beecher Stowe's best-seller brought the American
paradox home to many.*

conviction of slaveowners that Africans were inferior was essential to
rationalizing such a massively discriminatory system. Just as important, however, was the economic factor.[23]

The economic factor in U.S. definitions of slavery has been aptly
depicted as reflecting "the dynamics of unopposed capitalism." Latin
American slavery, which was defined earlier than in the United States,
was based more on a medieval model, with some affinities to serfdom.
Slaves were recognized as persons by the church, even if they were

• • •

bound in servitude. In America, however, settled at the beginning of the modern capitalist era, there were no other strong institutions or traditions to oppose the capitalist motives. So, as has been true in important segments of American life, the question was resolved on purely technical grounds, rather than on religious, moral, or even personal ones. Ultimately, the economic dimension of life, combined with the rationalization supplied by racism, defined the status of blacks.[24]

The irony of this arrangement reveals a deeper irony in Western civilization. Modern economic and technological superiority has depended on the ability to differentiate and isolate areas of life that can be treated on a purely rational basis. In contrast to medieval and most other periods in which spiritual considerations can pervade everything, modern Westerners have almost entirely rationalized some major activities, such as economic life. The Reformation inadvertently contributed to this by despiritualizing the medieval world of saints, sacred places, and miraculous powers. In general, the more rationalized outlook has helped the Protestant nations economically.[25] The price, however, was that Westerners were removing spiritual considerations from certain aspects of their lives and the price was vast.

The Western world, especially those parts with a Protestant heritage, however, were also producing revolutionary views of humanity and human rights that would eventually provide a counterforce to some of the depersonalizing tendencies of modern rationalized civilization.

So by the end of the eighteenth century, with changing views of the rights of individuals, reinforced by revolutionary ideology, many Americans began to question the anomaly of slavery. After the Revolution, some churches in both the North and South took stands condemning slavery and slaveowning. However, such stands prevailed only in areas where the economic and social reasons for perpetuating slavery were not strong. Hence, slavery was gradually eliminated in the North after the Revolution. But in the upper South, where antislavery sentiment was strong for a time, both churches and politicians soon found that they would lose their constituencies if they took a strong stance. In the deep South, more economically dependent on the slavery system, abolitionism never had a chance. After Nat Turner's slave insurrection in Virginia in 1831 and the rise of militant abolitionism in the North, most white southerners retreated to defenses of slavery as a God-ordained social system. By the 1840s the differing

• • •

moral perceptions in the two regions were so strong that the major churches split.

Slave Religion

Because of their harsh treatment in Christendom, the slaves themselves eventually made a sharp distinction between Christianity and Christendom and adopted the former as the central basis for their culture.[26] While Christianity became important to preserving the identities of many other immigrant groups, the Africans who were brought to North America were removed as far as possible from their African religious heritages. Members of tribes were scattered, so that formal religious practices varied for Africans on any given plantation and were difficult to retain. What they preserved longest were African styles and practices that various local African religions had in common. Eventually, many of these were incorporated into their Christianity. Afro-Americans, like many white Americans, also retained interest in occult magical practices such as voodoo. However, unlike some Latin American and Caribbean slave communities where African religions survived intact, by the time of the emancipation in the United States virtually the only organized religion among blacks was Christianity. Not all blacks were religious, of course, and black culture contained as many paradoxes between Christian practices and their opposites as white culture. Nonetheless, by the time of the Civil War, Christianity was overwhelmingly the religion of the blacks.

This remarkable cultural development, like so much else in American history, dates back to the Great Awakening. The openness and expressiveness of the Baptist and later the Methodist services had some affinities to African religious styles and allowed for the introduction of more demonstrative and ecstatic practices. Moreover, while more traditional Protestantism tended to emphasize hierarchical order and deference to authority, evangelicalism, while not being socially revolutionary, presented Christianity as a religion of the poor in which values would be reordered. According to evangelicalism, the life-styles of the aristocracy were evidence of moral degeneracy. The simple Christian, no matter how poor materially, could be morally and spiritually superior in a higher realm of reality.[27]

The first substantial numbers of blacks were converted to Christianity during the eighteenth-century awakenings, especially in the South during the 1750s and 1760s. Though blacks usually attended

• • •

churches with whites, a number of independent black preachers emerged, in both the North and the South by the end of the eighteenth century.

The most famous of these was Richard Allen (1760–1831). Born a slave in Pennsylvania, Allen was converted to Methodism, earned his freedom, and in 1794 founded an independent black congregation. In 1816 he and other black preachers in Philadelphia took the further revolutionary step of establishing a black denomination, the African Methodist Episcopal Church. Allen thus helped set an American pattern in which the church would be the most important agency for establishing black leadership and independence.

Although in the South there were sometimes a few independent black churches, most black churchgoers sat in separate sections of white churches. On slave plantations, where the majority of blacks lived, formal church activity was usually under white supervision. Nevertheless, increasingly during the nineteenth century and especially in the two decades preceding the Civil War, blacks were adopting evangelical Christianity.

The major impetus for this transformation of black culture came from within their own communities. Once Christianity was adopted on a wide scale, it became extraordinarily important for binding the black community together, introducing a new sense of communal identity. The most meaningful worship for plantation blacks often took place in secret meetings in cabins or "hush harbors," to which they would "steal away." Spirituals, which were composed and sung communally, became a leading cultural expression.[28] During the Civil War, a white Union officer observed of black regiments that, with a few exceptions, the only songs they would sing were spirituals.[29]

In the spirituals and throughout their religious expressions blacks typically saw themselves as a biblical people. This belief, found in the popular religion of many other Americans, was accentuated and shaped in unique ways by the black experience. For one thing, black culture was of necessity oral. The biblical narrative, eloquently repeated and sung, became accordingly a primary means of building self-identity. Typically, the slaves saw themselves as new Israelites, enslaved in Egypt. They celebrated their own version of a millennial hope when they preached or sang of the coming day of God's deliverance, when a new Moses would rise up to lead them out of Egypt,

· · ·

or Joshua would lead them to the promised land. They could rejoice in the hope of the "day of jubilee" when Jesus would deliver them or they would be released to heaven.

Such understandings had double meanings. Their primary meaning was clearly spiritual and otherworldly. For an oppressed people the hope of heaven where one could "lay my burden down" is not to be treated lightly.[30] The overwhelming testimony of the slaves themselves was that the heavenly hope had a real literal meaning. Nonetheless, such hope is by no means incompatible with hope for deliverance in this life also, just as the Israelites were literally rescued by God.

Only occasionally in North America did this hope take revolutionary form. When it did, as most famously in Nat Turner's brief insurrection in 1831, biblical imagery was central. Turner saw himself as literally a new prophet of God.

Totally denied access to political power, black culture in North America developed around the churches and leadership among the clergy. On the plantations black preachers often became the respected leaders of the community, and among free blacks both North and South, black leadership emerged in churches. Deprived of so much else, Bible religion for blacks—even more than for most of their white contemporaries—provided crucial resources to shape their views.

NONEVANGELICAL AMERICA

A Central Theme

For better or for worse, evangelical Protestantism, because of its dominant role at a formative stage, is crucial to understanding the role of religion in shaping mainstream American culture.

On the other hand, just as crucial is the counterpoint that American culture is uniquely pluralistic. One of the most pivotal themes in American religious and cultural history is the interplay between these two motifs, Protestantism and pluralism. Neither makes sense in the American experience without the other.

. . .

Sequoyah, inventor of a Cherokee alphabet, opposed missions to his people.

Native Americans as Outsiders

Even though evangelical Protestantism—while sometimes an ally of oppression—transformed much of black culture in North America, among native Americans both evangelicals and other Christians had a more peripheral, though equally ironic, impact.

During the colonial era, Catholic missions to the Indians were the most extensive in areas that eventually became the United States. Jesuit missionaries, of whom Father Jacques Marquette (1637–1675)

• • •

A newspaper printed in Sequoyah's Cherokee alphabet and in English.

is best remembered, made heroic efforts, sometimes with modest success, to evangelize the tribes of the upper Midwest. The most tangible artifacts of Catholic missionary endeavors is the chain of Franciscan missions in California, begun in the late eighteenth century by Junipero Serra (1713–1784). These missions were built as part of an effort to establish a Spanish presence in California, but also won substantial number of converts.

Protestant missions to the Indians increased with the Great Awakening of the eighteenth century and enjoyed occasional success. Nonetheless, most native Americans resisted Christian incursions and continued their traditional religious practices.

The native Americans generally perceived that, when missionaries

• • •

appeared, invasion could not be far behind. In fact, individual missionaries, although certainly trying to change Indian culture by the introduction of Christianity, were also attempting to provide an alternative to the more violent imperialism of the white peoples. White culture, as we have seen, was never simply Christian, or simply aggressive-acquisitive, but always a paradoxical mix. Time and again the story of Christian missions in North America was the story of some missionary successes, establishment of relatively stable communities of Christian Indians, and then the destruction of those communities by other white settlers; whites and Indians were frequently at war, ever renewed by the whites' insatiable quest for new settlements. War barbarizes the outlook of everyone involved, so that large numbers of white Americans came to believe that "the only good Indian is a dead Indian."

A striking example of the injustices arising even from the most controlled of such encounters is the nineteenth-century mission to the Cherokees. During the early decades of the century, missionaries successfully evangelized large numbers of Cherokees living in eastern Tennessee, western North Carolina, and northern Georgia. The mission became a model for Christian civilization-building. The Cherokees patterned their government on the United States Constitution, built schools and churches, and were developing an educated native leadership. Nonetheless, other whites not interested in the mission wanted the Cherokee territories and insisted that the Cherokees be displaced to the West. The president of the United States was Andrew Jackson, a Presbyterian who made a name for himself partly by fighting Indians; he shared the dominant views of white westerners that they were always in a virtual state of war with all Indians. Jackson accordingly ignored the Indians' rights. In the face of an adverse ruling from Chief Justice Marshall's Supreme Court, Jackson reportedly quipped: "John Marshall has made his decision; now let him enforce it." Despite the bitter protests both of missionaries and Indians, most of the Cherokees were removed to what is now Oklahoma, amid much suffering along a "Trail of Tears."

Such treatment of the Indians meant that, even when the missionaries were most successful, the majority of Indians would remain outside the dominant culture. For most of the native Americans, their traditional religions would increasingly become important in attempting to preserve tribal identity.

• • •

The Catholic Church: Outsiders with an Insider Heritage

Much of American history and politics has revolved around ethno-religious conflicts, although the mythology of the dominant Protestant groups who emphasize assimilation and consensus has played this down in the retelling of the nation's history. Nonetheless, except for the native Americans, the United States is a nation of immigrants and much of the nation's political history can be understood as efforts of the earliest dominant groups to keep control. Race, ethnicity, economics, and religion are all major forces in these struggles; but their interrelationships follow no simple pattern. The elimination of substantial religious differences between the dominant white community and the black community did little to alter blacks' social and economic subordination. On the other hand, in the case of Roman Catholics, religious prejudices were more important than race and often more important than nationality. So, for example, German Protestants could assimilate more quickly into the mainstream Anglo-Protestant culture than could German Catholics. Moreover, the long-standing Protestant versus Catholic cold war had helped create some deep national antagonisms that were carried over to America.

Catholics themselves were divided ethnically, so that a good bit of Catholic history in America is a combination of external struggles against dominant Protestant culture and internal frictions among competing Catholic national traditions.

The Catholic church in America through the early national era was small and dominated by English gentry from Maryland. Despite the anti-Catholicism implicit in the American republican tradition, many of these English Catholics supported the American Revolution. The promise of religious freedom in the United States was preferable to legal restrictions for Catholics under British law. Because of the lack of adequate numbers of priests, this early American Catholic church developed its own style, including "lay trustees" providing some congregational governance over their own affairs, and a "plain style" of worship.

Such early trends in American Catholicism were, however, soon overwhelmed by massive immigration. Between 1790 and 1830 the Catholic population grew almost ten times to about three hundred thousand and then between 1830 and 1860 grew ten more times to over three million, almost a hundred-fold increase in seventy years.

· · ·

By the end of this period the Catholic church was larger than any single Protestant denomination, although Catholics represented only about one-tenth of the total American population.

Because the overwhelming numbers of Catholics in this era were foreign-born, the position of Catholics in American life was largely that of insecure outsiders. Nonetheless, the Catholic heritage was an insider one, since Catholicism was the official state religion in most of the nations from which Catholics emigrated. The political dimensions of international Catholicism helped keep long-standing Protestant religious prejudices alive. The recently arrived Catholic immigrants in America had to face not only these prejudices but also ethnic resentments and biases against the poor.

Poverty was especially an issue with regard to the Irish immigrants who began to flood Northeastern cities in increasingly large numbers beginning in the 1820s. Most of the Irish were fleeing their native country because of a famine which became especially severe in the 1840s. Their poverty compounded resentments, both within and outside the Catholic church, regarding their ethnic ways. Within the churches they brought an authoritarian style and an emphasis on ritual, devotion, and elaborate decoration with artifacts dedicated to saints. Irish Catholics also brought with them a tradition of political authoritarianism, often supported by the church, and thus, despite their deep loyalty to their new land, were soon perceived by established Protestants as a threat to American ways. Prejudices against Irish Catholics were sometimes almost as severe as prejudices against blacks.

The other major immigrant group swelling the Catholic population at this time was the Germans. The massive German Catholic immigration tended to be farmers who moved to the Midwest in the "German triangle" area from Cincinnati to St. Louis to Milwaukee. Although typically not so poor as the Irish, they were separated from mainstream America not only by their religion and ethnicity, but also by their language. For many in the German communities this was an important source of pride and identity. They were in general not eagerly awaiting the day when they would become like Protestant Americans, but proud of what they regarded as cultural and religious superiority. Preserving their language was hence an important ingredient in preserving the faith. "Language saves faith" was a typical slogan. Consistent with this outlook, Germans were leaders among American Catholics in insisting on building parochial school systems

. . .

as alternatives to the essentially Protestant public schools. Such policies helped maintain closely knit ethno-religious communities that preserved solid German and Catholic identity for generations.[31]

Sociologically, people in immigrant communities were very dependent on each other, and churches in such communities were important social centers, often more important than their churches were in their native countries. Such communities and churches also tended to be conservative, placing a strong emphasis on preserving ethnic and religious traditions as a means of maintaining identity and communal cohesiveness.[32]

Protestant Outsiders

Such characteristics were not unique to Catholic immigrant communities. For instance, many German immigrants were Protestant, mostly Lutheran, but many were Reformed church members (Calvinists). Although for Protestants it was somewhat easier, especially in the second generation, to leave the immigrant community and to blend with the larger American society, many German settlers, especially in the Midwest, retained their ethno-religious communities and identities in much the same way as German Catholics. This was especially true of groups with strong Lutheran heritages, which did not have an exact British counterpart. The Missouri Synod Lutherans, founded in 1847, preserved use of the German language, separate school systems at all levels, and a strongly conservative theological tradition. Many other Lutheran groups, such as the Scandinavians who later settled Minnesota, did much the same. So did most other ethno-religious communities, including various ethnic Reformed, Methodists, and Baptists. As Garrison Keillor exemplified in his radio show, "A Prairie Home Companion," even in the late twentieth century the best way to understand many American communities, especially in the Midwest, is to find out their ethno-religious identities.

Common Values

Despite these ethnic and religious diversities, most of the population subscribed to many common values. Almost all had inherited largely the same Judeo-Christian heritage and believed in a moral system built upon the Ten Commandments. God was to be reverenced and worshipped; parents and those in authority were to be respected. They believed people should control their passions and desires, not

• • •

commit murder or adultery, steal, lie, or succumb to envy and greed. In general, these precepts were interpreted in a typically early modern republican fashion, emphasizing in moderate ways the rights and responsibilities of individuals. Individual character was seen as the chief force in history, and virtue of the individual was seen as the key to a healthy society.

The conventionally shared outlook of the day was in many ways conservative, more conservative than we might expect from reading the literary leaders of the era. A study of the letters and diaries of ordinary Americans reveals a considerable commonality in religious outlook, regardless of denomination or religion. Religion, which was prominent in these ordinary private expressions, was largely a matter of accepting God's providence. One should not expect to control one's destiny; but rather, one should learn to accept what God willed. Nineteenth-century Americans, for whom life was dramatically precarious, were closer to the Puritan attitudes of learning how to die and how to cultivate a submissive spirit in the meantime, than to what later developed as emphases on personal fulfillment and control. These earlier attitudes were strikingly different from later times in that the self was seen as a spiritual entity to be controlled and overcome, rather than celebrated. The individual was important in the sense that one had no one to blame but oneself for one's actions. But personal success was often judged in terms of overcoming overly ambitious aspirations, rather than, as in the twentieth century, being able to surmount any obstacle.[33]

Diversity: A Changing America

While such commonalities crossed many traditional religious lines, tradition itself was beginning to be challenged in pre-Civil War America. New alternative views seemed present everywhere. This was especially true of religion, which was the principal channel for ideological innovation. Nineteenth-century America was in the forefront of nations in allowing religious freedom. The ideologies of the new republic encouraged new beginnings. And vast tracts of land offered space for religious and practical experimentation.

The result was that the United States was remarkable not only in providing a haven to preserve many imported traditions; it was also remarkably fertile soil for the growth of new religious movements. Most of the variations developed within the older Anglo-Protes-

• • •

tant communities. These communities were dominated religiously by evangelicalism which generated a constant religious intensity. Part of this intensity focused on renewals of, and attempted improvements on, more-or-less traditional evangelicalism itself; another part sparked new religious emphases or movements.

Among these were some liberal or progressive movements. As a rule, such views usually develop among well-established elites, whose social position is secure enough to seek change without fearing ostracism. In general, groups in firm control can afford to be liberal or tolerant, while less secure groups will tend to enforce strict doctrinal or behavioral codes as a means to preserve their distinct identities. Because of their elite statuses, liberal groups in America, despite relatively small size, have had disproportional influence on the public culture.

The Literary Renaissance

Such disproportional influence is particularly true of a small group, mostly New Englanders, who were associated with the American literary renaissance in the mid-nineteenth century: Ralph Waldo Emerson, Henry David Thoreau, Nathaniel Hawthorne, Herman Melville, Margaret Fuller, and Walt Whitman.

In their day, most of them were so progressive that they were outsiders intellectually, even if insiders socially. It is true that Emerson became very popular on the polite lecture circuit and Whitman's poetry was sometimes patriotic or sentimental enough to gain a following. But most of American intellectual life was considerably more conservative. So the talents of Thoreau or Melville, for instance, were not appreciated much in their day. American academic life was still dominated by the churches. Nevertheless, the literary elite, because of their talents and an openness that made them forerunners of future trends, have been far better remembered than those, mostly theologians, who were considered the intellectual powers of their day.[34]

Romanticism and Transcendentalism

The American literary renaissance in the decades following 1830 was shaped especially by European romanticism. Romanticism took many forms, but for our purposes its most important emphasis was the primacy of the spiritual over the material dimension of ordinary reality. American culture was intensely practical, built primarily on

• • •

technical mastery of the material world. So most Americans valued
the scientific ways of looking at things emphasized during the Enlightenment. They looked for fixed laws of nature that could be ob-
jectively discovered, which could be supplemented by various traditional
Christian beliefs and experiences to bring one in touch with another
higher supernatural or spiritual realm. So the usual outlook was that
of a two-layered reality: the natural and the supernatural. Romanticism, a broad mood with many varieties, typically stressed that the
superior spiritual dimension of reality could be discovered in ordinary
experience only if individuals remained open to the subjective, intu-
itive, imaginative, and emotive dimensions of their experience. One
could intuitively see through the natural to the transcendent. Thus,
special revelations became relatively less important, while the creative dimensions of each unique individual became relatively more
important.

The archetypical American romantic of the most progressive or
transcendentalist variety was Ralph Waldo Emerson (1803–1882).
Emerson was reared in the progressive part of New England around
Boston, where by the early 1800s many people had already turned
from Puritan Calvinism to Unitarianism. Developing about the same
time as the American Revolution, Unitarians combined an Enlightenment optimism concerning human abilities with more-or-less traditional Protestant teachings. Such moderate liberals were influential in
the cultural center around Boston and controlled Harvard College, for
instance. Emerson became a Unitarian minister, but in the 1830s he
resigned. His turn from rational Enlightenment optimism to more
radical transcendentalism in fact shocked his moderate Unitarian friends.
When at the Harvard Divinity School commencement in 1838 Emerson declared that each individual could be a "newborn bard of the
Holy Ghost," Harvard professor Andrews Norton felt it necessary to
publish a scathing disclaimer. Nonetheless, Emerson preached his
radical doctrines of the ability of each individual to know the divine
directly. This was an exciting doctrine in the emerging democratic
culture in which deference to spiritual authority remained strong. In
contrast to the self-deprecating conventional piety of the day, "self-
reliance" was the watchword of Emerson's gospel.

Somewhat like the earlier outbursts of spiritual egalitarianism during the English Civil Wars and the later countercultural movement of
the 1960s, radical American romanticism came at a time of unusual

• • •

upheaval and openness. The 1840s, especially, was a decade of unrest and experimentation. Spiritually motivated groups formed experimental communities, such as the transcendentalists' Brook Farm, established near Boston in the 1840s. People wanted to go back to nature, as Henry David Thoreau did at Walden Pond. Others from the well-to-do classes were looking for spiritual realities in more exotic movements. Many middle-class people were experimenting with mesmerism, or hypnotism, which was believed to provide access to spiritual reality. Other sorts of spiritualism that were widely popular, especially among middle-class New England women, involved mediums who could make contact with spirits from the past and control other psychic phenomena. Often related to this innovative religious spirit were health regimens, including looser clothes (such as bloomers) for women, water cures, and vegetarian diets.

Sectarian Innovations

Though such religious and quasireligious experimentation was found primarily in the older Anglo-Protestant communities, it was not confined to the leisure classes. Less educated and less prosperous people provided the primary constituencies for alternative sets of religious innovations, departing from the evangelical mainstream by moving in a sectarian direction. A sect is a religious group that has very sharp boundaries of belief and behavior separating its members from the larger society. In general, such movements appeal to poorer and less educated people who are more likely to feel alienated from the prevailing order and hence open to a radically new value system.

The general rule one can glean from American history is that more sectarian and economically poorer groups preach doctrines that heighten emphasis on spectacular and miraculous divine interventions in history, through special exclusive revelations, promise of a dramatic end to the present age, and the inauguration of a millennial kingdom. Innovations among the more well-to-do classes tend, on the other hand, to be inclusive, emphasizing the availability of spiritual forces to all people, as in transcendentalism or spiritualism.

A classic example of American sectarian innovation are the Seventh-Day Adventists. The Adventist movement developed among followers of William Miller (1782–1849), who predicted that the end of the world and the return of Christ would take place between March 21, 1843 and March 21, 1844. Miller's teachings were accentuations

• • •

of many typical American evangelical traits. His millennial calculations were based on quasi-scientific mathematical calculations and literal interpretations of biblical prophecies. As the days for the predicted end approached, Miller's teachings created sensation in evangelical America. He gained perhaps 100,000 followers, some of whom sold their goods and ascended mountains for the final hours of the wait. When Jesus failed to materialize by March 21, 1844, Miller recalculated and discovered that October 22, 1844 was the correct deadline. With the world still intact after that date, many followers dispersed. Some, however, remained true believers. The most significant group of Seventh-Day Adventists eventually followed the leadership of Ellen White (1827–1915), a prophetess who incorporated many of the popular health regimens of the day into church teachings.[35] Sylvester Graham of graham cracker fame, and John Harvey Kellogg of cereal fame, became the most successful advocates of the Adventist meatless health diet programs.

Politically, the most significant sectarian innovators were the Mormons, organized by Joseph Smith (1805–1844) in New York state in 1830. Whereas Adventists accentuated evangelical Protestant themes, Mormonism, or the Church of Jesus Christ of Latter-day Saints, was a new religion combining previous Christian elements with unique teachings. Smith taught, for instance, that there was more than one god, and that the principal deity who ruled the universe had a body. Through direct revelations Smith found resolutions to the competing religious claims of the day. He claimed that an angel led him to a set of inscribed golden tablets deposited in the fourth century A.D. by American Indian descendants of the lost tribes of Israel. Smith translated these, which became the Book of Mormon, one of the bases for unique Mormon teachings. Smith and his followers soon established a community in Kirtland, Ohio. Another group moved to Independence, Missouri, which Smith claimed was revealed to him to be the site of the original Garden of Eden and center for a coming millennial age. There, on the frontier, they were severely persecuted by other settlers.

The Mormons then consolidated their efforts in Nauvoo, Illinois. Voting as a block, they became a significant political force in the state. In 1844 (the same year the Adventists were ascending to mountaintops) Smith announced his candidacy for president of the United States. He continued to have revelations, and secretly taught that he and some

• • •

Salt Lake City in the 1860s provided an alternative version of America as the new Israel.

other Mormon leaders were allowed to have several wives. Threatened with exposure (his own first wife apparently did not know), Smith closed a dissident press in Nauvoo. This violation of the freedom of the press led neighboring Illinoisans to abandon whatever commitment they had to freedom of religion. Smith and his brother were arrested, but an irate mob dragged them from jail and murdered them.

The main body of Mormons then made a trek to Utah under the leadership of Brigham Young (1801–1877). There they found for themselves a promised land which they turned into an ordered and stable new "Zion." While many other American religious groups talked of a return to biblical models, Mormons acted it out. They lived in what amounted to a continuing biblical time, with ongoing prophets, priesthoods, and miracles and promises of a millennial age when they would rule the earth.[36]

Even at a distance, American tolerance of Mormonism was strained. In 1857 President James Buchanan sent a military expedition to bring the territory under more than nominal federal control. One motive was pressure to eliminate polygyny. The Mormons resisted and the United States backed away from full-fledged war. Not until after dealing

• • •

with slavery and reconstruction in the South did the government return to the "Mormon problem." During the 1880s the government enforced antipolygamy legislation and threw some Mormon leaders in jail. In 1890, the Mormon church president announced a divinely sanctioned end to polygyny. By the twentieth century Mormons became some of the most patriotic of Americans and champions of traditional values.[37]

In the mid-nineteenth century, however, not only the Mormons, but a number of other American religious groups attempted to radically redefine what many regarded as the most sacred institution of Victorian society—the monogamous family. One group that was already doing so for close to a century was Shakers. Founded around the time of the American Revolution by Mother Ann Lee (1736–1784), Shaker communities did away with the traditional family entirely, insisting on celibacy for communal members.

At the other end of the spectrum was John Humphrey Noyes's Oneida community in upstate New York. Noyes (1811–1886), a radical Christian perfectionist, taught that perfect love should allow "complex marriage" and sexual relations between all the men and women in the community. Noyes's radical notions on sexuality were formulated in the 1840s, about the same time that those of the Mormon's were also made public. Like the Mormons, Noyes's community was constantly harassed by outraged Victorians, and by 1879 Noyes had to give up teaching complex marriage.[38]

The Age of the Spirit and the Woman's Place

All three of these communal groups were millennialists, announcing dramatic versions of the prevalent evangelical doctrines that a new age of the spirit was at hand. In the millennial age traditional relationships would be restructured or done away with as humanity discovered a whole new value system. Quakers had already announced such teaching in the 1600s. Radical sects of the nineteenth century suggested variations on the theme.

Such trends had particular significance for revaluing of roles of women. Some of the sects, notably the Shakers and the Seventh-day Adventists, had women leaders. Others, such as the Mormons, taught a rigid doctrine of the subordination of women. More important in a broad cultural sense than these particulars, however, was the mainstream evangelical belief that civilization was on the verge of a new

• • •

spiritual or millennial age, encouraging some pioneering rethinking about social relationships, especially of women's roles. Such trends which were supported by democratic rhetoric of human equality also fit well with and augmented the more open romantic spirit in many segments of America from the 1830s to the 1850s.

The prevailing view of women, however, was conservative and this view was reinforced by both Christianity and a romantic spirit. Western civilization was built around ordered hierarchical relationships. In such hierarchies women were almost always subordinated to men. Families, not individuals, were the basic unit of society, and men were the legal heads of families. Christianity, although in principle limiting the harshness of the subordination, generally was used to support these social arrangements. Moreover, because of explicit New Testament statements and tradition, the governance of the church was almost always confined to men, and in almost all Christian groups women were not ordained into the ministry or allowed to preach. Such traditions were particularly strong among the major outsider groups in the nineteenth century, including Catholics, other non-Anglo immigrant groups, and in the South. In the influential Anglo community of the North, patriarchy, or the dominance by males, was overwhelmingly the prevailing view as well. The difference, however, was that in these communities some alternatives were being suggested.

Though women were subordinated, their importance to society was celebrated in what has been called the "cult of domesticity." Middle-class Victorians lauded the women's calling to be wives, mothers, and homemakers. By making the family strong, women were considered the backbone of society. This ideal had a strong spiritual component. In an expansion of their roles, women were expected to be the spiritual leaders in the home. They were the guardians of traditional Christian virtues such as service and self-sacrifice. Men, on the other hand, were regarded in the popular literature of the day as prone to violence and lust. As mothers, women were to train their sons in more Christian virtues, and as wives they were to save their husbands from their selfish passions and vices.[39]

This mythology had some basis in reality. One of the social realities was that, for the middle class, economic activities were increasingly moving away from the home and family, becoming exclusively male domains. These areas of life were also becoming increasingly rationalized; that is, they were being conducted more on the scien-

• • •

tific-technological assumption that tended to lessen the importance of personal relationships and increase emphases on the impersonal considerations of efficiency and maximizing profits. So, increasingly larger areas of male activity were being depersonalized and hence exempted from traditional factors of moral review.[40]

In addition, warfare was always an exclusively male domain which, to say the least, did not encourage Christian virtues. Nineteenth-century society with its large frontier was a society in which ordinary men were often armed and dangerous. After the election of General Jackson in 1828 (who had earlier killed a man in a duel), the typical profile for the presidential candidates turned from the educated intellectual to the fighting man. American male pastimes typically included drinking, gambling, and violence. Churches strongly opposed most forms of violence, drinking, gambling, sexual promiscuity, and other perceived vices. Women, who were often victimized by these activities, were the strongest allies of clergy in opposing them.

In this society, women were carving out a spiritual domain in church and developing power domestically which provided them with meaning, vocation, and a sense of moral superiority to those who held formal power in society.[41] By the moral standards of the day, the destiny and even the survival of Christian civilization depended largely on the work of women, who constituted the majority of Protestant church membership and who often took over spiritual and moral leadership in the home.

New Public Roles

The openness to spiritual innovation in mid-nineteenth century America also began to provide some more public roles for women. As in the Quaker movement two centuries earlier, openness to an age of the spirit suggested that old barriers would be removed. This was true not only of radical movements that departed from traditional Christianity, such as Transcendentalism, Spiritualism, and Christian Science, in which women's leadership was prominent; it was also true of the spiritually radical evangelical right. The dominance of Ellen White among the strict Seventh-day Adventists is the most striking example.

Closer to the Anglo-evangelical mainstream, there was the holiness movement that developed in mid-century, particularly among American Methodists. Phoebe Palmer (1807–1874), for instance, led

• • •

influential Tuesday prayer meetings in New York City for over thirty-five years. Teaching a rigorous "holiness" doctrine, that every believer should experience a "second blessing" leading to a holy life, she became the chief spokesperson for a major movement within the denomination. Palmer also kept up a strenuous schedule as a travelling evangelist, although she did not call her sermons "preaching" and never sought ordination.

Meanwhile, a few traditional Protestant groups were moving toward ordination of women clergy. The first in a fully traditional group was Antoinette Brown (1825–1921), ordained by New England Congregationalists in 1853. Baptists and Methodists, who allowed lay exhorters, occasionally had lay women preachers. Jarena Lee (1783–?), for example, was a noted early black preacher in the African Methodist Episcopal Church.[42] The greatest changes on this front, however, came in small new separatist holiness denominations, where ordination of women first became fairly common, especially after the Civil War. The Salvation Army, an English import, is the best known example of such a theologically strict group with room for women's leadership in the post-war era.

The most broadly based advances in public roles for women in pre-Civil War America were in the many reform and missionary societies of the time. Since most of these societies were interdenominational rather than under direct church control, women could find in them substantial outlets for expressing their expanding roles as allies of the clergy, as the spiritual and moral guardians of society.

Promoting the public roles of women was among the many reforms proposed. While the vast majority of women subscribed to the cult of domesticity, some visionaries campaigned for seemingly radical proposals such as legal equality and the right to vote. As with the other reform movements, religious motives provided some substantial impetus to these campaigns.

While most of the dramatic changes in public roles for women came from within the reform societies themselves and in a few churches, another foundation was being laid in new educational ventures, one of the components of the voluntary reform movements. Although it was rare and radical to attempt coeducation—as at Charles Finney's Oberlin College—other schools for women, though usually more domestically oriented than men's colleges, provided the beginnings for women's higher education.

• • •

Literature was becoming another important avenue for women's expression. While women were not formally trained in theology and usually were not permitted the public forum, in writing popular educational literature they were finding an acceptable means to express some religious leadership.

Religion and American Politics

We can see from the foregoing discussion that religion was a strong influence in shaping American culture, its values, its institutions, its reforms, and the ways that people thought about reality. It is not surprising, then, that we should see its impact on politics, which rightly or wrongly is often taken to be the center of American life, or at least of American history. In politics, the impact of religion is usually indirect and difficult to measure. The separation of church and state meant the institutional distancing of religion and politics. The two, however, were always connected both in the rhetoric of civil religion and more substantially by the fact that they both dealt with the same questions of morality. "Religion in America," Tocqueville observed, "takes no direct part in the government of society, but [nevertheless] it must be regarded as the first of their political institutions."[43]

Religion's importance in politics is indicated by the religious divisions in pluralistic America that have often been the best predictors of voting behavior.[44] This striking, but largely ignored, correlation should not be so surprising since religious affiliation and political behavior both tend to reflect a number of the same variables: ethnicity, class, and region. Even though social forces and interests are major determinants in political behavior, religion has often shaped or reinforced the values that determine larger political goals.

In general, the religious dimensions of American political behavior can be viewed as a contest between those who see themselves in the Puritan-evangelical tradition and those who do not. The Puritan-evangelicals are usually of older British stock, strongest in the East and especially New England, and belong to mainstream denominations, such as Congregationalist, Presbyterian, and some types of Baptist and Methodist. They are Puritan primarily in the sense of applying religious principles to shaping the social order. In the nineteenth century they were usually evangelical or conversionist, emphasizing that changed individuals are the key to a changed society. They also emphasized that individuals must cultivate the expounded virtues of self-

• • •

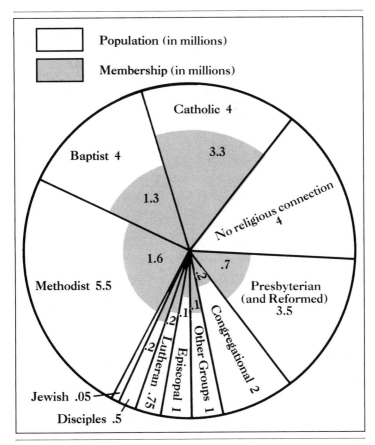

Population (in millions)

Membership (in millions)

Catholic 4

Baptist 4

3.3

1.3

No religious connection 4

Methodist 5.5

1.6

.7

.2

Presbyterian (and Reformed) 3.5

.1

.1

Congregational 2

.2

Lutheran .75

.2

Episcopal 1

Other Groups 1

Jewish .05

Disciples .5

Approximate church membership and affiliations in 1855.

This chart is adapted from figures compiled by Robert Baird in Religion in America *(rev. ed. 1856). His "population" figures were broad estimates to include children and occasional church attenders. The Catholic "population" was added, since Baird did not estimate it. In the nineteenth century, church membership requirements were usually considerably more rigorous than they are today, so many regular attenders were not full members.*

discipline, such as industry, thrift, and sexual purity. Converted individuals, they believed, should band together in their denominations, in voluntary societies, and in political parties to promote such values in all levels of society, through educational institutions and social reforms.

From the founding of the nation, other Americans resisted this broadly Puritan agenda. Jeffersonians, for instance, did not share New Englanders' zeal for making the government the regulator of morality. Such differing moral agendas help account for the early split between Jefferson and New Englander John Adams.

Religion was not always the primary variable in determining such lineups. By the mid-nineteenth century, white Southerners, many of whom shared the evangelical heritage, were forced by their defense of slavery to reject the Puritan belief in federal regulation of society's morality.

In general, however, religion was one of the significant determinants of where Americans would line up politically, especially when combined with ethnicity.

By about the 1840s, the classic patterns of American politics were taking shape. The massive numbers of Catholic immigrants were not likely to affiliate with political parties that had a strongly reformist Protestant agenda. They, accordingly, soon became the backbone of the Democratic party. Protestant religious groups who were also outsiders in the sense of not identifying themselves with the Puritan heritage tended in the same direction. Some strictly confessional Lutherans, such as the Missouri Synod in the Midwest, did not think America was likely to become a Christian nation, and so tended to vote Democratic. Similarly, even among a seemingly insider group such as the Presbyterians, the more strictly confessional Calvinist group ("the Old School") tended to vote Democratic. This was related to their strong Scotch-Irish ethnic identity, since the Scotch-Irish did not always get along well with New Englanders. The other main group of Presbyterians ("the New School"), on the other hand, were closely allied to New England Congregationalists and usually voted for the Whig party, which promoted the Puritan-evangelical ideals of virtue and hard work.[45]

Some other smaller sects were evangelical, but did not share the Puritan vision of Christianizing America. Rather, these groups, such as some Baptists and primitivists, stood closer to the tradition of Roger

• • •

Williams, seeing the civilization as more like Babylon than the new Israel. They, too, tended to vote Democratic. At the other end of the ecclesiastical spectrum, Episcopalians had a long history of antagonism to Puritanism and often did not share the Puritan-evangelical political agenda.[46]

These lineups help explain what otherwise might seem a total aberration in American political history: the Antimason party of the 1820s and 1830s. Antimasons consolidated around the indignation—especially in New York State—toward the influential Masons for the apparent murder in 1826 of William Morgan, an ex-Mason who threatened to reveal secrets of the order. In 1828 the Antimasons delivered nearly half of New York's electoral votes to John Quincy Adams. In 1831 they held the first American political convention, patterned after a convention of a religious voluntary society. They soon merged with the new Whig party, of which they became an important "conscience wing," and included strong proponents for antislavery such as Thaddeus Stevens (1792–1868) and William H. Seward (1801–1872).

This crusading impulse was largely an expression of culturally reformist Protestantism. The secret order of the Masons, which had elaborate rituals and covenants within its brotherhood, appeared to them to be a competing religion appealing to freethinkers. Radical nineteenth-century evangelicals thus attacked Masonry as a false religion, much as later twentieth-century fundamentalists attacked "secular humanism." Such attacks fit with antislavery, since the goal for evangelicals was to build a culture in which reforming evangelical morality would prevail. A telling example of the connection is Charles G. Finney, a long-standing evangelical proponent of abolitionism. Once the emancipation of the slaves was accomplished in the 1860s, he turned his political energies back to the now outdated agenda of the 1820s, Antimasonry.[47]

The evangelical connections to shaping American political patterns were more than a curiosity, however. They were central to the Whig party from the 1830s to 1850s. The Whigs had a strong moral agenda, and a strong Anglo-Protestant and Yankee constituency (although they had a Southern wing as well). Whigs cultivated the ideal that the "virtuous" middle class should take responsibility for building a society based on individual morality, self-help, and education. Though the party was shaped by the business concerns of this class also, its elitist evangelical-Puritan connections were so strong that it

• • •

has been aptly characterized as "in many ways the evangelical united front at the polling place."[48]

The next major political party on the scene in the turbulent years of the midcentury was more purely of this ilk, but without the dignity of the Whigs. The American or Know-Nothing Party was a resurgent political expression of nativism and anti-Catholicism. The huge Catholic immigration at that time brought such long-standing antagonisms once again to a head. Protestant leaders had been warning for decades that Catholic immigration could lead to a political takeover. One reason for building Protestant colleges throughout the nation was to counter Catholic expansion. Public schools also taught broadly Protestant doctrine and included Protestant religious exercises. When Catholics asked for equal tax support for their schools, they were denied.

By the early 1830s a number of prominent Protestants, such as Samuel F. B. Morse (1791–1872), inventor of the telegraph, and Lyman Beecher (1755–1863), the New England evangelical and father of a family of reformers (including Harriet Beecher Stowe), were issuing dire warnings concerning a growing Catholic power in America. The more popular counterparts were sensational anti-Catholic books that anticipated the standards of the twentieth century's *National Enquirer*. Marie Monk's *Awful Disclosures of the Hôtel Dieu Nunnery of Montreal*, a Protestant best-seller in 1836, for instance, told how a girl from a Protestant family was converted to Catholicism and then was enslaved in prostitution in a convent. A secret tunnel connected the nunnery to the priests' residence and babies were buried in the cellar.[49]

In the 1840s violence replaced sex as the most conspicuous motif in anti-Catholicism. In a number of eastern cities rioting broke out between Protestant laborers and the newer Catholic immigrants. The most serious was in Philadelphia, where St. Michael's and St. Augustine's churches in the industrial suburb of Kensington were burned to the ground.[50]

Such sentiments spawned nativist anti-Catholic protection societies and local political parties. In the early 1850s these consolidated into the Know-Nothing Party. In the off-year election of 1854 this nativist group seemed on the verge of becoming a new national party replacing the collapsing Whigs. It included Southerners as well as Northerners, swept the elections in Massachusetts, and gained other local congressional victories. In 1856, then known as the American

• • •

Party, its candidate Millard Fillmore carried twenty-one percent of the popular vote.

The slavery issue, however, overwhelmed anti-Catholicism and the American Party quickly disappeared. Its Northern antislavery members merged into the new Republican party.

The Republican party, which emerged from indignation over the Kansas-Nebraska Act of 1854 and the threatened expansion of slavery, brought together many of the reforming sentiments, although on a regional basis. Though antislavery overshadowed all other issues, Protestant reformers saw in this party a new hope to build a Christian America. Former anti-Masons, anti-Catholics, prohibition campaigners, and other champions of a national morality helped shape the new Republican ethos, which dominated American politics from 1860 to 1912 and reemerged again at least as late as the Reagan administration. Though Republicanism involves a philosophy of support for big business (also dominated in the nineteenth century by Protestants), its moral stance was integral to its platform.

A famous political blunder of the next era illustrates the point. In the election of 1884 the Republican candidate, James G. Blaine, remarked that the Democratic party was the party of "Rum, Romanism, and Rebellion." Ironically, the quip may have mobilized the Catholic opposition and cost the Republicans a rare defeat. Blaine's remark overstepped the bounds of explicitness with which the religious issue could be mentioned in public. Nonetheless, the fact was that the Republicans were the party opposing rum, Romanism (i.e., Catholicism), and rebellion.

The ironic fusion of antislavery and anti-Catholicism in the Republican party is a poignant one. It aptly illustrates that the issues surrounding the relationship of religion and public life are not simple. Religion is one, albeit not the only one, force that attempts to impose moral standards for national life. Yet moral codes that are appropriately defined within a religious system may not be appropriate standards to apply publicly in a pluralistic society. Anti-Catholicism or anti-Protestantism are attitudes that most people would deplore today. Prohibition of alcoholic beverages, although it was popular enough by the early twentieth century to become national policy, is also today considered to have been a failure. On the other hand, most people today think that their nineteenth-century forebears should have taken a more aggressive stance toward outlawing slavery.

• • •

White Southerners, on the other hand, viewed antislavery much
the way that Catholics viewed Protestant nativism. They saw themselves as every bit as Christian as their abolitionist Northern counterparts; in fact, more so. Our own moral indignation at their tragic
disregard of the rights of an entire people should not obscure our
understanding of how they viewed the matter. To them, defense of
the white Southern way of life was the defense of Christian civilization, a civilization in which Christianity and the republican virtue of
limited central government were ideally combined. They could also
see more clearly than the Northerners themselves that the supposed
"free" society of the North was oppressive in many ways, economically and socially, and far from truly Christian.[51] Hence, they saw the
abolitionist reformers as self-righteous and hypocritical imperialists.

To the black American slaves, the abolitionists appeared to be
nothing less than prophets of the Lord and the Northern armies seemed
sent from Jehovah to rescue his people. The black version of evangelical millennialism included the literal expectation that his faithful
people would be freed from bondage in Egypt. The seeming fulfillment of this biblical promise increased their commitment to their faith.

Whites in the North were, in the meantime, more ambivalent.
Radical abolitionism had the support of only a small minority. John
Brown (1800–1859), a militant Calvinist who believed he had a call
from God to raise an army and personally free the slaves, was executed after his failed attempt to mount an insurrection in 1858. Although he became an important symbol for abolitionists, most Northern
whites were far more conservative. Abolitionists, while influential, were
also controversial. In 1837 Elisha Lovejoy (1802–1837), an abolitionist
editor and a protégé of Charles Finney, was murdered by an angry
mob in Illinois. Other abolitionists often were attacked by irate Northern
mobs as well.

Nonetheless, by 1860 the North strongly supported Abraham Lincoln's moderate policy of containing slavery within its present territories without abolishing it. Even such a restrained stance, however,
presented by a president elected by a purely sectional vote, was sufficient to convince Southern leadership of the necessity of secession
to preserve their way of life.

Once the war broke out, the dominant view in the North took on
a strong crusading tone. Even though slavery was not abolished until
1863, they saw the war as a sacred cause with explicit millennial over-

• • •

tones. In the dominant rhetoric the Union itself was a sacred object essential to the advance of Christ's kingdom, "the coming of the glory of the Lord." The Union represented the culmination of the long tradition of Protestant-republican hopes to build a virtuous civilization.

In such conflicting views of Christian-republican civilization, North and South, we can see the agony of the Civil War generation. Major moral issues were at stake and, as Lincoln observed in the Gettysburg Address, the world was watching to see whether the American experiment of republican government would work. Because the American people were so religious and because the issues were of such monumental moral significance, it was inevitable that the republic's intractable social and political problems would be raised to cosmic dimensions. Religious commitments, rather than helping to unify the nation, now reinforced both sides' resolve to persevere in a torturous civil war.

• • •

CHAPTER THREE

Protestant and Progressive America: 1860–1917

The grandfather, who was in college sixty years ago, asked in dread and fear, "Is my soul saved?" . . . The father, who was in college thirty years ago, . . . asked, "Is your soul saved?" The son does not ask either question. He is content to live the life of the Christian. Salvation is taken for granted in a world of, by, and full of goodness.

C. F. Thwing (president of Western Reserve University), *The American College: What It Is and What It May Become* (1914)

*I*f one had visited the United States on the eve of the Civil War, then returned a half-century later at the height of the Progressive Era, one would have seen many continuities in the dominant culture. Political power was still held firmly by white Protestants who had every intention of keeping it that way. Their crusading spirit was as strong as ever. Sentiment was growing in the Protestant-Republican North for national legislation prohibiting the sale of alcoholic beverages. Protestant Southerners were willing to forget deep regional antagonisms long enough to join in this crusade, which was directed in part against perceived threats about new immigrant populations, especially Catholics, but also Jews, and perhaps even German Lutherans. A parallel effort at Anglo-Protestant dominance was the "blue laws" forbidding commerce in many localities on Sundays, a practice important to moralistic Anglo-Protestants, but not to most Lutherans or Catholics, and directly discriminatory against Jews because they observed a different sabbath.

At the same time Protestants had some reason to be proud of the civilization they dominated. The United States was viewed by much of the world as a model society where people from many nations could live together in relative peace, and with unusual opportunities for economic success. Whatever injustices, discriminations, and poverty were in the United States, one could find far worse in other quarters of the globe. Among the essential premises of the dominant American thought of the era were: (1) the superiority of Western civilization, (2) that Anglo-American democratic principles were the highest political expression of that civilization, (3) and that these principles were almost bound to triumph throughout the earth.[1] Without necessarily saying so explicitly, Protestants saw these ideals as an outgrowth of their heritage.

Moreover, Protestant moral reformers—women as much as men—could claim leadership in the major efforts to make the United States a more just society. Almost all the Progressive reform measures of the day were brought in by prodding the conscience of the dominant middle class. One estimate suggests that eighty-five percent of all social reformers of the era had some connection with evangelical Protestantism.[2] Catholics and Jews might also have been ardent champions of reform, but Protestants held the leadership and the power.

Prohibition and Sabbath legislation could even be seen as social reforms aimed at drug and labor problems. But Progressive reformers

• • •

Protestant America was confronted by urban masses and ethnic diversity.

had a much longer moral agenda for cleaning up government, regulating big business, protecting consumers, fighting poverty and the vast inequities in wealth, and building a more participatory democracy. All these reforms had strong middle-class Protestant support and reflected an ongoing Puritan spirit of civic responsibility. Their impetus came not primarily from class or religious conflict but from appeals to conscience, that people from most traditions might share.[3] Given the upbeat and often successful reforming ethos of the day, it did not seem incongruous that the theme song of Teddy Roosevelt's Bull Moose party convention was "Onward Christian Soldiers."

Despite such continuities with themes from 1860, the observant visitor to the United States of the end of this era would also be struck by some vast differences. The dominant Protestant culture, despite its increasing enthusiasm, was struggling to keep control. Though it was not obvious to most participants that they were at the end of the

• • •

era, realities were threatening to make the rhetoric hollow and obsolete.

The changes were vast. The most obvious were urbanization, industrialization and immigration, all of which threatened to undermine the dominant ethos which was implicitly built around the assumption that the world was made up of communities something like the New England town. Also, growing sentiments favored drastic limitation of immigration to keep ethnic ratios at their current proportions.

Threats to the Protestant cultural establishment were not simply external. Within the establishment the forces of change were taking their toll. Intellectual changes were especially important for many individuals because they led to practical changes in belief and value systems. Increasing numbers of educated people abandoned traditional Protestant teaching and trust in the authority of the Bible. Others modified traditional doctrine to accommodate modern thought. Debates over these issues were threatening to split the Protestant community from within.

So while the dominant American culture around 1910 in many ways resembled that of 1860, it was being pushed near the breaking point by both external and internal pressures of momentous proportions. This chapter and the next will examine the tensions this culture faced, looking first at the successes and changes within the dominant Anglo culture. Then we will consider how this world looked to other Americans who were still kept away from most centers of cultural power.

The Golden Age

Northern evangelical clergy typically described the Civil War in both covenantal and millennial terms. In speaking of this covenant they looked back to their Puritan heritage which they had thoroughly blended with the American principles of government. "While the Union is all in all, the very ark of the covenant to us and our children," went a typical statement from a leading New York Presbyterian in 1862, "it is everything to the race. It is freighted with better hopes for freedom and humanity than any other nation in existence."

With victory the nation could look forward to "millennial days"[4] when peace, justice, and the principles of Christ would reign. Once they abolished one of history's most spectacular injustices, they believed, the future of moral reform seemed unlimited. Even "govern-

• • •

ment," said the well-known theologian Horace Bushnell at the end of the war, "is now become Providential—no more a mere creature of our human will, but a grandly moral affair."[5]

The golden age of the reign of morality did not arrive. Instead, the nation experienced what Mark Twain and Charles Dudley Warner aptly characterized as "the Gilded Age." The rhetoric of a Christian civilization, Twain and Warner were suggesting, was a thin veneer hiding secular and immoral realities. In their novel, *The Gilded Age* (1873) the leading character, Senator Dilworthy, is involved in endless circles of corruption. Yet when he runs for reelection he waxes eloquent as a Christian statesman, addresses Sunday schools and ladies missionary societies, "and even took a needle now and then and made a stitch or two upon a calico shirt for some Bibleless pagan of the South Seas, and this act enchanted the ladies, who regard the garments thus honored as in a manner sanctified."[6]

The period that began with the assassination of Lincoln and included the trumped-up impeachment of President Andrew Johnson, Black Friday, the Credit Mobilier Scandal, the Whiskey Ring and other corruption in the Grant administration, the corruptions of Reconstruction, the reneging on the promise of equality for blacks, the possible stealing of the election of 1876, and the assassination of President Garfield (to mention only highlights) invited such characterizations. Henry Adams, the grandson of John Quincy Adams, scion of the best of the heritage of New England civic responsibility, anonymously published the novel *Democracy* in 1880. In it the heroine, seeking the virtue that should be at the heart of a republic, finds instead that her principal suitor, a Republican leader, is like a "moral lunatic," who "talked about virtue and vice as a man who is colour-blind talks about red and green."[7]

Mark Twain and Henry Adams were, of course, not typical figures of the era. Yet each was reared in the prevailing Anglo-Protestant culture, although at opposite ends of it. Adams was in New England aristocracy, Twain in the new west. Twain's character Aunt Polly from the novel *Tom Sawyer* seemed a universal character in Protestant America. Almost everyone, it seems, had encountered in their upbringing such strict evangelical Puritan piety. Writers such as Twain and Adams, who rejected the religious heritage and felt alienated from it, were perhaps in the best position to see its contradictions from within.

• • •

Adams (1838–1918), a historian by profession, provided the most profound overall analysis. In his autobiography, *The Education of Henry Adams* (1907), there is a famous passage entitled "The Dynamo and the Virgin." In it Adams reflects on his experience while visiting the Paris Exposition of 1900. At the center of this world's fair was a great dynamo, which Adams thought represented the power of modern culture, epitomized by American industrial civilization, since modern technological civilization was built on harnessing physical energy. From Paris Adams travelled to Chartes, where he saw the spectacular medieval cathedral that dominates the landscape. What sort of force, asked Adams, did it take for such an economically and technologically limited civilization to produce such a magnificent work of art? That civilization, he said, was run by a spiritual power, the power of dedication to the Virgin. "All the steam in the world," he remarked, "could not, like the Virgin, build Charters." American civilization, by contrast, had a superficial spirituality in Adams's view. Its real power was in brute force. The idea of great art in America, Adams observed, was General Sherman on a horse.

It was not that traditional Christianity was declining in America by any usual standard of measure. Churches of all sorts were growing and Protestant churches were keeping up with population increases, even though much of the new immigration was not Protestant. Major Protestant groups, such as the Methodists, Baptists, Presbyterians, Disciples, and Congregationalists tripled their combined memberships in the period from 1860 to 1900. In 1880 Robert Ingersoll, the most famous skeptic of the post-Civil War era, who travelled the country attacking the Bible and Christian teaching, announced that "the churches are dying out all over the land." Charles McCabe, head of the Methodist Church Extension Society, wired to Ingersoll:

> "All hail the power of Jesus' name—we are building more than one Methodist church for every day in the year, and propose to make it two a day!"

McCabe had reason to be optimistic, as indeed most Protestant leaders were in his day. The statistical strength of the churches could be matched with their continuing moral impact. James Bryce, a British visitor in the 1800s, observed that the clergy were America's "first citizens" and that they extorted "an influence often wider and more powerful than that of any layman." They seemed to be, as much as

• • •

anyone, the shapers of the value systems that made up the culture. It was an era of Christian crusades. Theodore Roosevelt remarked that he "would rather address a Methodist audience than any other audience in America" for "the Methodists represent the great middle class and in consequence are the most representative church in America." As historian Winthrop Hudson writes in his fine survey of this era, "In 1900 few would have disputed the contention that the United States was a Protestant nation."[8]

How are we to resolve these strikingly conflicting estimates? What was Henry Adams seeing that most of his contemporaries in 1900 were ignoring?

In essence the differing estimates reflect the two sides of what we have and will observe throughout this study as an essential paradox in American civilization: it is both intensely spiritual and intensely materialistic. In part this combination is an inevitable one which can be found in all so-called "Christian" civilizations throughout the ages. The spiritual dimensions never cut as deep as some of the public expressions of the civilization would suggest. This is true even of medieval Western civilization, of which Henry Adams held a somewhat romanticized view. The paradox in Western civilizations reflects a paradox deep in human nature.

Nonetheless, Adams was pointing to a real difference and for us what he points to suggests that whatever the perennial paradox, in modern American civilization it has been especially intensified.

Understanding Secularization

To understand this intensification of the paradox, we have to consider the way secularization has taken place in America. By secularization we simply mean the removal of some area of human activity from the domain, or significant influence, of organized or traditional religion. In the modern world, this has happened for two primary reasons. First, secularization has been promoted by those who have been hostile to traditional religion, especially Christianity. This hostility might take the form of resistance to the practical ethical restraints of Christian teaching; for instance, from the business person, the soldier, the politician, or the libertine who wants to carve out an area of life governed by principles other than those of Judeo-Christian morality. Or the hostility may arise primarily from ideological commitments to an alternative secular belief system. As we shall see,

. . .

especially after 1865 in America, increasing numbers of ideological secularists appeared who insisted that traditional Christian (or other theistic) teachings were untenable and should be replaced by higher principles that frankly were based on human inquiry alone.

But secularization might also be promoted by traditional Christians, practicing Jews, and other ardent theists. In fact, one of the most important characteristics of the modern world since about 1700 is the promotion of such secularization by traditional religionists. The reasons for this are closely related to the characteristics of the eighteenth-century Enlightenment, which we have considered earlier. It was essential to eighteenth-century thought to apply the inductive scientific model, so successful in the areas of physical science and technology, as the basis for understanding other domains of human activity. Christians as well as non-Christians saw the advantages of this approach. If areas of reality could be analyzed and organized rationally and free from prejudice—it was widely held—they could be vastly improved. Most modern people accept this principle with respect to technology. Even though they may have deep religious commitments, they want to keep certain technical areas free from religious influences. To make a simple contemporary example, most strongly religious people would not be happy with a car mechanic who told them the trouble with their car was a devil in the carburetor.

So in modern America, Christians and other religious traditionalists have often adopted a stance that we can call "methodological secularity" for an increasing number of their activities. Scientists and technicians of all sorts, no matter how religious, are expected to check their religious beliefs at the door when they enter the laboratory. Of course, they may pray about their work, and perhaps when they are done ponder how nature reflects God's design; but the activity itself will be, for methodological purposes, essentially secular.

One of the best examples of this technological principle being applied beyond the simply physical world is the design of the U. S. government. The Constitution is, in a sense, a technical mechanism to regulate potentially conflicting forces. Many Christian groups, notably the Baptists, were fervent proponents of such secularization, which involves simply separating out areas of religious and nonreligious activity. Religion would inevitably influence legislation, but the moral principles involved could be argued on the basis of natural law

• • •

Sometimes almost everyone would favor more secularization.

in public forums. Government could also sponsor formal ceremonial religious activities, although (like the technician who prays before entering the lab) these were expected not to have substantive bearing on the business of governing.

Crucial to the development of America was, as we saw in our discussion of the U. S. Constitution, that such applications of technological principles did not involve any essential hostility toward traditional Christianity. This contrasts importantly with the experience of the French Revolution, which became the chief symbol of modern

• • •

politics and the model for much later sociological thinking on the subject of secularization. In France and in much of Europe liberal politics came to be associated with direct opposition to the clergy and Christianity. The secularization of the government, or the removal of direct religious influences on it, had definite anti-Christian implications.

The American development was far different. Secularization of many areas of American life accelerated during the nineteenth century; but most often it followed the model of a methodological secularization set by the establishment of the U. S. Constitution— essentially friendly to traditional religion. Dominant Protestantism, in turn, was essentially friendly to such secularization and, as it generally did toward the U. S. government, could even bless it and celebrate it.

What was taking place was a gradual and largely peaceful differentiation of religious and secular domains. One of the important factors that eased this transition and even made it difficult to perceive was that as areas of life were removed from substantive religious influences, they might well at the same time continue to be baptized in more superficial ways in harmony with the general principles of Christian civilization. So one could not plot a neat contraction of religious influence in America. Rather, in many ways, religion could be seen spreading its influence, even if, as in the singing of "Onward Christian Soldiers" at the Progressive Convention in 1912, that influence might be increasingly thin.[9]

Religion and Politics: The Link Continues

One area in which the phenomena and paradoxes of the simultaneously religious and secular occur in American life is politics. Religion continued to be one of the best indicators of political behavior, especially when religion was combined with ethnicity, as it almost always was. In general, the Republican party remained predominantly the party of Northerners affiliated with the mainstream evangelical denominations, such as Methodist, Baptist, Presbyterian, and Congregationalist. These were groups with evangelical traditions, emphasizing the conversion of individuals who live in personal piety. These concerns were still connected with something broadly like the Puritan ideal of building a Christian society. Hence, they encouraged govern-

• • •

ment regulation of personal behavior according to evangelical standards, as the proposed prohibition of alcoholic beverages best symbolized. In general, this evangelical political program was opposed by more liturgically minded religious groups, such as Catholics, Episcopalians, and some Lutherans. While there were many exceptions, this was the general rule.[10]

Religion had a lot to do with politics since it helped shape and reinforce competing moral visions that infused political debates. Religion was far from everything, though; the firmest political alliance of the era was that within the Democratic party, between Catholics and white Southerners. The latter generally belonged to evangelical denominations and had strong interests in pietistic social legislation.

The role that religion played did not have to be explicit. In fact, it generally had to be subtle, since both parties wanted to recruit supporters from the other's constituency. So, for instance, Republican candidate James G. Blaine's notorious remark about "Rum, Romanism, and Rebellion" on the eve of the election of 1884 was thought to have cost him the presidency. Republicans needed to court Catholic support and occasionally got it. Archbishop John Ireland (1838–1918) of St. Paul, Minnesota, one of the leading Catholic "Americanizers" of the era, for instance, was an active Republican.

Democrats were also trying to broaden their constituency by cutting into the Republican evangelical base. In 1896 they fostered an important party realignment by nominating dark horse agrarian William Jennings Bryan, an ardent evangelical. He was also a prohibitionist, thus taking from the Republicans one of their traditional distinctions.[11] With the fervor of an evangelist, Bryan preached the need for social reform as an urgent ethical demand. By the Progressive Era, both parties were preaching moral reform and each presented a vision of America as the land where God's will should be done.

What we can see, then, is a pattern where both parties reached for a consensus built on moral claims that could bring people of all religions into what was regarded as essentially a melting-pot ideal. Despite the public toning down of the religious factors and emphasis on moral commonalities, the basic patterns of the differing religious (and regional) platforms of the two parties persisted until new ideological and moral issues began to displace them in the 1960s.

· · ·

The Republican Party and the Incorporation of America

While the religious factor promoting various moral visions in politics is undeniable, the basically paradoxical character of religion and culture can be seen by looking more closely at the development of the Republican party which was usually dominant from the Civil War to World War I.

In addition to emerging from the Civil War as the party of the Northern pietist moral reform, the Republicans were also the champions of rising big business. Business is a realm that tends to have a logic of its own, built upon the principle of maximizing profits. Individual and social moral demands may restrain business to a degree; but these weaken especially as businesses become larger and more depersonalized and in boom times when huge financial rewards come to those who can most efficiently organize and mobilize. Such forces were strong in America after the Civil War and for some they were irresistible, hence giving the Gilded Age its notorious reputation for political and economic corruption.

In addition to mere greed, however, there were more fundamental changes in the fabric of American economic life. Most important was the mammoth industrialization accompanied by the social revolution of urbanization and the economic revolution of incorporation.

Both of these forces created vast new areas of life that were less susceptible to religious and moral control. The teaming cities, despite the presence of ethnic enclaves, fostered large populations who were detached from religious communities. Since religions are sustained primarily through communities, this led simply to more unchurched people in urban areas. Anonymity was possible that had not been possible in small towns and rural America. Organizations such as the YMCA and YWCA, which once were evangelical agencies, and urban revivals tried to counter these trends, but the sheer size of cities made them centers for secularity.

At the same time, the incorporation of American business, much of which took place in the decades between 1865 and 1900, created another largely secular domain. In incorporation, the state grants a business the status of a "person" so it has an ongoing life of its own, is owned by stockholders, and is run by an essentially self-perpetuating board of directors. Owners (stockholders) are not personally liable for the debts of the corporation—only for their investments. As

• • •

Trinity Church in Copley Square dominated the Boston horizon in 1896. In 1979 it was dwarfed by an insurance building.

the new captains of industry mobilized resources during this volatile period of growth, the corporation was the preferred method of organization. Though individuals, such as John D. Rockefeller, Andrew Carnegie, and John Pierpont Morgan were prominent in this process, eventually it made the corporate "person" a less personalized entity; that is, identified less with any individual. This distancing of businesses from their owners also made them less susceptible to moral standards that would normally be expected of individuals.

Most of the mainline Protestant churches (such as Presbyterian, Congregationalist, Methodist, and Baptist) who had solid middle-class constituencies supported such trends. Churches tend to follow the mood of their constituents. So when after the Civil War much of the same constituency that had agitated for antislavery and other causes became disillusioned with reform, their churches followed suit, in

• • •

general supporting the social status quo and whatever seemed to favor business.

As industry, urbanization, and immigration expanded, the most pressing social problems of the day had to do with the relationships of capital to labor. Laborers were organizing, striking, and agitating for better working conditions. Occasionally, there were riots as in the 1886 Haymarket affair. The Chicago police tried to break up a labor rally, someone tossed a bomb at them, and the police fired back, killing some protesters. Then a number of anarchists, some of whom were not present at the incident, were convicted and condemned for agitation that was believed to have lead to the bombing.

Many mainline churchpeople reacted to such violence with alarm. The *Congregationalist,* one of the most respected New England religious papers commented: ". . . when anarchy gathers its deluded disciples into a mob, as at Chicago, a Gatling gun or two, swiftly brought into position and well served, offers on the whole, the most merciful as well as effectual remedy."[12] One senses in such remarks that the quality of Protestant mercy had become strained.

Nevertheless, we can understand such overreactions better if we see them in terms of the broader ideal for civilization that they reflected. Fear concerning anarchists was built on the deep commitment of the Anglo-Protestant establishment (and of Catholic leaders, for that matter) to law and order as the basis for a free society. New socialist and anarchist ideas were usually promoted by recent immigrants, so that Protestants saw in them a foreign threat to their civilization.

Beneath such issues were economic views that led many Protestant Republicans (and many others, of course) to oppose labor strikes of any sort and also to oppose government regulation of industry. The self-interest of their class was, of course, an incentive to promote such views. On the other hand, it should not be supposed, as is sometimes remarked, that they lacked genuine social concern. They had very strong concerns for the welfare of society, but had a much more individualistic theory of how that welfare could be accomplished.

Hard Work as a Social Program

Essentially, their outlook reflected a self-help ideal that—as with most American beliefs—combined Enlightenment ideals with some Christian principles. This outlook was based on the belief, wide-

• • •

spread in the eighteenth and nineteenth centuries, that human agency
was central to historical change. This same outlook produced the popular theory of the time that history is determined by "great men" and
that the great issues in history therefore concern morality. All the
American revolutionaries had held such views. In the nineteenth century most Americans still believed that what applied to the great applied as much to ordinary people: individual choices were crucial to
success or failure.

The standard view, still taught both in college economics texts
and in popular literature after the Civil War, was built upon the premise that God created the world with a system of rewards and punishments. People who worked were rewarded, while lazy or profligate
people suffered from poverty. The right to own private property was
considered a sacred right, since it was essential to the operation of
the reward system. It was important also not to interfere with the
natural mechanism, as in strikes or government interference. Charity
was an important duty toward the truly needy, such as the disabled,
widows, and orphans, who could not help themselves. But to artifi-
cially aid the able-bodied was simply to destroy individual initiative.
The logic of the system made it seem God-ordained.[13]

The question in the late nineteenth century was whether this outlook, which had some obviously beneficial applications in small town
settings that were economically rather simple, would work in the
emerging mass societies of the cities. Protestant leaders insisted that
it would. Henry Ward Beecher (1813–1887), the best known preacher
of the post-Civil War era, for instance, was confident that, "Even in
the most compact and closely-populated portions of the East, he that
will be frugal, and save continuously, living every day within the bounds
of his means, can scarcely help accumulating."[14]

The key to success and social welfare, then, was in this view for
individuals to work hard and help themselves. Conversion to Christianity could be an important first step toward such discipline. In any
case, the ethic was a gospel of work.

The McGuffey Readers, still the standard reading text in thirty-seven
states in 1890, helped transmit these values to the next generation
and to new Americans. Honesty, kindness, thrift, industry, and patriotism were recurrent themes. The lessons included stories like "The
Little Idle Boy," "The Idle Boy Reformed," and "The Advantages
of Industry." The latter concludes with the idle boy, named George

• • •

Jones, seen years later "a poor wanderer, without money and without friends." The narrator admonishes: "The story of George Jones, which is a true one, shows how sinful and ruinous it is to be idle. Every child who would be a Christian, and have a home in heaven, must guard against this sin." [15]

The emphases on hard work and self-reliance could be valuable ones in a society where most people started poor, but many white people had unparalleled opportunities for economic advance. However, the worldview included lessons on the dangers of riches, emphasizing that the virtuous poor were happier than the greedy rich; it also focused on the importance of charity.

Acres of Diamonds

Opportunity in America often was interpreted as a gift from God. The most famous clerical promoter of this view was Russell H. Conwell (1843–1925). Conwell, a Baptist preacher in Philadelphia, was a self-made man who amassed a fortune as well as establishing an "institutional church" that served the local community not only by religious services, but as a community center. Among Conwell's projects was the founding of Temple University. His fame, however, rested on the speech "Acres of Diamonds," which he delivered an astounding 6,000 times. Everyone had acres of diamonds of opportunity in their own back yards, he proclaimed. When asked why he did not preach the gospel instead of preaching how people could get rich, Conwell replied, "Because to make money honestly is to preach the gospel." [16]

Conwell and others in the tradition emphasized honesty, charity, civic responsibility, and other virtues; but as American industry burgeoned, that aspect of the individualistic ethic supporting unrestrained expansion driven by the inexorable goal of maximizing profits tended to overwhelm such moral restraints. In practice, this meant that expanding areas in American life were free from the religious and moral restraints that might be expected in more personal relationships.

A classic illustration of the tensions involved is seen in the career of John D. Rockefeller, Sr. (1839–1937). The Standard Oil magnate was a devout Baptist who prided himself on his personal integrity. Yet in the fierce competition for control of the oil industry, Standard Oil used ruthless tactics to drive its competitors out of business. The

• • •

Rockefeller Chapel symbolized the one-time religious tradition at the University of Chicago.

muckraking journalists, who by the 1890s were exposing business corruption, saw Rockefeller as the chief among the "robber barons." Part of the problem was that American monopolies were developing techniques that would outrage moral sensibilities in personal relationships, such as exploiting a weakness to drive a struggling neighbor out of business. Yet given the internal logic of the emerging competition, Rockefeller himself was convinced that "the Lord gave me my money." Like other captains of industry, Rockefeller followed the logic of the

• • •

individualistic ethic to share some of the excess of his profits with the community. Notably, he endowed the University of Chicago, founded in 1890, to be a great center for Baptist learning.[17]

AN AGE OF REFORM

The Middle-Class Protestant Consciousness

There was another side to the picture, however, that tempered the trend of letting freewheeling capitalism shape American society regardless of ethical consequences. Americans from the dominant classes were intensely moralistic, with a strong sense of civic responsibility. Civic responsibility and charity were, in fact, lessons that were always taught alongside the work ethic and tempered its individualism. Such sensitivities can be traced back to the Puritan heritage of a covenanted nation.[18] So reform in America often has a middle-class base, appealing to the Judeo-Christian principles that each person has responsibilities for the welfare of all their neighbors.

Since the middle decades of the nineteenth century, when business expansion became a major political issue, the mood of America has tended to oscillate between eras of reform when moral restraints are prominent and eras when the quest for material advance more often overrides such restraints.[19] So the Gilded Age, following the pre-Civil War age of reform, was succeeded by the Progressive Era of reform, which emerged in the 1890s and was dominant through World War I.

Women and Reform

As in the pre-Civil War reforms, women played a prominent, though still not controlling, role in the demands for moral reform. While most women accepted their assigned primary role as guardians of the home and, secondarily, as subordinate partners in the churches, their situation was changing. Increasingly, women were developing their own networks of organizations. By far the largest number of these were local church organizations, such as women's societies for charity and especially for missions. These were supplemented by nondenominational voluntary reform societies which continued to provide women

• • •

with their most important public role—as moral guardians of society, an extension of the widespread nineteenth-century expectation that women would be the moral guardians of the home.

That women had a significant social role to guard the moral sector (although part of a package that usually limited full-time career opportunities for women), was based on more than mythology. Since men held exclusive sway in industry, which was increasingly dominated by rationalized principles of seeking efficiency, male roles operating under rules of ruthless competition and survival of the fittest were accentuated. Most women, on the other hand, continued to operate largely in the home sphere and the neighborhood, where traditional standards of personal ethics were appropriate.

As in the society at large, religious options for women were broadening. After the Civil War many middle-class women turned to spiritualism and the occult, sometimes as ways of communicating with the dead, especially those lost in the war. Though such views led to exotic new sects such as Theosophy, founded by Madame Helena P. Blavatsky (1831–1891) and Henry Olcott (1832–1907) in 1872 in New York, or Mary Baker Eddy's Christian Science, most of the new spiritualistic experimentation probably supplemented more-or-less-traditional Christian beliefs. The reign of dogmatic systematic theologies, controlled by male theologians, was beginning to wane in many of the Northern Protestant denominations; the women's counterpart was often a more romanticized version of Christianity open to innovation.

The Christian dimensions of the women's reform efforts remained conspicuous. The most striking example was Frances E. Willard (1839–1898), leader of the most influential women's movement of the era. Willard was reared in a pious family of evangelical New Englanders, transplanted to Wisconsin. Part of her early inspiration came from hearing Charles G. Finney preach. In her own work Willard, a devout Methodist, likewise combined traditional evangelical theology, an emphasis on holiness, and ardent social reform. She worked principally with the Women's Christian Temperance Union (WCTU), the largest women's organization of the time. Assuming the presidency in 1879, Willard pushed the WCTU toward supplementing its preeminent temperance concerns with other reform interests, such as support of labor unions and especially women's right to vote. Willard was one of those who effectively turned the arguments for women's domesticity around by accepting the stereotypical image of women as

• • •

Frances E. Willard (center) and other officers of the W.C.T.U.

naturally more virtuous than men. Rather than see this as a reason for women to stay home, it became an argument for women to save society. "What the world most needs is mothering," said Willard.[20]

Willard and other activist women also pushed for women's equality in the churches. Here they met stiff opposition from the established Protestant denominations. The Methodist General Conference denied Willard the privilege to address them in 1880 and in 1888 refused to seat Willard and other elected women delegates. Nonethe-

• • •

less, the effective organization of women was helping pave the way for new policies in the mainline churches as elsewhere in American society. Just as within a generation, by 1920, women were granted the vote at the national level, so mainline Protestant churches began opening up at least some offices to women.

Missions

The period from the Civil War to World War I was the great age for American Protestant missions, an enterprise in which women played a major role, both in the field and supporting societies. In 1869 American world missions were about the same size as the total for continental European countries and half the size of British missions. By 1910 the Americans outnumbered continentals by over two to one and had surpassed even the British.[21] Counting those who were married, women made up about sixty percent of the missionaries. Meanwhile, women's supporting agencies at home had a membership of some two million.[22]

Enthusiasm for missions reflected a combination of motives. The primary motive arose from the traditional Protestant and revivalist belief that without faith in Christ the heathen would spend eternity suffering in hell. People who do not hold such a worldview may dismiss this motive; but if one took this view absolutely literally, as many Americans did, it was easily a sufficient motive for highminded people to give up their earthly comforts and risk their lives to bring the Gospel to a distant land. Added to this motive was the further conviction that Christianity was not simply an otherworldly religion, but a civilizing benefit to all people. Even some who by the end of this era may have doubted the exclusiveness of Christianity as a means of eternal salvation could continue to support a worldwide social gospel dedicated to transforming humanity through the principles of Jesus.

Moody and the Shaping of the Missionary Ideal

We can get some sense of the missionary fervor if we look at the most prominent promoter of American missions of the time. Dwight L. Moody (1837–1899) was to the generation from the 1870s through the 1890s what Charles Finney had been to the pre-Civil War era— America's chief evangelist. Moody was a homey, self-educated and self-made man, the epitome of the American Horatio Alger figure, the

• • •

boy who through luck and pluck rose from modest beginnings to fame and fortune. Converted through the work of the Young Men's Christian Association (then a leading evangelistic agency), Moody eventually gave up a lucrative career as a shoe salesman in Chicago, and turned to evangelistic work. After effective local ministries in Chicago during the 1860s, Moody and his song leader, Ira Sankey, toured the British Isles from 1873 to 1875. Success abroad catapulted them to immense fame and popularity at home. During the next quarter century Moody held revivals in American cities. Preaching a simple old-time Gospel of salvation through rebirth in Christ, Moody charmed audiences with sentimental stories and the conventional moralism of middle-class Victorian Protestantism.

In 1886 Moody made a tour of college campuses that led to a dramatic summer gathering of students at Moody's campground in Northfield, Massachusetts. There a hundred top collegians pledged their lives to missions. Their enthusiasm spread quickly to their campuses so that in two years, when they formed the Student Volunteer Movement, the number who pledged had grown to thousands. Out of the SVM arose most of the Protestant missionary leadership of the next generation. The watchword of the SVM—"The Evangelization of the World in This Generation"—matched the crusading and ebullient spirit of the day.

"Our Country"

Though Moody's message of the salvation of souls was a primary inspiration for young men and women to give their lives to missions, those who supported missions stressed its civilizing benefits as well. Most prominent of these was Josiah Strong (1847–1916), who in 1885 published the best-selling volume, *Our Country*. Strong, a proponent both of missions and social reform, firmly proclaimed that the world's destiny lay with the Anglo-Saxon race. Anglo-Saxons had two great contributions to offer the world: love of liberty and a "pure spiritual Christianity."[23] Missionary efforts promoted both of these.

Strong, like many of his contemporaries, held views that now seem outdated and racist. In part they based such views on what they saw as the proven moral superiority of civilizations, and in part on the social science of the day which included "social Darwinist" views on

• • •

race. According to such views, races or national groupings were always locked in struggles for superiority and dominance. Some races were past their prime and had reached a sort of racial senility. According to the Anglo-Protestants, the Latin races, or southern European Catholics, were of this sort. In Roman times they represented a great civilization. Now they were being surpassed by more vigorous Anglo-Protestantism. On the other hand, other races, such as the blacks, were seen as being in their infancy. To lift up and help such peoples was, as Rudyard Kipling put it, "the white man's burden."

Such views fit American foreign policy exactly at the time of the Spanish-American War in 1898. Americans saw themselves dealing with "savage and senile races."[24] Spain represented decadent Catholic civilization. The Filipinos, freed from Spanish rule by the Americans, needed American guidance. As President McKinley explained to a Methodist audience, he reached his decision to acquire the Philippines after spending many evenings on his knees praying for divine guidance: "And one night late it came to me this way. . . . There was nothing left for us to do but to take them all and to educate the Filipinos and uplift and civilize and Christianize them, and by God's grace do the very best we could by them, as our fellow men for whom Christ also died."[25]

Americans as a nation were beginning to encounter the rest of the world, but usually with the confident sense of their cultural superiority. In 1893 progressive religious leaders sponsored, in conjunction with the World's Columbian Exposition in Chicago, a World's Parliament of Religion. To the consternation of some conservatives, representatives of many of the world's faiths gathered and even bowed their heads together as the Roman Catholic prelate, James Cardinal Gibbons, recited the Lord's Prayer. Despite the new respect for other faiths that such a gathering inevitably engendered, even the most progressive Americans did not abandon their sense of cultural superiority. As John Henry Barrows, one of the principal organizers of the parliament put it, "Civilization is the secular name for Christianity."[26]

From such sentiments, which so thoroughly blended the dominant American secular and religious goals, it was not a far step to Woodrow Wilson's motto that World War I was "to make the world safe for democracy."

. . .

The Social Gospel

In the meantime, middle-class Protestant sentiments for reforming American civilization itself were growing. The Progressive impulse, however, was too broad to be attributed to any one social group or tradition. Some of it had grass roots origins in the Populist movement, but Progressivism reflected a change of mood in America in the two decades before World War I. Most simply, this change of mood seems to have involved a collective awakening of national conscience. As Richard Hofstadter has pointed out, key words in the national vocabulary of the Progressives included law, character, conscience, soul, morals, service, duty, shame, disgrace, sin, and selfishness.[27] Progressives typically attributed the evil in society to violations of moral law.

Since much of American society was professedly Christian, these moral appeals often had strong Christian overtones. Jacob Riis, whose photographs and narrative in *How the Other Half Lives* (1890) helped arouse the nation to the urgency of its urban problems, was an active churchman. Henry Demarest Lloyd's *Wealth Against Commonwealth* (1894), an effective exposé of the ruthlessness of modern monopolies such as Rockefeller's mentioned previously, had an explicitly Christian message. Lincoln Steffens, in *The Shame of the Cities* (1897), advocated the Golden Rule as the key to social progress. One of the most popular novels of the whole era, and one of the most revealing of the moral sensibilities that could be aroused among middle-class Americans, was *In His Steps* (1896), authored by Charles M. Sheldon, a Kansas Congregationalist pastor. Sheldon envisioned what it would be like if the people of a small city consistently asked, "What would Jesus do?" Just by following this simple rule, Sheldon suggested, business and personal relationships could be revolutionized, and American civilization would move into a golden age.

The emerging social gospel movement, of which Sheldon's book was an early popular expression, can best be understood if we recall that it appeared only thirty years after American Protestants in the North were making the most extravagant predictions about the onset of a millennial age. The social gospel, which in many ways was "the Progressive movement at prayer," revived this millennial vision, though in a more moderate form. Whereas the earlier social millennialism grew out of revivalism (such as Charles Finney's), the millennialism

• • •

Photograph of a sweatshop by Jacob Riis, whose work aroused concern for the urban poor.

of the new social gospel earned its name as *social* gospel because it focused more strictly on saving the social order than on saving individual souls. "The kingdom of God" that Jesus had preached about was central to the social gospel. Social gospelers played down the otherworldly aspects of understanding the kingdom and emphasized its relevance to the social problems of the day.

The two most important spokespersons for the social gospel were Washington Gladden (1836–1918) and Walter Rauschenbusch (1861–1918). Gladden, the pastor of a Congregational church in Columbus, Ohio, pointed out that the mainline Protestant churches were failing to reach the working classes. The reason, he thought, was that the laissez-faire economic theories of the day perpetrated injustice and hence alienated laborers. The ethics of Jesus, he insisted, would lead to economic theories that were more just to all classes of society.

Rauschenbusch was a middle-class Baptist whose social conscience was quickened by work in a New York City church near the infamous Hell's Kitchen neighborhood. In 1897 he joined the faculty

• • •

of Rochester Theological Seminary, where he produced major theoretical justifications for the social gospel. Rauschenbusch explicitly rejected traditional theologies for blinding Christians to their social obligations. Even more strongly than Gladden, he rejected laissez-faire ethics as un-Christian and advocated moderate socialistic reforms. Concepts of God, he argued, had to be adjusted to the modern age. So in the democratic age, the true meaning of the "Kingdom of God" must be understood as a social system working for the equality of all people. Such reforms, Rauschenbusch proclaimed in broadly millennial terms still shared by many Americans, would lead to a "Christianizing of the social order."

Pragmatic Progressivism

While the moral impulse was central to Progressivism, and Christianity was explicitly or implicitly behind much of its moral fervor, another dimension of the Progressive outlook had almost nothing to do with religion. This was a scientific or social scientific attitude that, while subordinate before World War I, signalled the direction in which American public life would soon move.

Probably the clearest illustration of this outlook and its practical implications is in work of Oliver Wendell Holmes, Jr. (1841–1935), the most influential legal theorist of his day and a justice on the United States Supreme Court from 1902 to 1932. Holmes argued that it was a misconception to think of civil law either as a question of morality or as some natural law principles built into the scheme of the universe. Thus rejecting the characteristic eighteenth-century viewpoint with its implicitly religious assumptions, Holmes pointed the way to a typical twentieth-century outlook. The law, like everything else, was simply the product of social forces. Understanding it was a purely pragmatic exercise. "The object of our study," said Holmes, "is prediction, the prediction of the incidence of the public force through the instrumentality of the courts."[28] In other words, the lawyer was like a social scientist, who predicted what the courts would do and obtained the best for the client under the circumstances. The courts in turn could view the law as an evolving social experiment and use the best of modern social theory to improve its function. Moral absolutes were irrelevant.

A number of Progressives took a similar, purely pragmatic approach to reform. Among historians, for instance, one of the most

• • •

famous was Charles A. Beard (1874–1948). In 1913 Beard published *An Economic Interpretation of the Constitution of the United States* in which he argued that the Constitution, far from being a quasi-sacred embodiment of natural law, was largely the product of its originators' economic interests. By challenging the myth of the Constitution's sacred origins, Beard helped clear the way for reinterpretations of the Constitution based on modern pragmatic understanding of social needs. Though still a minority, influential writers in many fields were questioning traditional absolutes.[29]

A Revolution in Education

Views such as Holmes's and Beard's reflected a massive revolution in American education that had been taking place since just after the Civil War. Since schools are major transmitters of the society's values and train its most influential spokespersons, this revolution was of far more than academic interest.

This revolution had especially profound implications for mainline Protestants, since at the beginning of this era they controlled most of American education. In public education, as we have seen, this control was substantial earlier in the century. When the common school system spread during the first half of the century, most of the public schools were virtually Protestant.

Beginning in the middle decades of this century Catholic protests forced some secularization of the public schools. Protestants found this solution preferable to providing Catholics and other religious groups with tax support for their own schools. Protestants usually were satisfied with the more vaguely Christian ethos of the public schools. Although McGuffey's *Readers* continued as the most popular text throughout the century, the later editions contained little of explicit Protestantism. Comparing the 1836–37 and the 1879 editions, education historian John Westerhoff observed that "Calvinistic theology and ethics have been replaced by American middle-class civil religion, morality, and values."[30] Though concessions to a more pluralistic society were tempering explicitly religious teachings, Protestants generally were not alarmed by such secularization. As historian Robert Lynn put it, they simply had a firm belief in "the inherent and inevitable harmony of public education and the Protestant cause."[31]

During this same period, a similar process happened in American higher education, but with more ominous implications for a continu-

• • •

ing Protestant dominance. At the end of the Civil War most American colleges were explicitly Protestant. The vast majority had clergymen as presidents, required chapel, strict moral codes, and taught Protestant theology and Christian ethics in courses. In 1865 the book most highly regarded by the majority of American academics was the Bible.

By 1917 the situation changed drastically. Although many of the most respected schools still had some church control, the explicitly religious features of their programs had disappeared or become optional. Most professors would have been embarrassed to claim the Bible as an authority, except perhaps on ethical issues.

Revolution in Beliefs

At the heart of this transformation in collegiate education was a profound revolution in the fundamental beliefs that educated Americans took for granted. It would be difficult to overestimate the impact of this transformation, especially for religion. Traditional beliefs that were accepted as the height of educated respectability in 1865 seemed by 1917 badly out of step with intellectual fashion.

The specific changes in belief were almost all part of a greater pattern. Intellectual inquiry was shifting from concern with discovering fixed absolute truths toward looking for natural explanations of how change takes place. At a time when Western civilization was rapidly changing and diversifying, understanding the processes that caused change seemed especially intriguing. Such analysis was attractive because it employed the newly-revered scientific methodologies.

This transformation was a major turning point in Western thought. Ever since the Greeks, intellectual inquiry had been directed at discovering fixed truths that were assumed to be built into the scheme of things. Now the modern intellectuals were proclaiming that truth is culturally bound and always changing, and that we can only look at the forces that produce various beliefs.

The new social sciences were an important manifestation of this transition. Through them traditional norms could be relativized. Rather than inquire how civil law might reflect natural law (as America's founders had), the new social sciences could view social norms and laws as customs, explained by the social forces shaping a society. Auguste Comte (1798–1857), an early European prophet of social science, had proclaimed that human society went through three ascending

· · ·

stages. First was the theological stage, when the society claimed divine sanction for social laws. Second was the metaphysical stage, when it appealed to the philosophy of natural law. Finally, the highest or "positive" stage, was when social law would be based on scientific inquiry. Science thus promised a secular millennium.

William Graham Sumner (1840–1910) of Yale, an early proponent of social science in America, held a similar view. Trained for the ministry, Sumner found a new faith in scientific analysis of natural forces. Later in his career, he remarked that one day he had put his religious beliefs in a drawer; twenty years later he opened the drawer and the beliefs were gone. The conclusions of Sumner's social science reflected the rugged individualism of the Gilded Age. A champion of what had become known as "social Darwinism," he considered religious and moral factors "sentimental." In a striking depiction of humans as products solely of nature, he proclaimed that "man" had "no more right to life than a rattlesnake; he has no more right to liberty than any wild beast; his right to the pursuit of happiness is nothing but license to maintain the struggle for existence. . . ."[32]

As the Progressive Era approached, America's new social scientists turned from dog-eat-dog individualism toward a view that the government should employ the human mind, informed by social science, to control social developments for the good. Such reformist views took for granted moral values worth fighting for. Moreover, not all the early social scientists had abandoned explicit Christianity as thoroughly as Sumner, either. Richard T. Ely (1854–1943), for instance, the prime mover in the founding of the American Economics Association in 1886, was a champion of the social gospel. Modern economics, he held, could be used for Christianizing society.

Ely, however, represented a transitional stage. John Dewey (1859–1952) was more representative of the way American academia was moving. Dewey was a significant exponent of pragmatism and a promoter of influential modern educational theories. Until the 1890s, Dewey held definitely Christian views; but gradually, he adopted a social outlook that was essentially an updating of Auguste Comte. He believed that human society had long been enslaved by restrictive religious restraints. True progress was possible only if we recognized that we live in "an open world" where "change rather than fixity is the measure" and science is used to reach limited human goals.[33]

• • •

The Symbol of Darwinism

Darwinism both was part of this larger thought pattern and became its chief symbol. Charles Darwin's (1809–1882) views on biology, announced in *Origin of Species* in 1859, made the same move that was being made in many other fields at the time. Just as Karl Marx was explaining social change through the laws of "scientific socialism" and Sigmund Freud later explained psychological difficulties through childhood developments, Darwin explained biological species by a hypothesis based on the premise that changing natural forces were the only relevant considerations.

Darwinism was immensely important for Western thought since prior to that time no one proposed a plausible explanation for human origins that did not involve some sort of designer and creator. Although many intellectuals had doubted the truth of Christianity, few were atheists, since the design in the universe seemed to entail a designer. This was especially true in America, where there were almost no professed atheists.[34]

While Darwin left many questions unanswered, his explanation made it intellectually plausible to believe that human life was the product of a chance universe.

Darwin's explanation was offered at a time when many intellectuals were eager to break away from the constrictions of traditional Christianity. This was especially true in England, where the Anglican Church still had a firm control on university education and anticlerical feeling was strong among some intellectuals. Such intellectuals enthusiastically adopted Darwin's biology, in part because it supported their larger naturalistic worldview; that is, a view in which only natural explanations of things was allowed.[35] England's T. H. Huxley, nicknamed "Darwin's Bulldog," coined the word "agnostic" in 1869 to describe the new outlook. In contrast to atheists, who denied God's existence, agnostics said they simply did not know, since science could not answer such questions.

In the United States the advent of Darwinism and similar outlooks limiting explanations to scientific analyses of natural changes coincided with the transitions from colleges to universities. The old-time colleges were like advanced prep schools with strict discipline and a combination of classical and Christian learning. Professors, many

• • •

Illustration from Punch's Almanack *alluding to Isaac Watt's hymn that Jesus died "For such a worm as I." Darwin is center left.*

of whom were clergy, were often generalists. In order to transform these institutions into universities it was necessary to professionalize and to specialize. Similar developments were taking place in many areas of late nineteenth-century American life, including business, law, and medicine. For the developing universities, the new scientific learning was especially useful. The standards of natural science provided a model for establishing specialized expertise in other disciplines. The new science's bias against introducing explicitly religious concerns into learning offered a rationale for breaking with the older, sometimes amateurish, Christian learning.

• • •

Darwinism could be especially useful for such campaigns. Andrew Dixon White, for instance, was the first president of Cornell University, founded in 1868 as a center to train people in technical expertise. The university avoided religious connections, and was accused by some local clergy of being too secular. In 1869 White lectured to a New York audience on "The Battle-fields of Science." Eventually he published a two-volume *History of the Warfare of Science with Theology in Christendom,* one of a number of books promoting the warfare metaphor to understand the relationship between Christianity and science. Ignoring that Christians had been the leading proponents of modern science and that earlier battles were largely *among* Christians, White and others argued that science was on the side of modernity and progress and traditional Christianity represented the superstition and the prejudices of the Dark Ages.[36]

While Darwinism itself did not immediately create the sort of consternation among the clergy that is sometimes supposed, the ambivalence of the churches toward the new science lent some credibility to the warfare idea. Protestants typically cited the scientific evidence of design in the universe as a chief argument for a designer. Darwinism threatened this argument, putting the prestige of science on the opposing side. Moreover, in American folk Christianity, the Bible was often taken very literally. Especially in the South after the Civil War Darwinism was cited as evidence of growing apostasy in modern Yankee civilization and a turning from the Bible. In the latter decades of the nineteenth century a number of Southern professors lost their jobs for teaching that biblical creation and evolution could be harmonized.

Despite such opposition, the broader reaction of the Northern Protestant establishment to Darwinism was toward harmonizing the new science with Christianity. So long as one did not accept Darwin's premise that natural forces were *all* there were, evolution could be seen as God's method of creating, much as photosynthesis could be viewed as God's way of giving us crops. Conservative biblicists in the North often added that God could have intervened in the evolutionary process to create the human soul, as described in Genesis.[37] Such issues could seemingly be resolved. The more ominous question for the Protestant establishment was not so much Darwinism itself as the rise of an exclusively naturalistic worldview, of which Darwinism was an important part.

• • •

Higher Criticism of the Bible

The focal point for the encounter between the two world views was at first not so much biology as the Bible itself. At the same time that Darwinism and other new scientific outlooks were being debated, the educated American Protestant community was being hit with shock waves of new biblical criticism. Biblical criticism was already developed in the prestigious German universities during the first half of the nineteenth century; so when it was imported to America during the second half of the century it arrived in mature and formidable forms.

The new "higher criticism" was based on the same premises as the other nineteenth-century sciences. Modern scholarship, it was proclaimed, should consider only natural causes that explained change or development. This approach involved an entirely new way of looking at the Bible, which up to that time most Western scholars regarded as supernatural in origin. If viewed, on the other hand, as a purely natural product, the Bible appeared quite different. It was simply the product of the evolving religious experience of the Hebrew people and the early Christians. The miracles, which were always taken as evidence of the Bible's authenticity, now became problems.

The premises of the new scholarship also challenged the uniqueness of Christianity. In thoroughly nonsupernaturalistic explanations, Christianity would be viewed exactly like other world religions—the product of historical and cultural causes.

In the late nineteenth century the most serious social and intellectual challenge faced by the American Protestant establishment was what to do with the claims of this new scholarship. Although most of its conclusions were simply restatements of its radical naturalistic premises, it had the prestige of the best historical science of the day on its side. Moreover, some of the specific issues it raised about traditional understandings of the Bible, such as who authored some of the books, were difficult to answer on any premises.

The Modernist Impulse

This crisis over the Bible and the uniqueness of Christianity triggered a major shift in theology among some of the leadership in mainline Protestantism, especially at theological seminaries where clergy were trained.

· · ·

Although there were various solutions to the problems, the broad outline can be described as typically fitting the rise of the "modernist" principle. Although the term "modernism" did not arise until the early twentieth century, by the late nineteenth century American Protestant leaders were endorsing the idea. To save Christianity from historical criticism of the Bible, they asserted that Christianity was not as exclusively dependent on the authority and accuracy of the ancient book as had been previously supposed. Rather, the Bible was the seed from which a higher Christianity evolved in modern civilization. When we have the oaks of civilization, said Henry Ward Beecher, America's most famous preacher of the post-Civil War era, why should we "go back and talk about the acorns."[38] The modernist principle, then, reflected the optimistic and progressive principles of the era, that a higher Christianity had evolved from the Bible and could be found in the best of modern civilization.

New Theologies

Such emphases coincided with a growing reaction against traditional theologies. Since the days of the Puritans, American theology had been dominated by Calvinist groups. Calvinism emphasized the sovereignty of God and the absolute dependence of humanity on God's grace: God could save whomever he willed and was generous to be saving any of the race from the damnation they deserved for their incorrigible perversity. In the eighteenth and nineteenth centuries, popular Methodist theology tempered Calvinist teachings slightly by providing people with a more cooperative role in salvation; but the hard teachings that, except for God's saving grace in Christ, people would deservedly be damned, were still standard teaching.

The new views of the Bible triggered a reaction against such traditional theologies. For one thing, they suggested that the Bible need not be taken as literally as it traditionally was. Rather, the more positive essence of the Christian message could be emphasized. This essence would be more in harmony with the increasingly optimistic view of human nature that had been building in America since the Enlightenment and was reinforced during the romantic era. In these more modern views, humans were not regarded as naturally depraved or sinful. Rather, they were seen as potentially good, though often misguided. In the new liberal or modernist theologies, Christian teaching blended with such emphases.

• • •

Such a new theology gradually developed on the American Protestant scene in the decades up to World War I. Because the process was gradual and because it was generally an era of optimism and church growth, these new theologies did not precipitate a severe crisis. Continuing to use traditional biblical language, they gave it slightly new meanings that nonetheless had continuity with the traditional spirit of American Protestantism.

Two such emphases particularly helped theologians and preachers meet the challenge of the new science and biblical criticism. One was that Christianity was basically a matter of the heart. Hence, Christians who knew Jesus in their hearts did not need to fear modern scientific challenges. Religion dealt with a higher level of truth than science.

Secondly, and just as important, the new theologies emphasized that the essence of Christianity was morality. Like the emphasis on the heart, morality had always been strong in the American revivalist heritage. Popular Protestantism, moreover, was often antitheological, stressing that what you did was more important than the details of what you believed. Modern theology was thus a theology of action. The social gospel was one manifestation of its spirit. Cooperative action could unite Christians and transform the world.

Filled with such assurance, establishment Protestants, despite the deep challenges they faced, moved with confidence toward what to them looked like an unlimited future. The twentieth century would be "The Christian Century" as the title of one of their church magazines labelled it. Working together, the major denominations formed the Federal Council of Churches in 1908. The new federation immediately produced a progressive social creed and set up commissions for cooperative missions and evangelism. The era of "ecumenical" Christianity seemed well under way, and optimists talked of a full union of Protestant churches as older theological issues faded.

By dropping some of the offensive and exclusive features of the evangelical heritage, but retaining the moral fervor and some substantial symbols of piety, liberal Protestants were successfully drawing people from many of the diverse American "tribes" into their melting pot. Liberal Protestants still dominated American politics, education, and public life. In a pluralistic society such dominance would have been difficult to maintain if they had continued to preach the exclusivist dogmas of their evangelical forebears. Now, however, they could

• • •

control a broadly "Christian" civilization that emphasized common moral ideals that could be widely shared.

Their universities provided an important example. Most of the major private schools retained their church connections, even while direct religious reference was being removed from the curricula. Explicit religious options were readily available in chapel services and in voluntary religious activities on campus. These, however, were no longer central to the enterprise. Nevertheless, undergraduate education at the universities retained the goal of building moral character, which was presumed to be a way of advancing Christian civilization.

• • •

CHAPTER FOUR

Pluralistic America: 1860–1917

If there were one religion in England, its despotism would be terrible; if there were only two, they would destroy each other; but there are thirty, and therefore they live in peace and harmony.

Voltaire

---

*I*f one way to understand the United States is to look at the dominant culture that attempts to shape and control a national consensus, an equally important theme is that of America as a diverse pluralistic society. Much of American history reflects the on-going tensions between these centripetal and centrifugal forces shaping the culture. Moreover, for new subgroups that are not Anglo-Protestant, a major question concerns what will be central to their identity. To what extent will it conform to the Anglo model and to what extent will the subgroup retain another distinct identity? For answering such questions, religion often plays a crucial role.

The Catholic Experience

These themes were played out on the largest scale in the American Catholic communities, especially in the era from the Civil War to early twentieth century. During this time the Catholic population continued its amazing growth. In 1860, Catholic Americans numbered over three million; by 1930 the number had grown to almost twenty million or about one-sixth of the American population and one-third of church memberships. In numbers, the United States was not nearly as Protestant a country as it was in tradition. By 1928 a Catholic, Al Smith, was the Democratic nominee and made a serious run for the presidency.

Throughout this era American Catholicism was continually being shaped by ethnic communities made up largely of new immigrants. In such communities, religion often played a larger role than it had in the immigrants' native lands, since religion became one of the most tangible ways of retaining a distinct identity. Moreover, the church provided the principal social organizations for ethnic groups in cities. For instance, in a typical working-class Chicago Irish parish in 1896, the church sponsored twenty-five societies that provided everything from charitable organizations to baseball teams and enlisted well over ten thousand members.[1] Such networks were especially important for ethnic communities where English was a second language. Moreover, each of life's major turning points, from birth to death, were marked by solemn church sacraments and were occasions for the most important gatherings of family, friends, and neighbors.

Catholicism, embracing people from many nations and traditions, was far from monolithic; hence, it had its own internal versions of the perennial American problem of unity and diversity, and of relating

• • •

the many subtraditions to the one church. Ethnic loyalties continued to be the principal source of tensions among Catholics, and inevitably these tensions grew as new ethnic groups swelled American cities. In the mid-nineteenth century the principal rivalries were between the Germans and the Irish. By the later nineteenth century the Irish emerged as the dominant group in church hierarchy, a situation that was deeply resented by almost everyone else. In the late nineteenth and early twentieth centuries, millions of Italians and Poles emigrated to America, each creating major communities with distinctive religious styles and strong ethnic loyalties. French, French Canadians, Portuguese, Belgians, Slovaks, Croatians, Hungarians, and Spanish-speaking Catholics each built smaller communities as well.

Immigrant communities were often divided within themselves, not only over questions of how much to Americanize, but also by regional attitudes imported from their native countries. Italian-Americans, for instance, were deeply divided between northern Italians—who came from more urban industrial areas—and southern Italians and Sicilians—who had preserved a peasant culture. Northerners were especially critical of the southerners' festivals and folk religion, which they considered superstitious and feared gave all Italians an unfavorable "backward" image. Italians were also divided politically. Italy had just been united in the 1860s under a democratic and nationalist regime. This regime was bitterly opposed by the papacy, which lost most of its lands and political power to the unification movement. The papacy accordingly discouraged Catholics from participating in Italian politics. Such tensions between modern democratic secularism and the church were imported to America, dividing the immigrant community and complicating the processes of Americanization. Though the particular patterns were different in each case, every immigrant community embodied such serious internal divisions.

Despite this bewildering diversity both among and within ethnic groups, it is still possible to perceive an overall Catholic style as well. Most Catholic immigrants to America came from peasant backgrounds, sharing some common European heritages. So Catholic historian Jay Dolan, while noting varieties between older and newer American Catholics, and among the many imported traditions, still characterizes a "Catholic ethos."

While eighteenth-century American Catholics were influenced by the republican heritage, by the late nineteenth century Catholic com-

• • •

munities were conspicuous, first of all, in their emphasis on authority. The overriding authority of the church was one of the things that had always distinguished Catholicism from Protestantism. In the nineteenth century, Catholic authoritarianism was reinforced by the inherently conservative nature of immigrant communities. The church in America was technically a missionary church until 1908, and so was directly under the authority of the Vatican. The Vatican, in the meantime, had its own problems, making it more authoritarian than ever. When it lost its political power to Italian nationalism, the church responded at the first Vatican Council in 1870 by strengthening its spiritual authority. The council declared, among other things, the infallibility of the pope when officially speaking on spiritual matters. American Catholics were in general receptive to such declarations. *Roma locuta est; causa finita est* ("Rome has spoken; the case is closed") became a popular motto in America.[2]

The second feature of the Catholic ethos, an emphasis on sin, was one that would be shared by many nineteenth-century American Protestants as well. Christian Americans of all sorts would hear similar messages to avoid worldliness and sins such as drunkenness, violence (except in warfare), and personal impurity. Catholics, like Protestants, had periodic revivals, called "parish missions," in which visiting priests would warn them of the dangers of hell if their sins were not forgiven. The principal difference in the message was that, while Protestant preaching tended to emphasize individual experience of commitment and personal resolve to live a pure life, Catholic preaching stressed reliance on formal church practices, especially the regular confession of sin to one's priest and acts of penance and devotion. Salvation was believed to come from the grace of God in either case, and the life of faith for either Protestant or Catholic was largely a matter of self-discipline. But for Catholics, the institutional church was the reservoir of grace, so that grace was channeled through its sacraments and the life of faith was guided by following prescribed church practice.[3]

These theological understandings led to other distinctions of the Catholic ethos—emphasis on ritual and openness to the supernatural. Not only did typical Catholic spirituality involve faithful observance of the rituals and ceremonies, but it also usually involved personal devotional exercises, such as saying the rosary or prayers to an array of saints who had special functions to help the faithful in everyday

• • •

life. Although Protestants as well as Catholics would expect answers
to prayer, in general the Catholic emphases on numerous saints and
tangible rituals kept them more open to the supernatural dimensions
of reality than their Protestant counterparts. In either case, and especially among almost any people with agrarian ties, such beliefs were
often mixed with considerable folk religion that went beyond specific
church teachings.

The central theme for Catholicism in America remained that of
establishing their own identity in relation to the host culture.

One of the most practical areas where this question had to be
faced concerned the schools. Initially, almost all schools in America
were Protestant. A "public" school was simply a school that performed a public function; so religious agencies, private organizations,
or communities could all sponsor public schools and expect tax support. When Catholics became a sizeable religious group, they soon
found that they were not welcome to participate as equal partners in
this arrangement. When they suggested that their own Catholic schools
receive tax support, they were rejected.

The key battles over this issue were fought in New York City in
the 1830s and 1840s. The Public School Society, which operated the
public schools, was a private agency run by Protestants. The Catholic
bishop, John Hughes, insisted that Catholic schools should receive
equal support. He pointed out that the public schools taught Protestant doctrine and included Protestant religious exercises, such as reading
from the King James Version of the Bible. A political campaign to
obtain justice for Catholic schools failed. Protestants were forced to
make their schools somewhat less sectarian and more secular; but they
preferred to have more secular schools for everyone than allow any
tax support for Catholic schools.[5]

Bishop Hughes and other Catholics had little choice but to build
their own parochial school systems. This was a matter of some dispute
in the Catholic community, since some Catholics saw the alternative
schools as hindering the process of Americanization. Nonetheless, by
the late nineteenth century, Catholic parochial education became one
of the most important institutions perpetuating the identity of Catholic communities. The schools were especially important in non-English speaking communities, since they helped preserve ethnic and
religious identity as well. Some Protestant ethnic groups, especially
the Missouri Synod Lutheran and the Dutch-American Christian Re-

• • •

formed, who had strong confessional heritages that separated them from American evangelicalism, built their own school systems for similar reasons.

The "Americanist" Controversy

For Catholics, as for every immigrant community, the debate over how far to Americanize was an ongoing one. The Catholic situation was complicated by the politically conservative stance of the Vatican in reaction to nationalism and political liberalism. Some Catholics, by contrast, shared the more progressive American outlook of the day and thought that Catholicism should adjust to that spirit. One of the early leaders of this "Americanist" movement was Isaac Hecker (1819–1888), a mid-century convert to Catholicism who founded the Paulist Fathers, an order of priests. Throughout the rest of the century, a small but very influential group of Irish Catholic leaders, including most prominently James Cardinal Gibbons (1834–1921), archbishop of Baltimore, worked for modest changes in emphasis, such as less stress on devotional supernaturalism and more openness to political liberalism, which they thought would keep the church up-to-date with its American setting. Unlike the Protestant liberals of the day, they generally did not suggest departures from traditional doctrine—only changes in style and tone. One item, for instance, that brought opposition from German-American Catholics was that the Americanists joined the Protestants in advocating prohibition of alcoholic beverages, one of the leading progressive reforms.

The more basic stance of the Americanists, however, precipitated a serious crisis. Pope Leo XIII (1878–1903) had seemed a friend to progressive causes, particularly in his encyclical *Rerum Novarum* of 1891 which, while condemning socialism, called strongly for justice for organized labor. The pope, however, soon put the brakes on any incipient progressive American Catholicism, issuing another encyclical in 1895 declaring that American separation of church and state was not the ideal condition for the Catholic church. Rather, said the pope frankly, the church would be better off if "in addition to liberty, she enjoyed the favor of the laws and the patronage of public authority." Much to the chagrin of the Americanists, the pope was saying that the Catholic church ought to be established by the state.

The next incident increased the papal pressure against the Americanists, though in part it was based on a misunderstanding. In 1897

• • •

James Cardinal Gibbons was at the center of the "Americanist" controversy.

a translation of a biography of Isaac Hecker was published in France. The translator suggested that Hecker's less authoritarian American style should be the model for modern Catholicism. This provided fuel for some Catholic liberals in France who were unhappy with papal authority. The Spanish-American War in 1898 did not help enhance the pope's view of America. In 1899 he issued another encyclical, addressed directly to Cardinal Gibbons, condemning "Americanism." The pope's definition of Americanism fit the views of the French

• • •

theological liberals better than it did the American progressives, whose theology remained quite orthodox. Cardinal Gibbons replied that he knew of no American Catholic "who has ever uttered such enormities" as the pope condemned. Despite the fact that the pope was condemning what the American leaders called a "phantom heresy," their campaigns for an American church in tune with the spirit of the age were effectively intimated.

The Triumph of Catholic Conservatism

The sequel to this almost entirely shut down progressive Catholicism. The more basic issue when the popes talked about "Americanism" was theological liberalism, which they saw as the inevitable outgrowth of any general policy of adjusting religion to the spirit of the times. One manifestation of this concern was that in 1898, at the height of the Americanist furor, the Vatican condemned John C. Zahm, a Catholic professor of physics and chemistry at the University of Notre Dame, for teaching theistic evolution (that God could use evolutionary means as a method of creation). A broader step was the papal condemnation of theological "modernism," issued by Pius X in 1907. Modernism covered all the efforts to adjust Catholic doctrine to the spirit of the modern age, especially to modern science and biblical criticism. So while American Protestant churches were moving rapidly to new theologies, the early growth of Progressivism in American Catholicism was effectively nipped in the bud.

The outcome was thus a triumph for the conservative forces which had always been strong in the American churches in any case. In the battle for self-identity a more distinctly Catholic definition triumphed over a more typically American one. During the next generation, while many mainline Protestant institutions lost their distinctiveness, Catholics built a solid framework of their own institutions. The intellectual life of their universities was conservative, dominated by the classic medieval Catholic outlook of Thomas Aquinas. While during this time Catholic schools provided little intellectual leadership outside their immediate circles, nonetheless, unlike their mainline Protestant counterparts they retained schools at all levels with a distinctly Catholic outlook. This was just one manifestation of the wider American Catholic experience during the first half of the twentieth century. Ethnic neighborhoods in American cities retained their coherence and the church remained an important defining feature. Catholics were in

• • •

many ways becoming the most typical of Americans yet they knew they were Catholics. Through preservations of neighborhoods and through preservations of distinct practices, such as eating fish instead of meat on Fridays, they retained a Catholic identity.

Non-Anglo Protestants

The vast immigrations of the era from the Civil War to World War I included many Protestants as well as Catholics. Most were from non-English speaking regions such as Germany, Scandinavia, and the Netherlands. High percentages of these immigrants settled in the rich farmlands of the Midwest, though substantial numbers also crowded in ethnic ghettos in the cities, following the dominant Catholic pattern.

In each of these groups the tensions over Americanization were as strong as among Catholics. Retaining one's native language and an ethnic community were crucial to retaining identity, especially for first generation immigrants. A strong homogeneous religious heritage could strongly reinforce this impulse, since holding onto such a spiritual heritage was framed as a matter of loyalty to God himself.

The largest group of such non-Anglo Protestants was Lutheran, especially from Germany and Scandinavia. Substantial numbers of Germans had settled in the New World since the eighteenth century. Germany, however, before 1871 was a collection of separate states divided among Protestants and Catholics. Beginning around the 1840s German immigration to the United States vastly increased and, as among the Catholics, by the early twentieth century the numbers of new Lutheran immigrants overwhelmed the older Lutheran groups in America.

The result was that Lutheranism, while vigorous in America, was divided in a bewildering number of ways. Already, before the mass immigration at mid-century, Lutheran churches were divided between "American Lutherans," who emphasized affinities with the dominant evangelicals, and traditionalists, who stressed the uniqueness of the Lutheran confessions, a staid and nonrevivalist style, often in the German language. The new immigrant groups were already divided by additional language and ethnic differences. Moreover, in each of these communities the struggles over Americanization were recapitulated, often continuing well into the twentieth century. America's strife with Germany in World War I provided incentives for German-Americans to abandon the German language and to Ameri-

• • •

canize. Most other national groups were moving toward English worship services at about that same time. Some successful union efforts merged many of the smaller local Lutheran synods into national denominations, a process that has continued throughout this century. Nonetheless, some sizeable Lutheran groups retained their independence and others, especially those in rural areas with fairly stable populations, such as Minnesota, retained strong identities that were both ethnic and Lutheran.

Dutch immigration, while much smaller in numbers, provides a similar variation on the Americanization story. Most Dutch Protestants were Reformed, or Calvinist. The early Dutch Reformed church from the colonial era had by the nineteenth century come to look much like other American evangelical churches. When numbers of Dutch immigrants swelled after the Civil War, some of the Reformed immigrants joined the existing Dutch Reformed (Reformed Church in America). Others deemed that church much too "American" and formed their own Christian Reformed Church, which built its own complete educational system and carefully preserved its confessional and ethnic heritage.

Eastern Orthodox Churches

Some ethno-religious groups had less opportunity to blend into the American scene. This was especially true for later immigrants whose traditions were new to the United States. Asian immigrants, for instance, had little choice but to remain in separate enclaves where they were usually content to preserve their own religious heritages. Much less distinct, because there was no racial factor involved and their religion was Christian, was the experience of Eastern European immigrants who belonged to the Eastern Orthodox heritage. Nonetheless, their distinctive heritage made them seem outsiders much more than non-Anglo Protestants, or even Catholics.

The Eastern Orthodox church had roots directly back to the ancient churches of the Eastern Roman Empire. In medieval times, after the Eastern Empire was separated from the West, these Eastern churches and the Roman Catholic church separated. In the modern era Eastern Orthodox churches remained the official state churches of Greece, much of Eastern Europe, and Russia.

Eastern Orthodox churches seemed strange in the American setting largely because immigrants from these countries were relatively

• • •

Eastern Orthodoxy, like its architecture, remained distinctive in America.

rare before 1900. Since then several million Americans (about 3.5 million in the 1980s) are Orthodox Christians, almost all from ethnic groups such as Russians, Greeks, Ukranians, Albanians, Bulgarians, Serbians, and Rumanians.[6] Because of differences in national backgrounds and disputes about proper relations to the church abroad, these groups have had difficulty uniting. Hence, survival of the Orthodox churches has depended largely on survival of ethnic identity. By the nature of the case, preservation of ethnic identity requires some isolation, meaning that Orthodox Christians as such have had little impact on the wider American life. Lacking much theory or experience of regarding themselves as one denomination among many, they have had difficulty forging compromises between being Orthodox and Ameri-

• • •

can. Thus, even more than many other ethnic groups, as their populations have Americanized, large numbers have drifted away from active practice of the faith. Nonetheless, their highly distinctive worship represents one of the oldest traditions of Christendom and remains vital for sizeable, though somewhat isolated, American communities.[7]

Judaism in America

The role of Jews and Judaism in shaping mainstream American culture makes a startling contrast to that of Eastern Orthodoxy. Although the total numbers of the ethnic constituencies of the two groups have been comparable (there were an estimated 5.5 million Jews in America in 1980), and although there are parallels in times of immigration and areas of origin, the Jewish impact has been vastly disproportional relative to numbers. More than any non-Protestant immigrant group, Jews have become an integral part of the cultural activities of the nation; but at the same time they have retained their ethnic identity.

One reason for the contrast is that religion has played a different role in the Jewish community than it has for the other ethnic groups we have discussed. Most ethnic groups came from nations where their religion was dominant, usually established by law. In the new land traditional forms of that religion played a crucial role within the immigrant community, but provided little help in relating to the larger culture. Those from the ethnic group who wished to retain a clear ethnic identity were likely to be traditionally religious. The options were traditional religious practice, drifting away to occasional traditional practice, or a total Americanization that would involve leaving both the religion and the ethnic community.

Jews, on the other hand, had always lived as a minority group in lands dominated by someone else's religion and politics. They already had generations of the ghetto experience that other immigrants found new. And their ethnic identity was not dependent on their religious practice. While for the traditional observant Jew the religious practices of keeping the law and observing the proper ceremonies was central to one's membership in the community, one retained an identity with the community even if one were not observant. Jewishness was simultaneously an ethnic and religious status.

The unusually influential role of Jews in the United States also reflected an economic difference from most other non-Protestant im-

• • •

migrants. Jewish immigrants, although typically in poverty when they arrived in America, generally did not come from peasant backgrounds as most Catholic or Orthodox immigrants. Rather, Jews, who were exempted from laws against usury (lending money with an interest charge) in Europe, had long traditions as a commercial class. The early Jews who came to America, mostly from Spain and Portugal, were few, hardly more than 1,000 by the end of the colonial era, but many of them prospered. During the early nineteenth century most Jewish immigration, which did not bring the totals to over 100,000 until the 1850s, was from Germany, often peddlers and merchants. Some of these became part of a commercial elite. In the late nineteenth century, this group of prosperous Jews was overwhelmed in numbers by Jews from Eastern Europe, especially Poland and Russia. Economic and cultural differences separated the two groups and created rivalries. Nonetheless, the Eastern European Jewish men were predominantly skilled craftsmen who, after initial years of poverty, soon moved toward economic success.[8]

Another factor contributing to the remarkable integration of Jews into American life was their affinity to the dominant Protestant culture. As we have seen from the Puritan days, many of the dominant Anglo-Protestants in America thought they were establishing a Bible civilization. Both the Puritans and some of their influential successors in the national era spoke of America as a "new Israel." Calvinist culture, which shaped much of the early American religious heritage, was a culture especially shaped by the Old Testament, or the Jewish Scriptures. Calvinists, more than most Protestant groups, saw their religious task as building a Christian civilization. To do so, they looked especially to the Old Testament model. Hence, American culture, perhaps more than that of any other modern nation, was shaped by Old Testament ideals. Until the twentieth century (when they forgot most of both), most Americans knew the history of the Jewish patriarchs as well or better than they knew their own history.

These traditions not only meant that Jewish values and outlooks fit well with the dominant Americanism; they also helped mitigate the ever-present prejudice against Jews. Early Puritans, for instance, treated occasional Jewish visitors better than they treated other outsiders. And although there was real discrimination against Jews and against Jewish political and religious practice in colonial America, it was relatively mild compared with European counterparts. In Europe

• • •

the Jewish experience meant toleration in various nations for a time, but then to be subjected to severe waves of persecution and popular anti-Semitism. In the United States, although there was anti-Semitism and exclusion of Jews from most prestige organizations and schools, the discrimination was at least tempered by enough exceptions to provide attractive contrasts to the European alternatives.

In addition to a common biblical heritage, American Jews shared with Anglo-Protestants influences from the Enlightenment. Like the Calvinists, who also had disproportionate influence in shaping America, Jews valued education and the written word. So by the eighteenth century their religious heritage was supplemented by high respect for the reason of the day. As an oppressed people, they had a passionate commitment to American Enlightenment doctrines concerning equal rights for all.

The initially dominant thinking in the relatively small Jewish communities during the first half of the nineteenth century was to draw on these commonalities in order to blend in with the mainstream culture. Beginning as early as the 1820s there were efforts to reform ancient rites, such as dietary laws, and rituals of synagogue worship which enlightened American Jews found unsuited for modern times. Out of such sentiments, which had their origins among Jews in Germany, grew a major Reform movement, engineered primarily by Rabbi Isaac Mayer Wise (1819–1900). Though opposed by traditionalists, Wise and others built a Reform movement that made this type of Judaism strikingly like a Protestant denomination. Probably the closest parallel was the Unitarian movement that grew out of Calvinism at the same time and also flourished among the well-to-do in urban centers. For Judaism, practice is more central than doctrine, so the principal reforms came in vastly simplified requirements for Jewish observance. Services were held in English, they were shorter, worshippers sang hymns, choirs and organs were introduced, and in some cases services were even held on Sunday rather than Saturday, the traditional Jewish Sabbath.

The growing tensions between the leaders of Reform and traditionalists were brought to a head by a dramatic incident. In 1883 at a banquet honoring the first graduating class of Hebrew Union College in Cincinnati, the center for Reform, the menu announced an opening course of shellfish, an item forbidden by strict Jewish dietary laws. Traditionalists and moderates stormed out. The eventual result was a

• • •

three-way division of American Judaism into Reform, Conservative, and Orthodox. The Orthodox were those who strictly continued traditional practice. Conservatism was a moderate movement between the other two. It was conservative in the classic nineteenth-century sense of affirming the value of distinctly Jewish traditions, but it also allowed that these traditions must evolve over time. Hence, Conservatives preserved more traditional practices than did Reform, but allowed some updating in the forms of such observance.

One can see, for instance, the degrees of concession to modernity in the treatment of women during worship services of the three groups. Orthodox practice required strict separation of women from men in worship, which was conducted totally by males. Conservatives condoned family seating in worship and allowed women to participate alongside men in communal worship. Reform, like liberal Protestants, allowed women to read from the Torah and eventually took the lead in encouraging women to be rabbis.[9]

This three-way division came just as the Jewish situation was beginning to change dramatically through immigration. The latter decades of the nineteenth century were a time of increased racism and ethnic nationalism throughout the Western world. One reason for this was a reverence for the social science of the day, which seemed to provide a Darwinist basis for the superiority of certain races in the struggle for survival. Such factors only provided a rationale for unleashing ancient hostilities and modern rivalries. Jews were among the chief victims of such renewed hostility and in Eastern Europe and Russia they were often driven from their homes by popular pograms and persecutions. Between 1880 and 1900 over a half-million emigrated to America and by 1920 nearly two million more had made the journey. New York City became easily the largest center of Jewish population in the world.

The new immigrants were almost all Eastern European, speaking a Yiddish or Polish dialect, and initially very poor, bringing with them all the problems that poverty entails. The older Jewish population of well-to-do German Jews were often appalled and embarrassed by the conditions of their co-religionists and feared it would breed anti-Semitism. Sharp "uptown" versus "downtown" differences emerged, as the New York version of the issue was described. The well-to-do uptowners had ambivalent feelings toward the newcomers who crowded the Lower East Side. They organized charities for them; but most of

• • •

all they seemed to want them to get rid of their "foreign" ways as quickly as possible. As the title of Israel Zangwill's 1909 play, immensely popular among the uptowners, put it, they should merge into *The Melting-Pot*. Said Zangwill, "[Here] all the races of Europe are melting and reforming . . . God is making the American."[10]

The situation did not prove to be so simple. The Eastern European immigrants brought with them two principal tendencies. Many in the first generation reacted to their uprooting in the fashion typical of most immigrant groups, holding on tightly to their traditional religious practice. Another substantial group had already, in their homelands, become explicitly secular or anti-religious. These typically were champions of socialistic solutions to the world's problems. Even though most of the Jewish community tended not to be highly organized politically, partially in reaction to Irish Catholic power, these ideological socialists provided the immigrant community with an important secular alternative to the explicitly religious heritage.

This secularizing tendency was soon accentuated, consistent with a principle known as "Hansen's law" (named for the historian of immigration, Marcus Hansen): "What the son wishes to forget, the grandson wishes to remember."[11] While many of the first generation of Yiddish-speaking immigrants attempted to preserve their old world heritage and religious practice, many in the second generation attempted to get away from their traditions. During the early decades of the twentieth century, this law operated more conspicuously in the Jewish communities than any other. By the 1930s fewer than one-third of Jewish families were members of any congregation and three-fourths of Jewish young people between ages 15 and 20 had attended no services for a least at year.[12]

Nevertheless, this strong secular alternative did little to weaken Jewish identity, which had been established over millennia. Cultural identity could be sustained, at least for a time, even without religious practice. During the early decades of the twentieth century, the Jewish community built flourishing networks of organizations to care for almost every dimension of social life. At the same time, the secularization of the communities, as well as their growing affluence and high educational attainments, made it easier for Jews to enter the mainstream of American life, particularly the media and entertainment, without religious encumbrance. Rather than blend into a melting pot, however, they established a model for twentieth century American

• • •

pluralism in which a group could build a strong continuing identity while at the same time participate with civility in the mainstream of public life.

Christianity of Black Americans

The experience of blacks in America since the Civil War contrasts dramatically with that of Catholics and Jews. For Catholics and Jews, religious differences reinforced ethnic rivalries with the Anglo-Protestant establishment. Blacks, on the other hand, were kept outside the power structures more decisively than other groups, *despite* their religious stance. Blacks were overwhelmingly Protestant, almost all Baptist or Methodist, and their churches flourished and grew. Yet their theological affinities to white Protestantism provided them with little social advantage. There is probably no clearer illustration of the point that, while religion has been immensely important in shaping American life, it often is not the decisive force. Just as warfare often has brought co-religionists to the point of killing each other, so also have racial antagonisms outweighed religious affinities. To pick just one striking example, perhaps no two groups have been more deeply separated from each other socially than white Baptists and black Baptists in the South.

One way to understand the experience of the freed slaves is to consider the analogy to that of immigrant groups in America. Once slavery ended, the position of blacks in America was in principle similar to that of some new immigrants. Slavery, of course, had not been the blacks' only social problem. They still faced the deep poverty and economic dependence of unskilled laborers. Such problems were compounded by lack of education and the almost total illiteracy imposed by slavery. Although these obstacles were massive, they were not vastly different from those faced by many immigrants. They became almost insurmountable, however, when combined with a third factor—racial prejudice. Just as anti-Semitism intensified throughout the world in the late nineteenth and early twentieth centuries, so racism intensified against blacks in America. In the United States, racial prejudice simply replaced slavery as the central motif in white attitudes toward blacks, and kept blacks on the bottom economic and educational rungs of society.

During Reconstruction, so long as Northern moral and religious idealism remained strong, hopes were raised to give blacks a place in

• • •

political life and to build educational institutions so that blacks might eventually take their place as equals in American life. The majority of Northerners, however, soon reneged on any promise of equality. When Reconstruction was brought to an end, control of Southern society and politics soon reverted to Southern whites only. Having lost the war, most Southern whites were deeply determined that they would not give up the principles for which they fought. One of those principles was that the South would be a white man's country. Blacks were soon effectively eliminated from political influence and Jim Crow segregation laws soon gave legal sanction to white superiority. The South, which had always been a society in which evangelical religion and violence were dual motifs, continued in the same vein. During the 1890s there were an average of three lynchings of blacks per week.[13]

As in most immigrant groups, the churches became for blacks their principal institutions both for coping with the hard realities of life and for building up a sense of community. In fact, because of the always limited economic resources for building other institutions and because the churches were the one black institution over which whites allowed blacks full control, the church usually functioned as the central and only black institution in a community. Fine church buildings often were major sources of community pride. The churches also provided almost the only opportunity for black leadership. In fact, black churches typically had strong pastors who personally controlled the network of church organizations that served the black communities. W.E.B. DuBois, the famous black sociologist, at the turn of the century observed that the black pastors of his day were "among the most powerful Negro rulers in the world." He observed also that "in the South, at least, practically every American Negro is a church member. Some to be sure are not regularly enrolled, and a few do not habitually attend services; but, practically, a proscribed people must have a social center, and that center for this people is the Negro church."[14]

After the Civil War the organizational separation of blacks and whites into their own churches was welcomed by both groups. In the South, until the war, they worshiped together in the same churches, with blacks segregated to the balconies. Blacks now generally forsook the white denominations, preferring their organizations to servile roles in white organizations in which they were unwelcome. Many joined Northern Methodist denominations, including the predominantly white Northern Methodist church, but principally two Northern black

• • •

Methodist groups, the African Methodist Episcopal Church and the African Methodist Episcopal Zion Church. By 1870, the blacks remaining in the Southern Methodist church had organized into the separate Colored Methodist Episcopal Church (now Christian Methodist Episcopal Church).

Even more blacks formed their own Baptist churches. Baptist churches are controlled by local congregations and therefore very easy for a group of believers to establish. This strength could also be a weakness. It was much more difficult for Baptists to organize nationally. For several decades after the Civil War black Baptists struggled to unite as a national denomination. In the meantime they organized many of their churches into state conventions and formed national Baptist agencies to promote foreign missions, especially to Africa. But not until 1895 was the National Baptist Convention established as the largest organization of black Baptists. Tensions continued, however, and in 1916 the convention split in two, the larger group calling itself the National Baptist Convention, Inc. and the slightly smaller group keeping the name National Baptist Convention. Localism plus a perennial lack of surplus funds made it difficult for black churches to maintain effective national organization.[15]

A number of issues were strongly debated within the black communities. The most persistent were what their relationship should be to the white society, and to the support of friendly Northern churchpeople. Initially, during Reconstruction, newly freed blacks were largely dependent on support from Northern whites. Especially in the field of education many former abolitionists sacrificially dedicated themselves to building black schools and training a black leadership for subsequent generations. At the same time, some Northern black leaders promoted the cause. For instance, one of the most effective black educators of the day was Daniel Alexander Payne (1811–1883), bishop of the African Methodist Episcopal Church. Born free in Charleston, South Carolina, Payne was driven out in the 1830s for organizing education of blacks. After the Civil War he returned to South Carolina for the first South Carolina Annual Conference of the AME Church. Payne's principal leadership role, however, was as the first black president of a black-controlled college, Wilberforce University in Ohio. Payne's leadership at Wilberforce was an important model for building other black institutions. By the end of the century black Christians had established some two dozen black colleges and benefited

• • •

from other black institutions that had primarily Northern white support.

Despite gratitude for white support, dependency was not a comfortable position. Some black leaders called for strengthening their own black institutions and thus establishing true independence.

This tension was complicated by the deteriorating race relationships in the latter decades of the century. The dominant black spokesperson to emerge in the era was Booker T. Washington (1856–1915), a Baptist and head of Tuskegee Institute in Alabama. Washington accepted the dominant work ethic of the day, proclaiming that if blacks were to escape from their poverty, they would have to work their way out. The first step was learning practical industrial and agricultural skills. In the meantime, Washington proclaimed that blacks should accept their secondary status in society, and cultivate all the white help and goodwill they could get. Of the two races, he proclaimed in a famous speech in Atlanta in 1895, "in all things purely social we can be as separate as the fingers, yet one as the hand in all things essential to mutual progress." Not only was this music to the ears of white segregationists and even to white progressives who had given up on resolving America's race problem, but it was accepted by most blacks.

Unlike the experience of contemporary immigrant groups in America, integration and assimilation into American society was proving to be an illusory and a frustrating option for blacks. Washington's compromise thus seemed to most as far as they could go at the time. As in other communities, however, there were dissenters. During the early decades of the twentieth century these black leaders demanded that blacks pick up again the agenda of full participation in American society. At least they should be demanding their civil rights. Such demands did not come so much from the churches as from extraecclesiastical organizations, most notably the National Association for the Advancement of Colored People, founded in 1909. W.E.B. DuBois (1868–1963), who abandoned his earlier Christian faith, was the most prominent spokesperson calling for more radical demands to go beyond the status quo.

Within the black churches a parallel tension developed about the degree to which they should be affirming the distinctive black traditions of worship. Northern blacks who had New England mentors before the war and Northern white supporters who wanted to raise

• • •

black educational standards generally thought that the black churches should move beyond the patterns of folk religion that developed during the time of slavery. In the twentieth century, black sociologists, beginning with DuBois, uniformly said the same thing.

Nonetheless, black Christians developed a distinctive style of worship which was truly their own and which they were not willing to give up. This style, as we have seen, combined elements of evangelical revivalism with ecstatic African patterns of worship. Spirituals as a creative dialogue within the congregation (which anticipated the development of jazz) were particularly meaningful and uniquely black religious expressions. These patterns of worship, and the theologies they entailed, had served blacks well during times of intense hardship by giving them hope. So they persisted in the vast majority of black churches. As historian Lawrence Levine summarizes the contemporary reports of black worship during the three-quarters of a century after emancipation:

> All the traditional trappings were there: the ecstasy, the spirit possession, the shouts, the chanted sermons, the sacred sense of time and space, the immediacy, the feeling of familarity with God and the ancient heroes, the communal setting in which songs were created and recreated.[16]

This African-influenced black American style proved to be not only a preservation of the past, but also a building toward the future. When the pentecostal movement emerged in America at the beginning of the twentieth century (see discussion below), perhaps its most influential early leader was a black pastor, William J. Seymour, principal preacher at the famed Azuza Street revivals in Los Angeles beginning in 1906. Modern pentecostalism, which developed out of a number of traditions in white evangelicalism, also incorporated substantial elements of black styles of ecstatic worship. In the early decades, pentecostal churches and worship were, remarkably, often integrated; but soon the movement separated out into black and white denominations. The largest black pentecostal group was the Church of God in Christ.

Like the white American communities, black Americans, despite their flourishing churches, faced strong currents of secularization as they entered the twentieth century. By the turn of the century, this secularization was signalled by the emergence alongside the spir-

· · ·

ituals of new forms of black musical expression—jazz, ragtime, and the blues. Although jazz and the blues sometimes incorporated religious elements, they also marked the development of a black culture outside the churches.

Such secularizing tendencies were accelerated in the early twentieth century by massive black emigration to Northern cities. There they founded churches, both traditional Baptist and Methodist, and newer storefront pentecostal and sectarian. At the same time the forces of highly differentiated urban life were forcing a compartmentalization of the role of the church that would have been impossible in a Southern town. Perhaps even more sharply than in most other ethnic communities, church was largely a special activity or Sunday affair, divorced from highly secular everyday realities. The black communities, like most of America, were both intensely religious and intensely secular. The biggest difference was that for a disproportionate number of blacks the expressions of these polarities were limited to ghettoes perpetually kept impoverished by a discrimatory social and economic system.

WHITE PROTESTANT RELIGIOUS OUTSIDERS AND PROTESTERS

American culture has always included a strong democratic impulse. One of the areas of American life, perhaps *the* area, where this impulse has most often been expressed is religion. Historians of American democracy have been most interested in the rise of liberal politics and so have not much noticed the democratic tendencies in religion, which they often regard as reactionary. Nonetheless, some of the most frequent protests against the authority of elite power structures has been religious protest. Religious protest is, of course, easier to organize and carry out than political protest and perhaps is sometimes a substitute for it. Nonetheless, the protests are real and substantial. They are protests against those who define the values and the valuing of persons in a community. We have already encountered such movements in the first Great Awakening, in the democratic awakenings and sectarian movements of the national period, and in slave Christianity. As the United States entered the twentieth cen-

• • •

tury, such anti-elite movements continued to offer to white Protestants significant numbers of alternatives to the dominant denominational structures.

The issues involved in the formation of new sects were primarily spiritual issues rather than class issues, but the two were often intermixed. New groups invariably developed out of a conviction that the mainline denominations were not sufficiently spiritual. Though such opinions could have appeal to persons in any social class, most of the new movements that offered a more radical spirituality and new, conspicuously distinctive communities of faith were likely to flourish among people who for one reason or another felt on the fringes of society, whereas the mainline denominations by their very nature retained a hold on the more settled elements of the population.

The Holiness Movement

The best example of these dynamics is in the development of a striking number of holiness sects from Methodism during the nineteenth century. Methodism during this period was America's largest and most typical Protestant denomination. From 1865 to 1920 the Methodist Episcopal Church (Northern) grew from one million to four million and its Southern Methodist counterpart grew from half a million to two million. Methodism, like the other large denominational group, the Baptists, remained a popular and largely evangelical movement during this period. In the nineteenth-century South the saying was that, "A Methodist is a Baptist who wears shoes; a Presbyterian is a Methodist who has gone to college; an Episcopalian is a Presbyterian who lives off of his investments." By the late nineteenth century, especially in the North, such denominational stereotypes would not have applied either for Baptists or Methodists. Methodism was still the denomination of the modest middle classes; but it had also acquired considerable sophistication. Methodists, for instance, were becoming leaders in higher education, maintaining scores of colleges and a number of universities. Such gains were signs of respectability won over generations. Inevitably this meant that, despite vitality that fostered continued growth, the intensity of the early days of the movement was often missing.

Holiness movements, quite simply, called for renewal of this intensity. They especially called for renewal of emphasis on personal holiness, such as in Methodist founder John Wesley's teachings. Al-

• • •

ready we encounter these movements in speaking of midcentury evangelicalism. Charles Finney, although he was a Presbyterian and Congregationalist, taught holiness doctrines. Phoebe Palmer taught them in her holiness meetings. The Wesleyan Methodist Church (1843) and the Free Methodist Church (1860) split from the parent denomination since they extended personal holiness to include radical views on slavery.

Mention of Phoebe Palmer, a doctor's wife who held her holiness meetings in her spacious home, illustrates that the holiness protests were not primarily a matter of social class. In the latter part of the nineteenth century the movement continued to have well-to-do advocates, including some educated women leaders who took advantage of the movement's openness to spiritual authority regardless of gender.

Nonetheless, as the movement grew into something of a revival within Methodism, it spread furthest among simpler folk attracted to an old-time religious intensity. The principal expression of this movement was in "holiness camp meetings," which were organized into a national movement in Vineland, New Jersey in 1867. By the 1880s this developed into numerous regional holiness associations on the edge of Methodism. Holiness teaching reemphasized the separation of the Christian from the world, saying that a dramatic conversion experience of being born again was not enough. Rather, one should also expect a "second blessing" of being filled or baptized by the Holy Spirit, which involved the eradication of "inbred sin." In addition, holiness teachers stressed two other doctrines not typically emphasized in mainline Protestantism: the power of miraculous healing, and the expectation of Jesus' return at any moment to set up a millennial kingdom on earth. The holiness emphases were sometimes summarized as a fourfold or "foursquare" gospel of Christ as savior, as baptizer with the Holy Spirit, healer, and coming King.

By the 1890s the holiness teachings led to splits within the Methodist denomination and the formation of a number of small holiness denominations, most of which formed into either the Church of the Nazarene or the Pilgrim Holiness Church. In the meantime, other holiness groups emerged. The best known is the Salvation Army, founded by William Booth in England in 1865 and soon flourishing as an evangelistic ministry to the poor in the United States. The English origins point out a trans-Atlantic connection that still could be found

• • •

Free coal distribution by the Salvation Army.

in almost every evangelical development. The ministry to the poor both through charity as well as evangelism illustrates that such evangelistic movements were not concerned only with saving souls for the next life. Other new holiness organizations were the Christian and Missionary Alliance and the Church of God (Anderson, Indiana), one of a number of groups called the Church of God.

Pentecostalism

This quest to be set apart by spiritual intensity, a dramatic experience of the Holy Spirit, miraculous powers and expectations, and a holy life produced not only new holiness groups but what by the later twentieth century became their much larger worldwide offspring—modern pentecostalism. We have already noticed black contributions to pentecostalism, or at least affinities of black traditions to emerging pentecostalism, in an ecstatic style of worship. But the main roots are clearly traceable to the turbulent holiness revivals of the late nineteenth century.

Many of these late nineteenth-century holiness revivals were re-

• • •

ferred to as "pentecostal" outpourings, which it was believed marked a new age of the Holy Spirit. Occasionally at revival services persons spoke in strange tongues; but such phenomena were not considered to have unusual doctrinal significance.[17]

Modern pentecostalism is usually dated, conveniently enough, from the first day of the twentieth century, January 1, 1901, when tongues-speaking broke out at a holiness revival service in Topeka, Kansas, as predicted by its leader Charles Fox Parham (1873–1929). In 1906, William J. Seymour, a black who heard Parham teach, carried the new views to the Azuza Street revivals in Los Angeles, which sparked a nationwide movement. At first the speaking in tongues was interpreted as speaking actual foreign languages, such as Chinese. Later it was usually regarded as speaking in unknown tongues that required an interpreter.

Early pentecostalism appealed to disproportionate numbers of the economically poor, both white and black. During its formative stages many competing doctrines emerged and literally hundreds of small denominations eventually formed. The largest pentecostal groups to emerge were the predominantly black Church of God in Christ, the Church of God (Cleveland, Tennessee)—both organized earlier as holiness groups—and the Assemblies of God (organized in 1914).[18] This complex movement accentuated many developments that flourished first and best in the American environment. Lack of effective centralized church authority, and the ideal of equality for all persons in the spirit, opened room for spiritual innovation and enterprise among all classes of persons.

One sign of the new age of the Spirit was believed to be the fulfillment of the prophecy in the Book of Joel, repeated in the Book of Acts in the account of the first Christian Pentecost: "I will pour out my spirit upon all flesh; and your sons and your daughters shall prophesy." Holiness and pentecostal groups accordingly had fewer inhibitions about women leadership than did most Christian groups. Prominent among women was Aimee Semple McPherson (1890–1944), who organized and ran the International Church of the Foursquare Gospel, a pentecostal denomination headquartered in Los Angeles.

McPherson's career (while not typical of all pentecostalism) also underscored the tensions that have always troubled such free enterprise religious movements in which the leadership is subject to no

• • •

ecclesiastical authority. Although an impressive evangelist, Mc-Pherson was plagued by rumors of scandal, including in 1926 a dramatic "disappearance" into the sea, reported to be a cover for a rendezvous with her radio announcer. In 1944, while on an evangelistic campaign, she died of a barbiturate overdose.

Perhaps the most interesting cultural question suggested by the rise of holiness and pentecostal movements in the late nineteenth and early twentieth centuries is why such teaching began to spread widely just at the period when industrialization and new technology were revolutionizing the world. A parallel question is why the doctrine of miraculous healings spread among Protestants just at a time when modern medicine finally began to make some real progress in healing people. Part of the answer to these questions must be that many people were reacting to the growing materialistic definitions of reality in the modern world. Middle- and upper-class people at this time often turned to romantic and idealistic philosophies that affirmed the primacy of the spiritual. Holiness and pentecostal teachings, although not restricted to any class, and though (as in all religion) not always followed consistently by their adherents, provided another nonmaterialistic alternative with which to define reality.

Premillennialism

One of the four dogmas of the "four-square" gospel of many holiness and pentecostal groups was that Jesus would return to earth at any moment to set up a kingdom in Jerusalem for a millennium. This belief, known as premillennialism (Jesus will return *prior* to the millennium), was in the late nineteenth century becoming popular among a wide variety of renewal or sectarian groups on the revivalist side of American Protestantism. The view became so widespread, so little the property of any one group, and so often a badge of those who were unhappy with the moderate or liberal drift of mainline Protestantism, that its rise becomes important for understanding many twentieth-century American religious movements.

In the mid-nineteenth century, as we have seen, millennial views were common within mainstream Northern Protestantism. The dominant view, however, was "postmillennial," teaching that Jesus would return only *after* a golden age that would grow out of current cultural and social progress. Postmillennialists were thus optimistic about culture and fit with the dominant mood of nineteenth- and early twen-

• • •

tieth-century America. As observed earlier, the social gospel movement
was a theologically liberal version of this hope to Christianize the social order.

Premillennialism was an older Christian belief, but its most common modern form (found in holiness, pentecostal, and later fundamentalist and charismatic groups) grew out of a number of trends
particularly strong in revivalist Christianity. Probably the strongest
impulse was one found in all these renewal movements, a heighten-
ing of emphasis on the supernatural dimensions of Christianity. At
the same time that moderate and liberal Protestants were blessing
natural cultural and ethical developments and stressing adjustment to
modern secular ideals, other Protestants were reemphasizing the
supernatural.

Integral to this view was a strongly supernaturalistic interpretation
of the Bible, once more going against the modern scholarly trends to
look at the Bible as only a historical product. Premillennialist interpreters insisted that the Bible was truly the word of God and therefore accurate in every detail. This was not a new belief; but just as
papal infallibility was emphasized in 1870 when it was being challenged, so about the same time many Protestants began to insist on
the "inerrancy" of the Bible in historical and scientific detail.

For interpreters of Bible prophecies this doctrine was especially
important since they believed that the prophecies contained accurate,
even if mysterious, predictions about the future. For them, it was
crucial that the 1,000 years of the millennium be an actual 1,000 years
during which Christ would literally rule in Jerusalem, not a symbolic
reign of Christ as postmillennialists would say. Others of their prophecies hinged on literal interpretations of biblical numbers.

Such interpreters of Bible prophecy did not see themselves as rejecting the scientific principles of the day. Just the opposite—they
saw the Bible as a book of reliable facts and themselves as applying
scientific principles to arranging and understanding those facts. For
instance, the most common premillennial view, called "dispensation-
alism," divided world history into seven eras or dispensations. Correct
scientific reading of the Bible, they insisted, could demonstrate that
modern people were living at the end of the sixth dispensation of the
"church age." This age would see, as they were seeing, a decline of
the large established churches and of so-called "Christian civilization." Only a remnant of the churches would have true, born-again

• • •

and sanctified believers. At any moment, they predicted, Jesus would return to inaugurate a series of dramatic events. These would begin with the "secret rapture" of the church, in which true believers would suddenly disappear from earth. Then there would be seven years of wars and tribulations during which the Jews, returned to Palestine, would be converted to Christianity. These events would culminate with the return of Jesus and the saints, his victory over the Antichrist in a literal battle at Armageddon (in Israel), and his thousand-year rule in Jerusalem.

Mainstream America: Loving It or Leaving It?

Such views, widespread among revivalists, naturally created some tensions as to how Protestants were viewing their American heritage. On the one hand, they inherited the tradition going back to the Puritans that America was a Christian nation with a special destiny in history. On the other hand, premillennial views invited pessimistic readings of so-called Christian culture. Revivalists often wavered between these two views. Dwight L. Moody, for instance, was a premillennialist and many of his associates were the most prominent teachers of dispensational doctrines. With Moody's blessing, they founded Bible institutes where the new doctrines were taught, to train an army of lay Christian workers. At the same time, Moody was a loyal believer in the American way of life and a friend to the optimistic liberal Protestants. And liberal and premillennial revivalists could cooperate under Moody's inspiration in the missionary effort to "evangelize the world in this generation."

The fact is that in the era before World War I a serious crisis was building ominously in Protestantism concerning the proper relationship of converted Christians to American culture. Those who formed new holiness or pentecostal sects were separating themselves from the dominant mainstream culture. Such separatists, however, were only a minority uneasy with the dominant trends. Many others, including some of the premillennialists, continued in mainline denominations, but were beginning to be critical of liberal Protestantism's downplaying of some traditional supernatural aspects of Christianity and the liberal identification of spiritual progress with the advance of modern civilization. As in Moody's day, the more liberal and supernaturalistically oriented Protestants could still sometimes work together, as in the prohibition campaign. Nonetheless, beneath such activism was

• • •

the potential for an explosion at the center of the Protestant religious and cultural establishment.

New Religious Movements: Christian Science and Jehovah's Witnesses

One indicator of the religious tensions building in a culture is the types of new religious movements that spin off from it. In the late nineteenth century the United States saw the development of two major new religious groups that, while having Christian roots, departed significantly from traditional Christianity.

These groups, Christian Science and Jehovah's Witnesses, provide a revealing contrast. Sociologically, they have been at opposite ends of the spectrum. Christian Science has had its most appeal among the wealthiest and best educated. Jehovah's Witnesses flourish primarily among the economically and educationally deprived. Correspondingly, Christian Science might be seen as a radical departure from tradition in a liberal direction, while Jehovah's Witnesses are a similarly radical departure, but in a revivalist millennialist direction. Both groups were responding to modern secularism and materialism by asserting the primacy of the supernatural. But the types of supernaturalism were opposite. Christian Science, even more than liberal Protestantism, emphasized that all reality was spiritual. Discovery of such a principle would revolutionize human relationships and perceptions. Jehovah's Witnesses accentuated millennial Protestantism's tendencies to expect spectacular supernatural interventions. Its revivalist mores were strict almost to the point of being reactionary.

Christian Science went beyond liberal Protestantism in its tendency to use traditional Christian terminology; but to give it entirely new meanings. The particulars of the outlook grew from the experience of the movement's founder, Mary Baker Eddy (1821–1910). Eddy was a New Englander who intensely experienced the characteristic sense of loss that nineteenth-century New Englanders felt as Calvinism declined as the organizing principle giving the dominant culture its meaning and direction. As we have seen, many well-to-do Anglo Protestants of midcentury, especially women, turned to transcendental or other spiritualistic movements that regained spiritual intensity. Almost all of these movements emphasized the primacy of spiritual reality over the material. Many people from the same mid-nineteenth

• • •

century middle class were also preoccupied with new programs for promoting health.

The experience of Mary Baker Eddy incorporated all these tendencies. In 1862, after years of poor health and suffering, she was dramatically cured by mind cure specialist Phineas Parkhurst Quimby (1802–1866). Eddy adopted Quimby's views and reinterpreted them in terms of traditional Christian language. She taught that God constituted all reality, which was spiritual. Regeneration came from recognizing that empirical experience of the material world was illusory and hence allowed God through Christ to transform one's being. Recognition of the illusory character of the material world would also lead to physical health, without resorting to doctors or conventional medicine.

Eddy's Church of Christ (Scientist) was chartered in 1879 and by the latter decades of her life, she achieved wide success and fortune, if not total freedom herself from physical suffering. Most notably she attracted a devoted following and established in Boston a prosperous mother church as the headquarters of her movement. While the movement never gained much more than perhaps a quarter of a million adherents in the United States, because of its affluence it had influence disproportionate to its numbers. Today it is best known for its outstanding, largely secular newspaper, *The Christian Science Monitor.*[19]

The Jehovah's Witnesses were founded about the same time by Charles Taze Russell (1852–1916), a small-time merchant from Pennsylvania. Like many nineteenth-century Christians, he was preoccupied with the ideal that one should use scientific means for a personal study of the Bible, not relying on the authority of others. Russell concluded that the "millennial dawn" already occurred in 1874, although the end of all things would not come until 1914. "Millions now living will never die" was his watchword. In these respects his movement was similar to Seventh-day Adventism. However, Russell's biblical studies also led him to a number of unique doctrines that diverged from most Christian orthodoxy. For instance, he rejected the traditional doctrine of the Trinity, seeing Jesus, instead, as wholly distinct from God the Father. He also, like some of the liberals of the day, did away with the doctrine of Hell, substituting an elaborate scheme of an era of probation or second chance for salvation, with

• • •

annihilation as the alternative. Even though the literal end of the age apparently did not occur in 1914, the doctrine was reinterpreted and the movement was successfully reorganized under the leadership of "Judge" Joseph H. Rutherford (1869–1942). Since then its aggressive door-to-door and worldwide missionary efforts have led to a steady growth. As with most American-born millennial movements (such as Adventists, Mormons, pentecostals, and fundamentalist groups), its growth has accelerated in the later twentieth century.

One of the features that has distinguished Jehovah's Witnesses from most other millennial groups is that they specifically reject loyalty to government. Almost all American millennial groups have proclaimed that modern civilization is corrupt and that Christians must radically separate themselves from it. Few, however, have carried such doctrines to their logical conclusions. So, when the chips have been down, most of these groups are willing to put their country first and to make the "ultimate sacrifice" of risking their lives to fight the nation's wars. Before World War I, some dispensationalist premillennialists questioned whether Christians could fight in wars and a good many pentecostals refused military service prior to World War II; but few such millennialists have retained that heritage. Jehovah's Witnesses, on the other hand, have consistently taken literally the teaching that Christ's kingdom is not of this world. Accordingly, they have refused military service and refused to pledge allegiance to the American flag. Many suffered imprisonment for their unpopular stances during both World War I and World War II. In 1942 some Jehovah's Witnesses were finally granted recognition as conscientious objectors and in 1943 the Supreme Court ruled that their children could not be excluded from public schools for refusing to salute the flag.

Peace Churches

Ever since the pilgrims arrived on American shores, American Protestants have wrestled with the question of what allegiance they should give to the prevailing political establishment and in what ways they should separate themselves from the "world," or the dominant culture of their day. To what extent should the church be a sect separated from the world, based strictly on the model of the early church of the New Testament? Would too strict of a separation destroy the church's influence?

The usual response to this dilemma has been essentially the same

• • •

Old Order Mennonites.

as that suggested by the Puritans—to keep the church pure by retaining strict membership requirements, but at the same time to try to dominate and transform the culture, and build a Christian culture. By the early twentieth century, in mainline Protestant churches, one dimension of this solution (the strict membership requirements) was beginning to recede and the churches were increasingly blending in with the dominant culture.

Another tradition was represented early in America by Roger Williams, who denounced the possibility of a Christian civilization, emphasizing the separateness or sectarian nature of churches based on the New Testament pattern. Positions much like Williams's had already been developed during the Reformation by the Anabaptist sects, who insisted on adult baptism as a symbol of separation and who established Christian communities separate from the rest of society. Anabaptists insisted that allegiance to Christ superseded allegiance to

• • •

any earthly rulers, and so were strict pacifists. Quakers, arising out of the English Civil Wars of the 1650s, took a similar view.

Eighteenth-century America, especially Pennsylvania, became a haven for radical sectarian groups. The two best-known Anabaptist groups to establish communities in America were the Mennonites and the closely related Amish. These groups often divided into subgroups. Typically, they have lived in separate communities and have been pacifists. But as they developed in the United States, their internal differences divided them into a spectrum of views from the strictest separatism to some assimilation into the mainstream culture. The strictest groups are the Old Order Amish who live in tightly closed, but internally very supportive, communities and reject all outward signs of modernity. They dress plainly in a style from early modern times, reject the use of modern conveniences, such as electricity and automobiles, and retain their own German dialect. Some other Amish allow for modern conveniences. Mennonites are divided by similar patterns. Some are strict separatists; others have become much more like other American denominations, using the English language, and giving up all distinctive dress and communal practice. Most, but not all, remain pacifist.

Other peace groups in America have experienced similar tensions regarding how strictly they should remain as separate sects or how fully they could participate in the wider society as just another denomination. To be a sect meant to separate themselves and to try to remain pure.

The Quakers probably have experienced these tensions most sharply. Although founded as a radical sect, they became the first families of eastern Pennsylvania, and among the wealthiest and most influential. Still, they attempted to remain distinctive, even if not living in separate enclaves. Not until the 1830s, for instance, did they give up their scruples against higher education; but then they founded a number of outstanding colleges, beginning with Haverford in 1833. Like other distinctive immigrant groups, they were becoming acculturated. By the twentieth century Quakers around the country covered a considerable spectrum of largely broad-minded religious opinion. Many were still pacifists, though not so much because they were sectarian as because their views were so progressive. Others gave up their pacifism. America's two Quaker presidents, Herbert Hoover and Richard Nixon, were not especially known for their pacifism.

• • •

A Common Heritage in a Pluralistic Society

For almost every group in America, whether ethnic, sectarian, or both, the central theme in their development has been much the same. How does the group retain its identity, but still participate in society? Almost every variation on this theme has been played out somewhere in America. Differences among groups as well as differences within them, often heightened by religious overtones, have separated Americans. Yet at the same time this common dilemma has given many American's some commonality of heritage.

• • •

CHAPTER FIVE

Traditional Religion and Twentieth-Century American Culture

Our Country is filled with a Socialistic, I.W.W., Communistic, radical, lawless, anti-American, anti-church, anti-God, anti-marriage gang, and they are laying the eggs of rebellion and unrest in labor and capital and home, and we have some of them in our universities. . . . If this radical element could have their way, my friends, the laws of nature would be repealed, or they would reverse them; oil and water would mix; the turtle dove would marry the turkey buzzard; the sun would rise in the West and set in the East; chickens would crow and the roosters would squeal; cats would bark and dogs would mew; the least would be the greatest; a part would be greater than the whole; yesterday would be after tomorrow if this crowd were in control.

Billy Sunday (1925)

Both our practical morality and our emotional lives are adjusted to a world which no longer exists.

Joseph Wood Krutch, *The Modern Temper* (1929)

Traditional Protestantism, Cultural Dominance, or Both?

While outsider groups were debating how much to assimilate with mainstream American society, insider Protestants were struggling during the early twentieth century over how to relate to a *changing* American society. Even if one belonged to a long-established Protestant church, such as Methodist, Baptist, Presbyterian, or Congregationalist, and were from long-Americanized British, or perhaps German, ethnic stock, one was still confronted with the issue of how Christians should relate to an increasingly pluralistic and secular society. For the leadership in such groups one practical question was whether they could continue to dominate American life. If so, could they retain their traditional Protestant beliefs? Or would they have to modify and broaden those beliefs both in order to remain current with prevailing opinion and to continue their cultural influence?

The reason this was an either-or choice was simple. Traditional Protestantism, like almost all other Judeo-Christian religions, is exclusivist. It teaches that some people will be saved for eternal life and some will not. Moreover, differences regarding morality are not simply matters of preference, but reflect the will of God. The total dominance of such views in a society would lead to an exclusivist, God-centered society like early Puritanism. In the United States, however, Protestant views had a more informal dominance. They retained an impact on public life through some concessions to a limited pluralism. That is, within the boundaries of broadly Judeo-Christian moral consensus, some views were tolerated and civil government was not based explicitly on religion. So long as the national heritage was predominantly homogeneous and Protestant, religious and secular views could be easily blended together without great conflict. The public schools, for instance, could teach generally Protestant viewpoints, mixed with American Enlightenment ideals.

By the early twentieth century when the United States was one of the most pluralistic nations on earth, this stance was becoming awkward. What was especially awkward were Protestantism's exclusivist claims. If these were replaced with inclusivist teachings, for instance, by saying that Christianity is just one of the ways by which humans can find God, then such a broadened Protestantism could retain its cultural leadership. Such broadening was encouraged also by the intellectual outlook of the time, which challenged all claims to

· · ·

absolute truth and explained differences in belief in terms of differing historical circumstance.

A second alternative, especially for those who retained some form of the traditional supernaturalism, was to move in a sectarian direction, giving up aspirations to control the whole society, but remaining pure within one's own group.

A third alternative was not to give up either traditional Protestant belief or their aspirations for cultural dominance. Rather than withdraw from mainline churches into separate groups, they might continue to fight for traditional Protestant values in the culture, and against liberal theologies. The presence of such people, the first to be called "fundamentalists," in some of America's most influential denominations, led to some of the twentieth century's most dramatic conflicts regarding the role of religion in culture. Such conflicts have continued in a variety of forms throughout the century.

Prelude to Conflict: Southern Conservatism

Most of the issues that divided mainline Protestantism in the twentieth century were fought in the North; but these conflicts were anticipated by religious antagonisms between South and North arising from the Civil War. As white Southerners began reentering national life, especially after 1900, a number of them contributed significantly to mainline conflicts.

When the white South tasted the dregs of defeat in the Civil War, its people determined that they would still win the peace. They had fought for an ideal civilization, for what they considered a Christian civilization. A mere military defeat could not take away that ideal. The principles of the "lost cause," which they considered morally and spiritually superior to Yankee civilization, could be preserved in the hearts and minds of the people.

Preserving the lost cause meant romanticizing pre-Civil War Southern culture as a model for civilization. Any deviation from that model would be a decline. This outlook meant that a strong motif in dominant Southern thought was a resistance to post-Civil War modernity.

This stance had important religious implications. Preserving the ideals of pre-Civil War culture meant preserving the dominant reli-

• • •

gious outlook of the 1850s—essentially, revivalist evangelicalism. Since mainstream American Protestantism was changing rapidly in the late nineteenth century, this stance immediately put most white Southerners on the conservative side of the current theological debates. Furthermore, the Southern sectors of the largest Protestant denominations, such as the Methodists, Baptists, and Presbyterians, had separated into their own organizations and remained separate after the war. To justify such continued separation, they asserted their superiority to their Northern counterparts. Yankees, they said, were turning toward theological liberalism, while Southerners remained true to the faith. Such conservatism was reinforced by continuing revivalism in the South. During the Civil War there were remarkable revivals among the Southern troops and revival religion remained in style.

A significant minority of Southern Protestants resisted all these trends and worked toward building a new South that would be as progressive in its views as the North. Conservative influences, however, remained dominant. Conservatism was supported by the relative homogeneity of the white Southern population. Immigration to the South, which was largely rural and not prosperous, was slow. So the white population of most of the region remained overwhelmingly Anglo-Protestant.

One helpful way to look at the white South since the Civil War is as a new American ethnic group.[1] Like other ethnic groups it was shaped by a common heritage, but also by a very strong sense of national identity—in this case with the short-lived Confederate nation. This identity continued to be strong as Southerners found themselves in a partly alien environment in the decades after the Civil War. As in other American ethnic communities, some argued for more assimilation with the dominant culture, while others argued for preserving their heritage. Much like other ethnic groups, religion played an important role in defining Southernness, and a sense of Southernness, and helped preserve religious conservatism. They were preserving the ways of the "old country"—in this case, the antebellum South.

The result was that, as the South entered the twentieth century, its dominant religion still had almost all the traits that were characteristic of American evangelicalism generally in the mid-nineteenth century. It was strongly biblicist and revivalist, putting emphasis on traditional theologies and individual conversions.

· · ·

Whether such traits were superior or inferior to the more progressive Protestantism arising primarily in the North was a matter of debate. And a cultural explanation of why some trends prevailed in one part of the country and others prevailed in another does not settle such issues. For the people involved, traditional revivalism or progressive Protestantism were attractive for the merits of what they taught.

As with many issues in the South, religious issues were mixed with beliefs about race. Most white Southerners in this era were firmly committed to keeping the South a white man's country. The churches were no exception. White churches welcomed the exodus of blacks after the Civil War and supported the strict segregationist society. Typically, the white churches professed to hold to the doctrine of "the spirituality of the church," by which they meant that churches should stay out of politics. This doctrine arose in opposition to Northern church support of abolitionism. The doctrine was far, however, from a declaration that the church should not be tarnished by involvement with a cultural system. Rather, it was a doctrine for those who already dominated the culture politically. The social functions of being nonpolitical are apparent in a revealing statement by the Southern Methodist bishops in 1894:

> "Our Church is strictly a religious and in no wise a political body. The more closely we keep ourselves to the one work of testifying to all men repentance toward God and faith toward our Lord Jesus Christ, the better shall we promote the highest good of our country and race."[2]

For most white Southern Protestants the spirituality of the church was selective, not keeping the church from speaking out on what they considered moral issues, as opposed to purely political issues. On questions of traditional evangelical morality, such as Prohibition or Sabbath observance, they were quite ready to support political action.

So among Southern Protestant churches in the early twentieth century the dominant mood was both theologically and culturally conservative. An important segment of white Southerners did speak out for progressivism and for a social gospel; so the region was never all of one mind. Nonetheless, in the battles emerging over modernist theology and more secular and pluralist culture, Southerners were more likely to be on the side of the antimodernists.

. . .

The Last Crusade for Protestant Civilization

The impending crisis within the dominant American Protestantism was partially obscured by their common evangelical heritage and hence by their continuing ability to follow a common cause.

The most remarkable instance of the power of concerted Protestant effort was the campaign to prohibit the sale of alcoholic beverages. In the age of crusades prior to World War I, this was the Protestant crusade *par excellence*. Liberals and conservatives, social gospelers and evangelists, and Northerners and Southerners joined together in the cause. Some of the more progressive "Americanized" Catholic leaders also joined the campaign. But overall, Prohibition was the result of mobilizing the political potential of Protestant Christians. It marked the high-water mark for the usually elusive ideal of a unified evangelical civilization.

The reasons for the wide support are not hard to find. First of all, excessive consumption of alcohol was the first major modern drug problem. Many people today speak as though the whole idea of Prohibition was preposterous; but they should note that the United States today prohibits the use of all sorts of drugs and (as in the case of prohibition of alcohol) has had immense problems enforcing such laws. The more problematic question was whether alcohol would be an appropriate drug to put on the list of substances prohibited. At the time, it seemed plausible to many that it was. Its use to excess seemed to be encouraged both by frontier conditions and later by the tensions of the new urban industrial society. The extent of excessive use was sufficient that one later historian could appropriately characterize the United States as "the alcoholic republic."[3] Such excess undermined evangelical religion and other strict evangelical mores. Early nineteenth-century evangelicals accordingly latched onto alcohol as a chief vice to eradicate. They demanded total abstinence among their converts and worked to set a similar standard for society at large. By the late nineteenth century alcohol was a primary symbol of secular civilization and opposition to it was a chief symbol of evangelical civilization.

Theological liberals, Catholic Americanizers, and progressive social gospelers might adopt this cause also, since alcoholism was a major urban problem. Clearly it broke up families and contributed to other urban vices. The situation was complicated, however, by the

· · ·

insistence that total abstinence from alcohol was almost unique to American Protestantism. Recent immigrants, almost no matter what their Old World religious traditions, were unfamiliar with these ideals, and typically consumed some alcohol as a regular part of their diet. Prohibition thus involved an attempt by dominant Protestants to impose their standards on immigrants.

Often the favor was deeply resented. Those who opposed Prohibition pointed out that alcohol had been around since the dawn of civilization, had been consumed routinely in Puritan New England, was a benefit when used in moderation, was not condemned by Scripture or tradition (Jesus turned water into wine and instituted the use of wine as a holy sacrament), and its abuse could be limited by voluntary moderation, rather than by legislation.

The campaigns for Prohibition became a formidable political force with the formation in 1895 of the Anti-Saloon League, a largely Protestant organization. The two largest Protestant religious groups, the Methodists and the Baptists, both in the North and the South, provided the campaigns with fervent support. This zeal was complemented with effective political organization, directed by the Anti-Saloon League. Attacking the issue on a state and local level, champions of Prohibition won five states to their cause by 1900 and twenty-six by the outbreak of World War I in 1917. Many other localities were also "dry." Wartime fervor provided the last great impetus to put the crusade over the top. Legislation made the country virtually dry by the end of the war. Meanwhile, Congress adopted the Eighteenth Amendment, which went into effect in 1920, banning the commercial manufacture and sale (although not some private manufacture and use) of alcoholic beverages from the country. The millennium had not been brought in, but the dominant Protestants had gained what seemed, for a brief time, an important symbol of moral progress.

War and Peace

Perhaps the most difficult issue in relating churches to culture has been the issue of war and peace. The Christian church was initially an outsider sect in the Roman Empire and largely pacifist. After Constantine's conversion, and eventually becoming the official state church in the fourth century, the church almost always supported state war efforts. St. Augustine of Hippo (354–430), one of the early church fathers to face the new situation, proposed criteria for "just wars"—

• • •

the only wars, he said, that Christians could support. The cause, for instance, had to be just and the means of achieving that goal had to be proportional to the goal itself. Just wars should be fought by armies only and should not involve killing civilians.

Such just war policies have been the standards for most churches up to the present. However, nations have always claimed that their causes were just and churches' resistance to state wars have usually proved ineffective. This has been especially so in the case of churches officially established by the state. These have usually, almost as a matter of course, supported state policy. Sectarian groups reacted to such complicity by insisting on strict pacifism for their members.

The mainline Protestant churches in the United States stood in a peculiar position on such issues. Almost all of them had a sectarian heritage which demanded at least some symbolic separation from the world and encouraged some criticism of the state. Baptists, for instance, particularly prided themselves on being champions of "the separation of church and state." On the other hand, these denominations were unofficially established churches in a republic. Their members, like other Americans, were among the supporters of prevailing state policy. In times of war, except when regional differences are involved, American churches are almost always swept along with the enthusiasm for the cause.

Protestants, who especially saw themselves as the conscience of the nation, were troubled by such Christian enthusiasm for violence in the name of the Prince of Peace. In almost every era, thoughtful people agonized over this anomaly. Was it proper for a person to kill a member of one's own religious group for the cause of the nation? The brotherhood of the Masons could point to cases where officers had refused to order a firing squad to fire upon a prisoner seeing that the captive gave a Masonic sign. Why could not Methodists or Baptists do the same?

Mark Twain, having departed from his evangelical upbringing, but retaining its underlying moral sensibility, was free to state the paradox more sharply than most Americans. In his "The War Prayer" (1904) he presents a stranger who appears in a church and prays:

> O Lord our God, help us to tear their soldiers to bloody
> shreds with our shells; help us to cover their smiling fields with
> the pale forms of their patriot dead; help us to drown the thunder

• • •

of the guns with the shrieks of their wounded, writhing in pain; help us to lay waste their humble homes with a hurricane of fire; help us wring the hearts of their unoffending widows with unavailing grief; help us to turn them out roofless with their little children to wander unfriended the wastes of their desolated land in rags and hunger and thirst . . .

Twain added: "It was believed afterward that the man was a lunatic, because there was no sense in what he said."[4]

Campaigns for Peace

Though indeed most pious Americans would have shouted down any wartime suggestions that Christianity and the national cause were at odds, some nineteenth-century Protestant leaders did agonize over how the brutality of war betrayed their high hopes for Christian civilization. Without going to the sectarian alternative of the peace churches, the one recourse left was to work for reform from within the culture. This was the great hope for nineteenth-century American Protestants—that they could bring in the millennium by reform. This golden age would, among other things, be a time of perpetual peace. One of the reform movements of that era, accordingly, was a campaign for peace. Champions of the cause founded the American Peace Society in 1828. Consistent with the establishment stance, but trying to reform it at the same time, this campaign was not totally pacifist, but rather an effort to promote peace whenever possible.

Such efforts were overwhelmed by the Civil War, which captured the enthusiasm of almost all the reformers who championed peace. Even that war, however, was viewed as perhaps the bloody birth of a new age in which both peace and justice would prevail. Soon after the war, however, disillusion set in.

Yet peace reform continued. Frances Willard, for instance, in the 1880s persuaded the Women's Christian Temperance Union to include peace advocacy among its causes. But as in other areas, it was in the Progressive Era that the crusading spirit of the pre-Civil War days was revived.

Just before World War I, campaigns to work for world peace and arbitration reached their peak. Andrew Carnegie generously funded the leading American peace organizations and in 1911 the Federal Council of Churches formed a Commission on Peace and Arbitration.

• • •

Growing international peace efforts were interrupted, however, by the outbreak of the Great War in Europe in 1914. The United States at first resolved to stay out of this conflict. Nonetheless, the nation was drawn inexorably toward the conflict. The American secretary of state, William Jennings Bryan (1860–1925), was caught in the middle. Bryan, three-times Democratic presidential candidate, was both an ardent evangelical and an ardent champion of progressive causes, including the peace campaign. In 1915, after the German sinking of the Lusitania, a British ship with over a hundred Americans among its more than 1,200 lost passengers, President Wilson sent a sharp note to Germany demanding apology and reparations. Fearing this act would lead to war, Bryan followed his conscience and resigned from the cabinet.

When Woodrow Wilson finally did bring the United States into the war in 1917, most of the peace advocates, including Bryan, supported the decision. Universal peace, they reasoned, might be possible only by the victory of those who were principled and ultimately champions of peace. Wilson himself was a champion of arbitration and carefully provided just war rationale for entering the conflict. Consequently, they could join with Wilson in yet another millennial hope that this would be "the war to end all wars."

As Wilson recognized, the champions of restraint do not prevail in a time of war, when many people's relatives and friends are being killed. Even before Americans saw action, the wartime enthusiasm reached a height never surpassed in the nation's history. Congress soon passed the Alien Act and then the Sedition Act, which gave the government sweeping powers to suppress disloyal, profane, or scurrilous remarks about the U.S. cause, or even the flag. Civil religion, in the sense of popular and legally enforced demands for total loyalty, reached a peak. In Oregon in 1918 one Methodist clergyman told the Portland Rotary Club:

> "There is no place on the top side of American soil for a Pacifist. . . . If you have one, shoot him. Don't talk peace to me; I don't want peace, I want righteousness."[5]

Any meetings, including church services held in foreign languages, especially German, were suspect and sometimes outlawed. Towns with German names, such as Berlin, changed them to patriotic titles. Stories were circulated concerning German atrocities, rape, and pillage.

• • •

So misleading was such propaganda that, twenty-five years later during World War II, many thoughtful people were skeptical of reports of Nazi atrocities toward the Jews, thinking them repetitions of World War I extravagances.

America's churches, along with their constituents, were swept along by this wartime fervor. The clergy were probably no more or less extreme than most other Americans, which meant that some were cautious about unrestrained nationalism, while others endorsed the American cause with abandon. Some of the latter virtually draped the flag over the cross, so that one could no longer tell the difference. The consensus was simply stated by Frank Mason North, president of the Federal Council of the Church of Christ in America: "The war for righteousness will be won! Let the Church do her part."[6]

The patriotic enthusiasm, although only sometimes explicitly religious, nonetheless had causes closely related to the nation's religious heritage. The enthusiasm for the war was of the same ilk as the simultaneous enthusiasm for prohibition, progressive reform, or world missions. All these were part of an increasingly popular zeal for an American democratic way of life, a somewhat secularized form of the old ideal of Christian and republican civilization.

The difference was that, unlike most earlier American crusades, nearly every group of Americans except peace churches lent their support to the secularized version of the ideal of "making the world safe for democracy." Rather than drive insiders and outsiders apart, the war temporarily brought them together. Immigrant groups, Catholic, Protestant, Eastern Orthodox, and Jewish, were all especially eager to demonstrate their patriotism and dispel any aspersions on their loyalty and foreignness. Blacks, though severely discriminated against, retained a firm faith in the American way. White Southerners were reentering the mainstream and could point to one of their own in the White House. World War I marked a major step for many conservative Southerners in their transfer of loyalty from the Confederacy to eventually becoming among the nation's most fervent champions of national patriotism.

Conflict in the Mainstream: Fundamentalists versus Modernists

Wars are catalysts for social change. They speed up the processes of social development and conflict. So while World War I temporarily brought most of the nation together in an orgy of patriotism, the

• • •

morning after revealed open antagonisms that could not be healed. In the long run, none of these antagonisms were culturally more significant than that between fundamentalists and modernists in the mainline churches. At first, many observers thought this highly publicized conflict was a temporary aberration in the overall story of building consensus. Instead, it was the first uncovering of a major fault line that ran through that center. Only in the second half of the twentieth century would it become apparent that major cultural conflicts were coalescing around two competing moral visions of American life. These moral visions were grounded to a large extent in the nation's religious history.

Since Protestant Christianity stood so close to the centers of power in nineteenth-century America, one of the strong impulses for Protestants was to keep up with whatever changes were going on in the culture. This impulse was a major component in theological liberalism or modernism, which believed that Christianity should keep up with and provide leadership for modern cultural and intellectual change by reinterpreting its traditions to fit with modern ideals. Modernism, although by its nature having many varieties, thus could be very compatible with fervent wartime patriotism. Building a progressive democratic worldwide civilization based on brotherhood (as they put it) of all people under the fatherhood of God was close to the essence of the hopeful vision of liberal Protestants.

Premillennialists, on the other hand, taught that the hope for humanity was not in building a liberal civilization, but in the dramatic return of Jesus to set up a millennial kingdom. The more extreme premillennialists, such as Jehovah's Witnesses and some pentecostals, followed the implication of this view that America was not the hope of the world, and remained pacifists. Most of the premillennialist Protestants, such as those who were associated with Dwight L. Moody, were more moderate. The majority of these still remained in mainline denominations and, while occasionally entertaining pacifist views before World War I, became ardent American patriots once the war broke out.

Despite this essential commonality regarding the war itself, the sense of cultural crisis that the war precipitated turned growing conflict over theological questions into a major debate over the nature of American civilization itself.

Premillennial revivalists with mainstream Protestant connections

· · ·

and other mainline conservatives had been sniping away at modernist theology in their denominations for some years. From 1910 to 1915 they published a twelve-volume series of booklets called *The Fundamentals* in which conservative authors defended the traditional Protestant faith against theological liberalism and higher criticism of the Bible.

Billy Sunday

Such serious-minded attacks were amplified by revivalists who increasingly turned to the techniques of modern show business as a means of drumming up support. The most famous evangelist of this era was Billy Sunday (1862–1935). Sunday provides a revealing continuity and contrast to the great evangelists of previous eras—George Whitefield during the Great Awakening, Charles Finney during the Second Great Awakening, and Dwight L. Moody in the late nineteenth century. Each of the previous evangelists to some degree stood against the religious establishment of his day, but eventually were largely accepted. Sunday, although ordained a Presbyterian, remained more of an outsider. This was partly a matter of style. Sunday combined Finney's concern for technique with Moody's disinterest in deep theological discussion. A former major league baseball player, Sunday's style was essentially that of a showman, with shouting and well-timed acrobatic gestures, including sliding into the podium as though it were a base or, in a frenzy of patriotism, planting a flag on top of the pulpit. "I'd stand on my head in a mud puddle," he once quipped, "if I thought it would help me win souls to Christ."[7] His evident sincerity, as well as his showmanship, won him a wide audience. In fact, in 1915 the *New York Tribune* drama critic playfully compared Sunday to the great vaudeville actor of the era, George M. Cohan. "George Cohan has neither the punch nor the pace of Billy Sunday," he wrote. ". . . It is true that Cohan waved the flag first, but Billy Sunday has waved it harder. . . . All in all we believe that Sunday has more dramatic instinct than Cohan."[8]

Sunday's gospel can be best described as a combination of popular Americanism and revivalist Christianity. He preached for moral cleanness and "real manhood" (occasionally adding "real womanhood"). The saloon was a favorite target. And during the war his patriotism was second to none: "If you turn hell upside down," he said "you will find 'Made in Germany' stamped on the bottom."[9]

• • •

Despite this fusion of Christianity and Americanism, and hence such commonality with liberal Protestantism, Sunday did not hesitate to lambaste the liberals he thought had forsaken the old Gospel message of sin and salvation. Such attacks and such a message ensured that he would remain an outsider to the mainline religious establishment and reach audiences who, although largely white Protestant, for one reason or another also felt like outsiders. With the world changing rapidly, popular prophets such as Sunday could easily alarm them about ominous new trends.

The Post-War Cultural Crisis

The immediate aftermath of World War I increased the sense of cultural crisis. In 1918 the actual engagement of American troops in the war brought the nation to a fever pitch of patriotism. In November the war suddenly ended, leaving many Americans with undirected zeal to fight for a holy cause. Immediately, some saw an enemy within. The Bolshevik Revolution in Russia in 1917 and major labor strikes in America in 1919 led to the "red scare" and what became in some circles a permanent fear of a communist takeover. Revivalists such as Sunday, while not primarily responsible for such fears, fanned the flames as they added bolshevism to the threats to national morality.

At just the same time, however, hopes ran incredibly high in mainline Protestant denominations. The war effort brought them together and obscured theological differences of earlier times. The war was won. Prohibition was passed. People talked and laid plans for uniting all major American Protestant groups. In 1919 Protestants also launched the Interchurch World Movement, which was to be a colossal effort for worldwide Protestant cooperation in benevolence and missions. This was to be the Protestant equivalent to the League of Nations, which was to ensure world peace.

As with the League of Nations, intense opposition to such idealistic efforts quickly set in during 1919 and 1920. Though some old denominational antagonisms were forgotten by progressive church leaders, new and different ones were widening the faultline that separated theological liberals from conservatives and revivalists. These were exacerbated by a widespread, though ill-defined, sense of cultural crisis, a sense that things were changing too rapidly and that America might be losing its heritage. The plans to unite Protestantism and the Interchurch World Movement both soon collapsed.

. . .

Meanwhile, conservative Protestants and revivalists were providing a strong dissenting analysis of the perceived cultural crisis. The problem, they said, was primarily theological and moral; America was founded on the Bible. Liberal Protestants and secularists attacked the authenticity of the Bible, offering evolutionary-based philosophies as an alternative. Evidence of the consequences was a dramatic change in mores, sped up by the war. America was moving rapidly from the Victorian to the age of the flapper. Conservative church leaders deplored the new dances and short dresses, or the transition from "the bended knee to the bared knee." Such changes, they thought, were just a few signs that America was losing its moorings. Liberal theology and secularism, they said, were to blame.

Darwinism as Symbol

Such views gained in popularity when in 1919 one of the nation's best-known politicians, William Jennings Bryan, entered the fray. Bryan and a number of other conservative leaders concluded that evolutionary philosophies were at the root of the crisis in Western civilization. This theme emerged during the war, as Americans sought to explain how Germany turned to the barbarism that American propaganda described. One explanation was that German culture adopted the "might is right" philosophy of Friedrich Nietzsche (1844–1900). Conservative Christians immediately tied this to the fact that liberal theologies and higher criticism of the Bible were based on evolutionary views of how religions and the Bible itself evolved as cultural products. And liberal theologies were often "made in Germany" and imported to the United States.

The symbolic center for such views was Darwinism or biological evolution. Such views, Bryan and others pointed out, led people to believe that humans were nothing more than higher-order animals. Hence, there would be no basis for morality. Bryan was particularly impressed by a study published in 1916 by James H. Leuba showing that well over half of American biologists did not believe either in God or immorality.[10] Some conservatives also saw biological evolution as contradicting their literal interpretations of the creation account in Genesis. Bryan and others insisted that it was better simply to trust God and the Bible rather than what he saw as the speculations of modern science. "It is better to trust the Rock of Ages," he said, "than to know the ages of rocks."[11]

• • •

Evolution thus became a symbol that could put a lot of things together to explain the cultural crisis. On the one side, traditionalists could say, was civilization founded on the Bible and the belief in the Creator of the moral order. On the other side were atheistic and purely naturalistic explanations of the human condition, evolutionary sociologies, and psychologies, which made values relative to time, place, and individuals, offering schemes for reform or revolution with no firm foundations for a moral order. Astoundingly, according to the traditionalists, liberal theologians were more open to the evolutionary views than to the old-time biblical view.

This complex set of social-cultural issues could be boiled down most easily in public debate to the issue of biological evolution. Even though biological evolution was as much a product of the broader evolutionary outlook, it served as a handy symbol for the whole package. Opponents of traditional Christianity used the prestige of evolutionary theory as such a symbol for some time. It also served particularly well as a symbol for biblical literalists, such as premillennialists, Southern conservatives, many revivalists, certain ethnic Protestant conservatives, and some others. Genesis, they insisted, excluded the evolutionary origins of humanity. In 1919 William Jennings Bryan and others began campaigning to stop the spread of teaching biological evolution in America's public schools.

In the same year William B. Riley (1861–1947), the premillennialist Baptist pastor of a large church in Minneapolis, founded the World's Christian Fundamentals Association to support this and other militantly conservative revivalist Protestant causes. Major battles were brewing on a number of fronts.

Fundamentalism

In 1920 the word "fundamentalist" was first used to describe this coalition of militantly conservative Protestants who were trying to preserve the nineteenth-century revivalist Protestant establishment. The term was coined by a conservative Baptist editor, Curtis Lee Laws, to designate his party in a battle in the Northern Baptist Convention (the major Baptist denomination in the North). Defending "fundamentals" implied being willing to fight for certain fundamental doctrines that liberals denied. Lists of these varied, but usually they included beliefs in the inerrancy of the Bible, the virgin birth of Je-

• • •

sus, the authenticity of his miracles, atonement for sin through the death of Christ, Jesus' resurrection, and his coming again.

Fundamentalists were distinguished from other Protestant conservatives by their willingness to fight for these doctrines. Typically they saw the world through images of warfare. The war was on two fronts: they were fighting against modernist theology in their denominations and against some of the conspicuous trends toward secularism in their culture.

The denominational wars were fiercest in the Northern Baptist Convention and in the Presbyterian Church in the U.S.A., two of the major Northern denominations where militant conservatives and moderates were of roughly equal strength. In 1922 the most famous liberal preacher of the day, Harry Emerson Fosdick, became the center of the denominational struggles. A Baptist, but serving a large Presbyterian church in New York City, Fosdick preached a widely publicized sermon—"Shall the Fundamentalists Win?"—pleading for tolerance in the denomination. Presbyterian conservatives counterattacked, eventually forcing Fosdick to leave their denomination.

In 1923 the fundamentalist cause was strengthened by the appearance of J. Gresham Machen's *Christianity and Liberalism.* Machen was a New Testament scholar at Princeton Theological Seminary, a stronghold for dignified Presbyterian theological conservatism. Machen did not like to call himself a fundamentalist, and his emphasis on the intellect did not fit with popular revivalism. In fact, when he once spoke at Billy Sunday's Bible conference at Winona Lake, Indiana, he complained that his lectures were preceded by the "singing of some of the popular jingles, often accompanied by the blowing of enormous horns or other weird instruments of music."[12]

Nonetheless, in *Christianity and Liberalism* Machen provided fundamentalists with their strongest defense. His argument was that liberal Protestantism, despite using traditional terminology, was a new religion since it denied the most essential traditional doctrines, such as that Jesus died as an atonement for human sins and literally rose again. Liberals, he said, should be perfectly free to start their own churches; but since their religion was different from traditional Christianity, they should not remain in denominations that were based on traditional creeds. "A separation between the two parties in the Church," he declared, "is the crying need of the hour."[13]

• • •

Though some influential outside observers agreed with Machen's argument that extreme Protestant liberals believed in a religion other than traditional Christianity, most Protestants were not concerned enough for doctrine of any sort to have the stomach for grim theological warfare. Conservative and fundamentalist efforts to purge denominations of liberals, while creating a sensation for a few years, met with little success.

Bryan and the Scopes Trial

In the meantime, more Americans seemed ready to rally to the cause on the other front, in the battle to save America from the alleged threat of secularism. Here, in the public arena, symbols were more effective than substance and "evolution" became the chief symbol for a whole set of social changes that conservatives found ominous. The success of the anti-evolution crusade owed a lot to the leadership of William Jennings Bryan, always an effective orator. His campaigns had the most success in the South, where a number of state legislatures passed laws banning the teaching of biological evolution in public schools. Many other states were also considering such action. The scientific community, many secularists, liberal religionists, and champions of the freedom of expression were deeply alarmed at a sweeping national trend that looked to them like a return to the Dark Ages.

In the summer of 1925 the crisis came to a head in a scene that could not have been staged better to dramatize the tensions between the old evangelical culture and the new twentieth-century, more secular, outlook. John T. Scopes (1900–1970), a young high school teacher in rural Dayton, Tennessee, with the support of the American Civil Liberties Union, volunteered to defy a recently passed Tennessee law banning the teaching of the biological evolution of humans. The American Civil Liberties Union supplied skilled lawyers, including the most famous trial lawyer of the day, Clarence Darrow (1857–1938). The prosecution countered by accepting the services of William Jennings Bryan.

This was at the height of the age of ballyhoo, of media-generated national crazes, as well as controversies over changing mores, jazz, new dances, styles of dress for women, and sexually-suggestive Hollywood movies. Proponents of the new, more lenient culture were already deeply antagonistic toward defenders of the old-style Victo-

. . .

rian mores, and so made the most of a drama in which science could be pitted against religion, city against rural, and North against South.

The setting of the trial in rural Tennessee accentuated the urban versus rural theme. To sophisticated observers of the day, fundamentalism seemed to be a function of the countryside. As Richard Hofstadter later observed of this era, "The United States was born in the country and has moved to the city."[14] Cities were more secular than small towns because they were more impersonal and provided many organized alternatives to the life of piety. Because they were ethnically diverse, they were also less evangelical than the more Protestant countryside. Moreover, sociological theory reinforced the assumption that traditional religion went with traditional rural culture. Education and sophisticated modern urban industrial society were supposed to disabuse people of the pieties of a more primitive agrarian time.

William Jennings Bryan, who rose to fame in the election of 1896 as "the boy orator from the Platte," representing agrarian and populist impulses, could easily be fit into the bumpkin stereotype. H. L. Mencken, the acerbic critic of American foibles, wrote of Bryan at Dayton: "Making his progress up and down the main street of little Dayton, surrounded by gaping primates from the upland valleys of the Cumberland Range, his coat laid aside, his bare arms and hairy chest shining damply, his bald head sprinkled with dust—so accoutred and on display he was obviously happy."[15] The counterpart to Bryan was the urbane, sophisticated Darrow, representing sophisticated modern urban culture and right thinking.

Their actions amplified by the widest press coverage of any trial in history, the actors played their roles. The local judge, openly sympathetic to evangelical religion, allowed Bryan to testify on the Bible as an expert witness. Bryan's expertness consisted of years as a popular Sunday school lecturer. Darrow subjected him to withering and sarcastic cross-examination on village atheist-type questions such as where Cain, the son of the Bible's first humans, Adam and Eve, got his wife. The outcome of the trial itself was indecisive. Scopes was found guilty but given a token fine. The drama was heightened, however, when Bryan, who felt he performed well, died suddenly in Dayton five days after the trial. This underscored the aura of defeat for fundamentalism reported in the sophisticated press. It made H. L. Mencken "thank the inscrutable gods for Harding, even for Coolidge. . . . Dullness has got into the White House, and the smell of cab-

• • •

Bryan and Darrow at the Scopes trial.

bage boiling, but there is at least nothing to compare to the intolerable buffoonery that went on in Tennessee. The President of the United States may be an ass, but he at least doesn't believe that the earth is square, and that witches should be put to death, and that Jonah swallowed the whale. The Golden Text is not painted weekly on the White House wall, and there is no need to keep ambassadors waiting while Pastor Simpson, of Smithville, prays for rain in the Blue Room." [16]

The Image of Fundamentalist Defeat

The most important impact of the Scopes trial, one of the few twentieth-century religious events reported in most American history texts, was the image that it created. Fundamentalism, indeed all conservative Protestantism—it was easy to believe—had been thoroughly routed and discredited. Gradually it would disappear, so it was assumed, as education spread and the nation urbanized. Indeed, in many respects, fundamentalism was now on the defensive. Militant funda-

• • •

mentalists would no longer be welcome in American universities, and after Bryan, they would be subject to ridicule in public life.

In mainline denominations, fundamentalist and conservative hopes for control declined precipitously also after 1925. Moderates who tolerated liberals took the counteroffensive. J. Gresham Machen, for instance, was denied promotion at Princeton Theological Seminary and left to found his own theological school in 1929. A few years later, when he refused to support Presbyterian missions which included liberals and set up his own mission board, he was defrocked from the ministry and so started his own tiny denomination. Northern Baptist fundamentalists and conservatives experienced similar defeats.

Such events created the impression that conservative evangelical Protestantism was dying out. In fact, during the 1930s mainline observers spoke of an "American religious depression" since there was some decline in mainline church membership. But mainline Protestantism was not synonymous with American religion, not even with American Protestantism. Fundamentalists and other conservative and revivalist elements were regrouping. Many local congregations left mainline denominations to found independent Bible or Baptist churches. The Southern Baptist Convention, an overwhelmingly conservative group that intentionally remained outside mainline Protestantism, was growing rapidly and was becoming one of the nation's largest denominations. Smaller pentecostal, holiness, and other sectarian evangelical groups were also growing, although few at the centers of American life were paying attention. Such groups were building networks of Bible schools to train leadership and strong senses of identity that would serve them well in the latter half of the twentieth century.

In the wake of the fundamentalist-modernist controversies of the 1920s, however, such continuing evangelical strength seemed to most secular and mainstream Protestant observers not the wave of the future, but the vestige of a formidable, but dying, order.

Catholics and Fundamentalists: The Election of 1928

The evidence of continuing conservative Protestant strength as well as a pluralistic public life were most vividly apparent in the Al Smith campaign for the presidency in 1928. The Democratic party had long been primarily an alliance of groups outside the mainstream

. . .

Protestant Republican business establishment. Its two most loyal constituencies were Southerners and Roman Catholic immigrant communities, two groups that had very little in common except that they opposed mainstream Protestant Republicans. In fact, the South was far more overwhelmingly Protestant than most of the rest of the country, and anti-Catholic prejudices were strong.

Anti-Catholic prejudices were one contributor to the revival of the Ku Klux Klan after World War I. Although anti-black racism was the chief interest in the Klan, opposition to Catholics, Jews, and to other immigrants was also strong. The Klan, in fact, fit the image that critics attributed to fundamentalism. It appealed primarily to relatively poor or small town white Protestants, both in the South and the North, who unabashedly opposed the growing religious and ethnic pluralism in America. The Klan was an organization of Protestants with some religious ceremonies, but its cultural concerns were far more important than its ecclesiastical or theological interests. Many fundamentalist and conservative Protestant leaders denounced the Klan, although the Klan had cordial relations with some churches, especially in the South. By 1924 the Klan was a formidable political force, but declined sharply after 1925. Despite the decline of the organization, the racist and nativist attitudes that it reflected remained strong.

Though most white Southerners did not belong to the Klan, the overwhelming majority were ardently for racial separatism and were at least moderately anti-Catholic, thus making their alliance with the northeast, Catholic immigrant wing of the Democratic party highly artificial. Only the strong white Southern loyalty to the memory of the Confederacy, rendering them idelibly anti-Republican, kept them solidly in the Democratic ranks. The nomination of Al Smith, a Catholic, as the Democratic candidate for the presidency, severely tested this loyalty, and provided another symbolic moment in the contest between two definitions of Americanism emerging in the twentieth century.

Anti-Catholicism was by no means confined to the South or to conservative Protestants. Liberal Protestants, who sometimes virtually equated the Kingdom of God with the advance of democracy, were also fearful that Catholic influences in politics would lead to authoritarianism. Most liberal Protestants, however, were already Republican.

Smith was the popular governor of New York. Like almost all

· · ·

Al Smith, the first major challenger to the Protestant monopoly on the presidency.

Catholic politicians in America, he was a Catholic and a politician rather than a Catholic politician in the sense that he explicitly related his religious faith to his political outlook.[17] In the United States, such a stance was almost a prerequisite to Catholic political activity. This was so not only because of the traditional American distancing of religion and politics; but because of anti-Catholic prejudices compounded by international Roman Catholic policy. International Catholicism was premised on its being the official state religion, and that Catholic rulers should accept moral guidance from the church

• • •

hierarchy. Moreover, the papacy, despite the loss of almost all its lands, continued to operate as a civil power as well as an ecclesiastical power. When Protestant critics pointed out these factors, local Catholic politicians could reply quite accurately that these ancient Catholic policies had no effect whatsoever on their political behavior in America. Al Smith captured the attitude perfectly during the 1928 campaign when he quipped in reply to a question about the latest papal encyclical, "What the Hell's an encyclical?"[18]

Catholics also had an effective counterattack to Protestant criticisms. One Catholic author, for instance, asked the question, "Are Protestants Americans?" He argued that if Roman Catholics were not qualified to run for the presidency because of their alleged allegiance to the papacy, then Protestants were violating the Constitution by, in effect, imposing a religious test for office.[19]

The Catholic issue was a delicate one that no national politician could afford to say much about; it was complicated, however, by a major campaign debate over Prohibition, a major concern of most Protestants, whether liberal or conservative. Smith was avowedly a "wet," favoring the repeal of Prohibition. The largely Baptist and Methodist white South had been strong in supporting Prohibition. Especially for Methodists, who emphasized piety and practice more than theological debate, Prohibition was a counterpart to theological fundamentalism. Virginia Methodist Bishop James A. Cannon, Jr. led the Southern campaign against Smith and for Prohibition. Anti-Catholicism and prohibitionism were strong also in most Protestant areas of the North, where they helped cement the old Protestant-Republican alliance.

Neither the Catholic issue nor the Prohibition question was decisive in the election. Smith was overwhelmingly defeated; but probably so would have been any Democrat in the prosperous Republican days before the stock market crash of 1929. Smith lost his home state of New York by 100,000 votes. Remarkably, Republican Herbert Hoover broke into the "solid South" and carried the states of the upper South. The Catholic issue and Prohibition no doubt were factors here. Nonetheless, the counterpart is that the only region Smith carried entirely was the Deep South, the very region where one would expect Protestant and Prohibition forces to be the strongest. Distinctly religious issues were a factor in modifying the election pat-

• • •

terns; but, typical of American politics, they were only one factor among many.

Catholicism: Building an Identity

While in politics Catholic Americans were moving into the mainstream, the church itself was building a strong, distinct Catholic identity. As always, ethnicity was a primary factor. The era spanning the two world wars was the golden age of the urban Catholic ethnic neighborhood. Not everything was golden, of course. Every urban ethnic community had poverty and crime. Differing ethnic neighborhoods often developed strong rivalries and resentments of each other, which a common religion did little to quell. Nonetheless, ethnic neighborhoods offered many of the compensating features of close-knit communities in which family and church played major roles.

This was a great era of popular devotional Catholicism in America. Such activities would often be deeply connected with preserving old-world ways and reinforcing family ties. For instance, one event that has been studied closely is the annual *festa* of the Madonna of Mount Carmel on 115th Street in Italian East Harlem, New York. This religious festival was imported from southern Italy and extravagantly celebrated in East Harlem every July during this era. It was a time of family gatherings, of food, dancing, partying, and fireworks. The central event was a great parade following the image of the Madonna through the streets. The Madonna was believed to have powers of healing and the celebration, mixing what might seem like the sacred and the profane, reflected the preservation of an old-world sense that the spiritual and the mystical penetrates into everyday existence.[20]

Catholics were building strong religious identities in many other ways, too. Despite continuing ethnic rivalries, the national church organization was becoming more centralized and unified. One of the strongest forces was the parochial school systems, which were now almost universal in areas of concentrated Catholic settlement, and which ensured that Catholics would not become too homogenized into secular Americanism or forget their distinctive religious teachings and identity. Catholic higher education, concentrating mainly on liberal arts colleges, offered a church-controlled avenue for entry into American middle-class life. In some ways these institutions marked the entry of more Catholics into the mainstream. Catholics could take

• • •

Two heroes of Catholics in the 1920s—Knute Rockne and Thomas Aquinas.

pride in Notre Dame football as the best in the nation. Catholic academic thought, too, was quite distinctive, centering around neo-Thomism, the revival of the views of the great medieval thinker Thomas Aquinas. Arguing that reason provided a solid foundation for faith, neo-Thomists sharply challenged the prevailing secular assumptions of this positivist era that science and reason would conflict with classic Christianity. A formidable system of Catholic presses likewise provided the population with materials that reinforced their sense that Catholics, because of their religious commitments, were different. At all levels of sophistication Catholic magazines and books cultivated a separate identity. Catholic charitable institutions and hospitals provided a Catholic context for all life's major activities from birth to death, and beyond.

The sense of Catholic identity was also reinforced by continuing Protestant nativism, as seen in the anti-Catholicism of the revived Ku Klux Klan. The strict immigration quotas adopted in the 1920s also transparently reflected an attempt by the Anglo-Protestant establishment to limit further Catholic growth. In the state of Oregon there was even a law that required all children to attend public schools;

• • •

although the statute was finally struck down by a Supreme Court ruling in 1925.

While American Catholics after World War I were victims of the conservatism and reaction of the time, the same national trends were reflected within the Catholic community itself. The general Catholic conservatism of this era paralleled and drew from some of the same cultural trends as Protestant conservatism and fundamentalism. Strongly religious people of all sorts were alarmed at the cultural trends in modern America. In the Catholic churches, however, the leadership included no real modernist party. In part this reflected immigrant conservatism and in part it reflected the conservatism of the beleaguered international church. Catholics worldwide, for instance, were strongly anticommunist and tended to be so in America also.[21]

American Catholicism, in fact, generated its own brand of political fundamentalism, borrowing Protestant revivalist techniques of enterprising evangelism. In the early 1930s the most famous radio preacher in America was Father Charles E. Coughlin of Royal Oaks, Michigan, a Detroit suburb. In some Catholic communities Sunday afternoon ballgames were halted to hear Coughlin's broadcast. People could remember walking down the street and "hearing out of every window the voice of Father Coughlin blaring from the radio. You could walk for blocks, they recalled, and never miss a word."[22] Coughlin's message was a strange mixture of anticapitalism and anticommunism. At first he adamantly favored the election of Franklin D. Roosevelt. Soon, however, he turned on Roosevelt and attacked him as part of a Jewish and communist conspiracy. Eventually, his anti-Semitism and favorable views of Hitler forced him from public life in 1942.

Coughlin was only one of the extremist anti-Semitic, anticommunist, anti-New Deal preachers of the 1930s. Most of the others were Protestant fundamentalists, or simply demagogues, who were moving toward an American fascism. Coughlin, for instance, made common cause in 1936 with Gerald L. K. Smith, a Disciples of Christ preacher who had been a close associate of Louisiana's Huey Long, assassinated in 1935. In 1936 Coughlin and Smith's Michigan-based Union party gained nearly a million votes in the popular election. It marked, however, the high point of organized American political reaction, quickly declining after 1936 as many Americans became alert to the real dangers of European fascism and Nazism.

• • •

"THE ACIDS OF MODERNITY"

The sensational reactions that marked the whole era between the two world wars reflected the tensions of rapid cultural change. They also sometimes obscured the significance of the changes since they helped create the impression, eagerly promoted by media, that anyone who would express alarm at the transformation must be a bigot or fanatic.

Nonetheless, some sober observers recognized the revolutionary nature of the developments taking place within American society itself. One of the most astute of these was the famed journalist Walter Lippmann. In *A Preface to Morals*, appearing in 1929, Lippmann observed that the "irreligion of the modern world [is] . . . radical to a degree for which there is, I think, no counterpart." [23] Modern Americans, he said, had "defied the Methodist God and have become very nervous." [24] Lippmann, a secular Jew himself, was not recommending a return to old-time religion. Even though he thought that J. Gresham Machen had "the best popular argument produced by either side in the current controversy," [25] he was convinced that anti-intellectual popular fundamentalism and extremism had irremediably discredited traditional Protestantism among the thinking people in the community. Yet civilization could not go on without a shared morality. Lippmann's solution was to base such a moral consensus on a new humanism. "When men can no longer be theists, they must, if they are civilized, become humanists." [26]

Building a new humanist moral consensus was, of course, more easily said than done. And "the acids of modernity" that Lippmann described had sources that went beyond ideological or even religious change.

Perhaps most basically, the United States was increasingly becoming what the sociologist Pitirim A. Sorokin described a few years later as a "sensate society." [27] That is, the operative values for most Americans most of the time were increasingly defined by satisfaction of the senses—materialistic, hedonistic, or sensuous. This was an accentuation of the trend that Henry Adams pointed out at the end of the nineteenth century, that the United States was preeminently a materialistic civilization. It was materialistic philosophically in that it was built on a science and technology that regarded the material, empiri-

• • •

cally observable world as the "real" world. And it was practically materialistic in its efficient commercial and technological management of material culture.

Such broad cultural trends lay beneath the celebrated "revolution in morals" of the 1920s. Commercial interests particularly pushed Americans toward definitions of themselves in terms of things that they owned and pleasures they could enjoy. In the 1920s the wide promotion of such outlooks was relatively new. Commercial advertising was just emerging in its modern form. The commercial possibilities of sexual suggestion were just being developed. During the Victorian Era sex was a subject to be avoided in public. Once that taboo was broken, around World War I, advertisers made the most of it. As one observer put it, "Advertising, once pristine, began the transition which . . . was to transmute soap from a cleansing agent into an aphrodisiac." [28]

The commercial value of sexual suggestion also became a major force shaping much of American popular culture. Although relatively tame by later standards, popular songs celebrated "hot lips" or "burning kisses" or proclaimed, "I need lovin'." Hollywood movies, although threatened with censorship, made sex their leading motif with films like *Up in Mabel's Room*, *Her Purchase Price*, and *A Shocking Night*. The new dances, complained Southern Methodist Bishop James Cannon, brought "the bodies of men and women in unusual relations to each other." [29] Cannon and other traditionalists could do little, however, about the rumble seats of automobiles which were subject to similar objections.

The sexual revolution found its intellectual rationale in the new popularity of the psychological theories of Sigmund Freud in the 1920s. Freud, who developed his theories in nineteenth-century Vienna while working with patients who had upbringings in which sexuality was strictly suppressed, built his analysis around theories of broadly defined human sexuality. Americans of the 1920s, who typically had similar upbringings, eagerly latched onto popular versions of Freud's views as a rationale for open sexual expression. Freud provided the aura of scientific authority for new "healthy" standards of human behavior, radically different from the so-called "bluestocking Methodist" standards (or equally strict Catholic norms) typical in nineteenth-century America.

The revolution, of course, did not take place overnight. It had

• • •

Clara Bow: "It" girl. Everyone knew what "It" meant.

many precursors and the battle between the two standards continues to the present. In the 1920's, however, the encounter between the two moral ideals was probably as sharp as it ever was. In many ways the culture was still remarkably straight-laced. Buying alcoholic beverages was illegal. Strict observance of the Sabbath, a form of true asceticism in which children would be forced to renounce their daily games and pleasures and spend long afternoons in quiet, pious reading, was still the experience of most Americans who were reared as Protestants, and had not receded in some parts of the country, especially the South. Many in Catholic immigrant communities retained similarly strict religious disciplines and sexual mores, reinforced by

• • •

regular confession to a priest and appropriate acts of penance. In small-town America young women who dared to be seen in the swimwear of the day (excessively discreet by later standards) were liable to be warned by guardians of the old order that they were risking the flames of hell. Many strict evangelical groups, including many pentecostals, fundamentalists, Southern Baptists, and Southern Methodists, banned mixed bathing. But the cultural change was more complex than merely a conflict between the new sensate culture and the old-time religion. The changes were ones that internally were altering American Protestantism itself.

Such concessions were not so much to the new sensuality, which liberal Protestants generally condemned, as to a new view of human nature. Essentially, the belief growing within both wings of American Protestantism was that humans were free and largely in control of their destinies. Such changing views were reflected in the continuing decline of Calvinism, which emphasized that humans were ultimately neither free nor in control of their destinies. These latter doctrines had disappeared in liberal churches and were played down in much of revivalism at least since the time of Moody. The new revivalism emphasized instead the importance of individual choice and the ease with which it could be made. Simple decisions for Jesus made by raising a hand at the end of a revival service increased both the numbers of converts and the sense that human will was in control. Billy Sunday's ethical message to "be strong and show yourself a man" had similar import.[30] For both liberal and conservative Protestants, Christianity was increasingly a matter of building "character" through self-discipline.

The ideal of character challenged the dominant American cultural trends only partly. Perhaps because so many Protestants concentrated on symbolic behavioral issues, such as Prohibition, they directed little critique at the larger dimensions of the cultural revolution. The social gospel, which had been vigorous before the war, declined in the Republican 1920s. Relatively few mainstream Protestants questioned in any basic way the commercial character of the culture and the material and competitive values it was promoting. So, for instance, the best-selling nonfiction book in 1925 and 1926 was Bruce Barton's *The Man Nobody Knows* (1925). Barton, an advertising executive, presented Jesus as a master businessman who built an organization of only twelve men into the world's most successful enterprise. The book's

• • •

epigraph was the boy Jesus' statement to his parents after he remained teaching in the temple: "Wist ye not that I must be about my Father's *business.*"[31]

Disillusion

In the meantime, important literary figures of the generation of Americans coming of age were thoroughly disillusioned with the churches. Perhaps the most effective critique was novelist Sinclair Lewis's *Elmer Gantry* (1927). Gantry was a partly self-deceived, sometimes sincere, and sometimes shallow, religious enterpriser and charlatan. A clergyman moving through a variety of church posts and sexual liaisons, he could be a modernist, a fundamentalist-revivalist, and/or a civic reformer as the occasion demanded. His own success was paramount. Many in this time of sophisticated disillusion readily saw Gantry as representing the phoniness of the churches.

H. L Mencken captured the cynicism of the era with his suggestion that municipalities build giant stadiums in which clergymen could be turned loose on each other as a public display.

Many saw the crisis as a deeper illness in Western civilization itself. Young men had died, wrote poet Ezra Pound after World War I,

> For an old bitch gone in the teeth,
> For a botched civilization.[32]

People spoke knowingly of German author Oswald Spengler's *Decline of the West* (1918), though few read through his involved arguments. And American writers fled what they regarded as the stifling "Puritan" atmosphere of Prohibition America, setting up their own expatriate colony in Paris. Ernest Hemingway, for instance, represented well the outlook of this "lost generation." Subjected to a strong evangelical upbringing by his grandmother, Hemingway seemingly detached himself entirely from the traditional ideals and concerns of so-called Christian civilization.[33] Rather than moralize, his writing reflected a deep appreciation of style and sensitivity to the experience of the moment.

Joseph Wood Krutch, whose *The Modern Temper* (1929) was widely read at the end of the decade, addressed the philosophical issues behind this disillusion. True to his generation, he saw the findings of natural science, particularly evolutionary science, as the great challenge to traditional belief. Krutch, however, went beyond the com-

· · ·

monplace claim that natural science undermined Christian faith to point out that it undermined humanism as well. "The paradox of humanism" was that modern science provided for many people the leisure to enjoy humanistic pursuits. At the same time, however, modern science proclaimed that humans were no more than higher-order animals; and that love, beauty, and moral ideals, as well as religion, were all illusions, simply pleasing survival mechanisms.[34]

Perhaps the most powerful analysis of such pessimistic themes came from the historian Carl Becker. In his *The Heavenly City of the Eighteenth-Century Philosophers*, published in 1932, Becker argued that educated moderns were as far away from the worldview of the eighteenth century as they were from the Middle Ages.[35] The most enlightened eighteenth-century thinkers, such as Jefferson or Franklin, believed in reason as a sure guide to finding truth. They had such faith in reason, Becker pointed out, because they presumed that there was a Creator, and therefore an order of natural and moral laws to be discovered. Truly modern persons had no basis for such a belief in a purposeful and ordered universe. In a brilliant summary of the modern predicament, Becker (who like so many Americans had been reared in evangelical Protestantism) wrote:

> Edit and interpret the conclusions of modern science as tenderly as we like, it is still quite impossible for us to regard man as the child of God for whom the earth was created as a temporary habitation. Rather must we regard him as little more than a chance deposit on the surface of the world, carelessly thrown up between two ice ages by the same forces that rust iron and ripen corn, a sentient organism endowed by some happy or unhappy accident with intelligence indeed, but with an intelligence that is conditioned by the very forces that it seeks to understand and to control. The ultimate cause of this cosmic process . . . appears in its effects as neither benevolent nor malevolent, as neither kind nor unkind, but merely as indifferent to us. What is man that the electron should be mindful of him![36]

Most Americans, even most intellectuals, were not willing to follow the naturalistic worldview to conclusions so consistent with its premises. It was one thing to profess such a worldview; it was another to live consistently with its implications.

· · ·

Pragmatic Secularism: John Dewey

More typical was an effort to reconstruct meaning on a thoroughly naturalistic basis, such as that offered by John Dewey (1859–1952). Dewey was *the* representative American secular thinker of the first half of the twentieth century. According to Henry Steel Commager, who lived through the era, Dewey "became the guide, the mentor, and the conscience of the American people: it is scarcely an exaggeration to say that for a generation no major issue was clarified until Dewey had spoken."[37]

Dewey was a pragmatist, the most typical philosophy of the day, and offered the most plausible alternative to traditional religion for constructing values. Pragmatism was built on essentially naturalistic evolutionary principles. Rather than design a philosophy by first asking abstract questions about God or the nature of ultimate reality, the naturalistic worldview declared such questions to be ultimately unanswerable. So pragmatism started with what science can still observe and describe about human thought: how the mind works. In Dewey's version of pragmatism, the human mind was described essentially as an "instrument" which functioned for purposes of survival. In a famous summary he declared that "ideas . . . become true just in so far as they help us to get into satisfactory relation with other parts of our experience."[38] That is, we should not waste our time worrying about whether our ideas correspond to some absolute truth in the real world; but rather, consider how our beliefs actually function.

Such an instrumental view of belief, said Dewey, reveals that our ideals and values are shaped by our social settings. Various religious beliefs, for instance, were generated by societies to legitimize their social, political, and ethical order. Such religious beliefs, evolving over the centuries, were typically irrational, however, and therefore not always the most healthful adjustments to reality.

In the light of modern science then, Dewey continued, we ought to be able to construct new religious beliefs that more healthfully advance the human species. Defining religions functionally as people's highest ideals and values, Dewey proposed, in *A Common Faith* (1934), humanistic values on which people from all traditions ought to be able to unite. These were principles that promoted ideals like human community, justice, security, art, and knowledge.[39]

Dewey's widest impact came from applying similar principles to

• • •

American educational theory. Education, Dewey emphasized, should promote a social environment that allows the full development of each individual's potential. A fixed body of knowledge, although not irrelevant to education, was less important than learning that built character. Democratic values, such as those outlined in *A Common Faith*, should provide the ideals that individuals should internalize. Thus Dewey, having a functional definition of religion, was in effect promoting the public schools as the functional established churches of America in which would be taught common ideals promoting human growth.

Dewey is important both because of his wide influence and the way his thought illustrates an important transition in dominant American public philosophy. He was a New Englander and like so many of his nineteenth-century contemporaries was reared in an evangelical environment. During his early adult career as a professor, until the 1890s, he was active in church work and even taught Sunday school. Then, once again like so many of his academic contemporaries, he abandoned Christianity entirely. Nonetheless, Dewey retained the evangelical and old New England Calvinist zeal to transform the social order. Like the liberal Protestants and some of the conservatives, he concentrated on building character. He offered twentieth-century Americans a secular faith that promised to yield the highest moral ideals. Through such a faith Dewey and many of his contemporaries hoped that a scientifically based civilization could usher in an era when people of all traditional religious heritages could be brought together. The millennial dreams still persisted.

The Neo-Orthodox Critique

By the 1930s influential liberal Protestant spokespersons were questioning the degree to which their churches were identifying the cause of Christianity with increasingly secular American civilization. Because this critique was influenced by a "neo-orthodox" European reaction to liberal theology, beginning just after World War I, the American movement also became known as neo-orthodox. The American movement, however, did not necessarily repudiate theological liberalism as thoroughly as did the European movement.

European neo-orthodoxy was identified primarily with the work of the Swiss theologian Karl Barth (1886–1968), who in massive and impressive theological tomes reemphasized traditional doctrines such as

· · ·

the sovereignty of God, the depravity of humans, and the centrality of salvation in Christ, uniquely revealed through the witness of Scripture. Though Barth did not claim the historical and scientific accuracy of the Bible the way fundamentalists did, he asserted that there was a great gulf between what humans could learn by unaided reason and true knowledge of God, which could be learned only through Christ.

The leading spokesmen for American neo-orthodoxy were the remarkable brothers, H. Richard Niebuhr (1894–1962) and Reinhold Niebuhr (1892–1971). Reared in a conservative Protestant German-American community in the Midwest, and coming of age just when World War I placed German-Americans in an awkward position, demanding strong loyalty from them, the Niebuhrs both became intensely interested in questions concerning the relationship of Christianity to culture. Coming from outside the mainstream, they saw more vividly than their Anglo-Protestant counterparts the ambiguities and paradoxes of identifying Christianity with any national cultural norm.

H. Richard was the more theologically traditional of the two and one of the important articulators of an American neo-orthodoxy in the early 1930s. According to him the American Protestant churches had fallen into bondage to a corrupt civilization, one dominated by capitalism, humanism, liberalism, and nationalism. All these were human-centered doctrines. Christianity, he emphasized, must be centered on God. American Protestantism, he claimed in a famous statement, had de-theologized itself. The result was that it preached that "a God without wrath brought men without sin into a kingdom without judgments through the ministrations of a Christ without a cross."[40] To be truly the church, Christians must stand against the world. "If the church has no other plan of salvation," Niebuhr proclaimed, ". . . than one of deliverance by force, education, idealism or planned economy, it really has no existence as a church and needs to resolve itself into a political party or a school."[41]

Reinhold Niebuhr was more concerned with politics than his brother and perhaps for that reason became better known in the twentieth-century world, when politics was often the operative religion. Like many intellectuals of the generation between the world wars, he leaned toward socialism. But under the influence of neo-orthodoxy his principal contribution to Christian social thought was a Christian realism that warned against identifying the kingdom with any political ideol-

• • •

ogy. In his classic volume, *Moral Man and Immoral Society* (1932), he pointed out that we cannot apply the same moral standards to social and political institutions that we can to individuals. Governments, business, and labor unions are constructed essentially to promote self-interests. Hence, the impact of Christian ethics on them, although potentially important, will always be limited. Often in public policy, we will have to settle for what is relatively better. Therefore, we cannot identify the Kingdom of God with any social-political proposal.[42]

Theologically, Reinhold Niebuhr's major contribution was to revive the doctrine of Original Sin. This doctrine, which was a leading motif in early American Protestant thought, had been increasingly denied in the optimistic and romantic era of the nineteenth and early twentieth centuries. Humans, Americans were coming to believe, were capable of doing anything. Especially, they believed this when they thought they had science and technology on their side. John Dewey's philosophy was a good example. Liberal churches, however, were just as optimistic about human nature.

Reinhold Niebuhr argued that there was an essential flaw in human nature, which he equated with Original Sin. Because humans had the freedom to be creative, they rose above the animals. But their freedom and creativity also led them to overestimate themselves. They thought of themselves as the creators of their own destinies. The very virtues that made them great became their vices. The righteous man Jesus, Niebuhr observed, was crucified through the combination of the two great human achievements up to that time—Jewish religion and Roman law. So it was with all individuals and nations. They overestimate their virtues and turn them into vices. Only from the perspective of the Divine Creator can humans see themselves in their true, limited perspectives.[43]

Neo-orthodoxy had a significant impact on liberal Protestant thought for the next generation. Because of its sophisticated nature, its strength was found primarily in seminaries, through which it influenced many pulpits. Nonetheless, its subtle emphases on the ambiguities and paradoxes of the application of Christianity to the world prevented it from becoming a widely popular movement. Most twentieth-century Americans, if they were looking for religious answers, wanted simpler formulae. Nevertheless, the neo-orthodox critiques tempered theological liberalism for a generation. Liberal preacher Harry Emerson

• • •

Fosdick, for instance, declared in a much-noticed sermon of 1935 that "The Church Must Go Beyond Modernism." Modernism as a theological self-description went out of style, though various forms of liberalism continued to be popular among Protestant leadership and in mainline seminaries.

A Secular New Deal

One of the reasons why the neo-orthodox prophets were calling their mainline churches to stand against the world was that the world was becoming more overtly secular, even in the relatively religious United States. During the Progressive Era, when the only slightly secularized New England reforming culture experienced a triumph, it was still easy for Protestants to believe that progressive reform was essentially an expression of Christian civilization. By the 1930s an increasing number of leading American figures, especially in the arts, entertainment, and education were openly secular and the idea of Christian civilization was becoming more problematic.

The New Deal under Franklin Roosevelt was an important symbol of public secularity. Although Roosevelt himself was an active Episcopal layman and sometimes referred to God in his public utterances, his administration was presented frankly as an effort in pragmatism versus dogmatic moral principle. The immediate end of Prohibition helped provide a secular tone. More pervasive, however, was a pragmatic style. While the key words exciting social action in the Progressive Era had been "soul," "morals," "service," "duty," "shame," "disgrace," "sin," and "selfishness," during the New Deal they were "needs," "organization," "humanitarian," "results," "technique," "institution," "realistic," "discipline," "morale," "skill," "expert," "habits," "practical," and "leadership." [44]

Progressivism had embodied two major impulses. The dominant impulse was to apply moral fervor to politics, and the secondary theme was an emerging pragmatism, as represented, for instance, in the legal thought of Oliver Wendell Holmes, Jr. The New Deal represented the triumph of this latter ideal. It was, most simply, the triumph of technological principle applied to government. The technological principle states that the bottom line is finding the most efficient means to get the job done.

The view was articulated most clearly by one of Roosevelt's cabinet members, Thurman Arnold, in a widely read volume of 1937,

• • •

The Folklore of Capitalism. Arnold argued that the principles of modern business should be applied to government. Businesses are not run by ideologues with creeds; they are run by experts with slogans. Efficient organization is the goal. To keep public support, the principles of advertising should be applied to government.

What Arnold was promoting was a relatively benign American version of the principles of modern propaganda, being so skillfully and sinisterly promoted in Stalin's Russia and Hitler's Germany. The big difference, though, was that the totalitarian propaganda was used in the cause of rigid ideologies, while in America the government had a long tradition of nonideological pragmatism that the New Deal was accentuating. At the same time the American heritage also included a strong tradition of moral review of the government, and scrutiny by the press and public. So there were some culturally inbuilt restraints on how far the government could depart from taken-for-granted moral principles. Moreover, pragmatic organization has to be directed toward some goals. So the New Deal, despite playing down overt moralism, could draw on a heritage of shared humanitarian and democratic goals.

From the longer perspective of American cultural development, however, the rise of large, bureaucratic pragmatic government was, for better or worse, another step toward the secularization of modern public life.

• • •

CHAPTER SIX

Return to Faith and Quest for Consensus:
1941–1963

Now the trumpet summons us again—not as a call to bear arms, though arms we need—not as a call to battle, though embattled we are—but a call to bear the burden of a long twilight struggle, year in and year out, "rejoicing in hope, patient in tribulation"—a struggle against the common enemies of man: tyranny, poverty, disease, and war itself.

. . . With a good conscience our only sure reward, with history the final judge of our deeds, let us go forth to lead the land we love, asking His blessing and His help, but knowing that here on earth God's work must truly be our own.

President John F. Kennedy, Inaugural Address (1961)

orld War II marked another major turning point in American cultural history. Its impact was, however, almost the opposite of World War I. Whereas the First World War brought to the United States a temporary, wild enthusiasm for its international mission, it soon led to disillusion and a period of cultural pessimism. The Second World War, on the other hand, led not only to America's role as a world leader, but also to a widespread revival of faith in America and America's religions.

Taking a broad overview of the twentieth century, we can see that World War II represented an interruption of the sense of cultural crisis in the 1930s. In the Vietnam era of the 1960s and early 1970s, the sense of crisis resumed. The Reagan years of the 1980s then reflected an attempted return to the ideals of the World War II era. However, so much changed in the meantime that the return was only partial. Deep new divisions emerged in American society and the roots of these divisions were often found in new patterns of American religion.

World War II and American Faith

Between the world wars, many of America's Protestant leaders thought they had learned an important lesson about religion and culture. They endorsed the American cause in the First World War, sometimes with extravagant enthusiasm, only to find out afterward that they had been taken in by wartime propaganda. Looking back, it was difficult to see the war as the forces of light versus those of darkness. So they organized for lasting peace. These peace concerns paralleled optimistic international efforts, most notably the Kellogg-Briand Pact of 1928, in which fifteen major nations agreed to renounce warfare as a national policy. Many thousands of clergy, especially from mainline Protestant denominations, signed pledges never to support a war again.

Clerical opposition to American military intervention in the ever-worsening international situation continued right up to the bombing of Pearl Harbor in December 1941. That event brought a dramatic reversal and an almost universal willingness to support a war that seemed to be for the survival of democratic civilization itself. Compared with the ideal, American liberal culture seemed to many thoughtful people to be deeply flawed; compared with the alternatives—especially that presented by Adolf Hitler, who combined mod-

• • •

ern technology with a horrible lack of moral principle—the American way of life seemed worth fighting and even dying for.[1]

American church leaders and politicians, and President Roosevelt himself, sometimes spoke of the war as a struggle for "Christian civilization." Totalitarianism had suddenly spread worldwide and appeared poised to destroy democratic civilization. Most Americans saw the combination of republican government and a popular willingness to play by the rules as one of the great accomplishments of the British and the Judeo-Christian cultural heritage. The myth of a Christian republican heritage, although usually exaggerated and often used crassly, had some basis in reality.[2]

Nonetheless, the old paradoxes of fighting a war for a seemingly righteous cause crept up. As theologian Reinhold Niebuhr frequently observed, a too-confident sense of justice often leads to injustice. One did not have to look far from home to exemplify the point. An outstanding instance was that many Americans feared disloyalty from Japanese-Americans in their midst and so raised little objection to rounding up over 100,000 into concentration camps for most of the war.

While these were benign places compared with Hitler's incredibly sinister death camps for Jews and others in Europe, Americans and their allies were reduced to Hitler's standards on another score with more permanent consequences. One of the traditional criteria for a "just war" was that it be fought by armies, and that reasonable efforts be made to exempt civilian populations from the killing. With the bombing of Dutch and British cities, Hitler violated this principle on a scale unprecedented in modern times. The allies soon retaliated in kind. Americans at first were reluctant to engage in indiscriminate bombing of German cities, but by 1944 had lost their compunctions. With the British they engaged in horrifying firebombing of German cities, killing in the bombing of Dresden alone, on the night of February 13–14, 1945, 135,000 men, women, and children. Since it was the night (Shrove Tuesday or Mardi Gras) before the Christian observance of Ash Wednesday, many of the children were dressed in festival costumes. Even if Hitler was more barbaric, war barbarizes everyone, and the juxtaposition of the ideals of Christian civilization and the realities of human use of technology were now appearing starkly on both sides.[3]

At the point of the routine acceptance of firebombing, Western

• • •

Dresden after the British and American firebombing.

civilization abandoned an ancient principle and entered a new age, accepting almost as normal that war included terrorism against civilians. Another technical advance, the invention of the atomic bomb in 1944, came to symbolize what had happened. In August 1945, Americans used two of these to destroy the civilian populations of the Japanese cities of Hiroshima and Nagasaki. Thus, they brought the war to a close but introduced a new meaning for war.

The atom bombs underscored anew the dilemmas of war, peace, and justice among clergy. The pope condemned the bombings and so did some Catholic and liberal Protestant clergy. Others justified it as a lesser evil, since it saved lives by ending the war. Theologically conservative clergy more often tended toward this latter view. Fundamentalists often added that the bomb should remind us of the fragile character of all human civilization and that God would soon bring history to an end.

Despite the paradoxes, international tensions, and instabilities created by the wartime destruction, Americans emerged from the contest with renewed idealism. They believed especially in them-

• • •

selves as the last best hope for the world. America was less scathed by the war than other major nations and Americans now took seriously the nation's role as an international power. This again marked an important turning point, since from then on the United States would be defined, in part, by a consciousness that it was an integral part of the world community. The founding of the United Nations, with its headquarters in New York City, signalled this new role. American Protestant clergy followed the lead, playing a major part in founding the World Council of Churches in 1948. The American sense of world leadership was based in part on its economic and technological superiority after the war. It included also, however, a strong sense of mission to provide not only economic aid but also leadership to restore justice and establish democracy throughout the world. Many people from all faiths believed that religious values were important for promoting such goals.

The dark side of the picture was the overshadowing presence of the cold war in a nuclear age. World War II ended with political power in the world divided primarily between the United States—allied with Britain and France—and the Soviet Union. At the end of the war the Soviet Union consolidated a vast empire that included Eastern Europe. Stalin's Russia did not have a qualitatively better record than Hitler's Germany in employing modern technologies for the ruthless extermination of its enemies and for total suppression of dissent. To make matters more alarming, in 1949 an extended civil war in China ended with a Marxist victory. The U.S.S.R. and the People's Republic of China were allies, and in the United States international communism was widely believed to be one concerted force. By 1950 communist North Korean expansion into South Korea drew the United States, fighting under the official auspices of a United Nations peacekeeping force, into another war. Until this war was settled indecisively in 1953, a threat of World War III, with nuclear weapons on both sides, seemed particularly imminent.

Under a real threat of communist expansion, the imagined powers of the international movement were magnified. Led by Senator Joseph R. McCarthy, worried political conservatives attempted to rid the land of supposed communist sympathizers within. McCarthy was a Catholic from Wisconsin with a strong conservative Catholic constituency. Protestant fundamentalists and conservatives also tended to support militant anticommunism; but except in the South, Protestant

• • •

conservatives did not have much of a political base. One of the most colorful of the politically oriented fundamentalists was Carl McIntire (b. 1906). McIntire had a daily radio broadcast, carried on some 600 stations at its height, which emphasized anticommunism. McIntire argued that the mainline National Council of Churches (formerly the Federal Council of Churches) and the World Council of Churches (which included representatives from the Russian Orthodox Church) were hotbeds of communist subversion. According to McIntire and many fundamentalists and other conservative Protestants, the turn of mainline churches to modernist theology was leading to a relativistic world church and world government which would essentially be in sympathy with "godless communism." J. Edgar Hoover, head of the Federal Bureau of Investigation, and a strong foe of communist subversion, was a conservative Protestant who held similar views.

The Irony of American History

Such strong views from the religious right helped make more welcome the moderate views from the Protestant mainstream. Particularly, neo-orthodox theologian Reinhold Niebuhr reached the height of his popularity in the post-war era. Although not a media figure, Niebuhr was apparently the last major American Protestant theologian to be taken seriously outside of the churches. Some of his academic admirers called themselves "atheists for Niebuhr."

In the *Irony of American History* (1952) Niebuhr pointed out the ironic similarities between the United States and the dreaded Soviet Union. The two nations had similar origins in their enlightened confidence in the human ability to use scientific analysis to create an ideal society. Each had ultimately similar goals: that humans should be masters of their own destinies. Each proposed similar means to reach these goals, essentially through an economic system. Both tended to define humanity in terms of property; either the ownership of it or the lack thereof. Each reverenced a scientific elite. Each nation had similar mythologies asserting its own innocence and the corruption of its opponents. Ironically, for instance, while Americans took their economic prosperity to be evidence of their virtue, much of the rest of the world took it to be evidence of vice. Finally, each nation used the myth of the virtue of its intentions to justify the vices of its policies in reaching its goals.

Niebuhr was not endorsing the Soviet Union as being just as good

• • •

as America. Rather, he was for a realistic foreign policy that would stand up to the Soviet threat. However, at the same time he pointed out the irony that the Soviet vices Americans criticized—especially materialism and the belief that one could build a better society based simply on human mastery of science, technology, and economics—were in effect the principles that Americans most believed in. Moreover, to double the irony, Americans used their religious heritage simply to endorse this humanism and materialism. Rather than see themselves in the light of a transcendent God who laughs at all human pretentions to be able to manage their own destinies, Americans used their religion to rationalize for themselves unlimited powers and rights. By contrast, Niebuhr urged maintaining a sense of human limitations, even when we are sure we are in the right. Abraham Lincoln earlier epitomized such modesty when he observed in his second inaugural speech that both sides in the Civil War prayed to the same God and that the prayers of neither would be fully answered since "the Almighty has his own purposes." Such a stance, Niebuhr added, can proceed only from a "broken spirit and a contrite heart."[4]

The Post-War Revival

The United States from the 1940s until the early 1960s was in the midst of an extensive religious revival; but many observers, such as Niebuhr, questioned its depth. Religious groups of nearly all sorts were growing and prospering. A national survey, conducted shortly after World War II, revealed that two out of three Americans attended religious services at least once a month and forty-two percent attended every week. Other polls revealed that nineteen out of twenty Americans believed in God, nine out of ten said they engaged in prayer, six out of seven viewed the Bible as the divinely inspired word of God, and three out of four believed in life after death.[5] These figures were all substantially higher than in any other major industrialized country. On the other hand, lack of depth to some of this commitment was suggested by a poll revealing that over half of the adults could not name any one of the four gospels.[6]

Whatever the depth of the commitments or knowledge of the faith, unprecedented numbers of Americans were joining religious groups, with memberships rising from about fifty to over sixty percent of the population in the decade after the war.[7] As usual, when most people talked about the revival they thought first about the mainline North-

• • •

ern Protestants who still regarded themselves as representing a sort of all-American religion. Probably the belief of most laypeople within such churches was traditional Protestant; but critics were noticing how often it was vague and how much of it was mixed with seemingly secular Americanism. As historian Martin Marty observed at the time, more and more people seemed to have faith in faith itself. They were in favor of "religion-in-general" and believed in a God who was understandable, manageable, comforting, and ultimately a good-natured "man upstairs." Bible-believing actress Jane Russell, for example, described God as a "livin' Doll."[8] Apparently bland suburban religion was reinforced by a marked increase in public piety. President Eisenhower, who took office in 1953, came to be a symbol of American spiritual values. During this time, prayer breakfasts, special church services, and back-to-God and values crusades were conspicuous Washington activities.[9] Reflecting now more broadly and vaguely than ever the old Republican agenda to unite the nation under a moral-religious ideal, people were encouraged to go to the church of their choice and to pray for peace. The words "under God" were added to the hitherto secular Pledge of Allegiance. President Eisenhower encapsulated the prevailing view that religion was a "good thing" with his since-famous remark: "Our government makes no sense, unless it is founded in a deeply felt religious faith—*and I don't care what it is.*"[10]

The outlook of faith in faith was embodied in a runaway best-seller of the Eisenhower years, Norman Vincent Peale's *The Power of Positive Thinking* (1952). Peale, one of New York City's leading mainline Protestant preachers, proclaimed positive thinking as the "secret to success." All that was necessary was to "believe in yourself! Have faith in your abilities!" The book was filled with rules and formulas for overcoming negative attitudes and promised happy and productive lives.[11]

The most widely heralded analysis of this sort of popular American religion was Will Herberg's *Protestant-Catholic-Jew* (1955). Herberg, a Jewish scholar, argued that despite the differences among America's three major traditions, these were not the real religions of most Americans. He made a distinction between professed religion and "operative religion," the latter defined as the highest values that people actually live by. The operative religion of most Americans was

• • •

faith in the "American Way of Life." This religion involved a faith in democracy, individualism, optimism, idealism, humanitarianism, nationalism, and tolerance of other Americans.[12]

For instance, almost all Americans believed that one should love one's neighbor as oneself and over half believed they did follow this rule "all the way" in their lives. This in itself was a remarkable assertion of their own virtue for people formally professing religions that traditionally emphasized human sinfulness. Moreover, ninety percent claimed they truly "obeyed the law of love" toward people of other religions, and eighty percent toward those of other races. Yet, Herberg observed, many of these same Americans did not extend the law of love to communists or to enemies of one's country. So, said Herberg, "Where the American Way of Life approves of love of one's fellow man, most Americans confidently assert that they pratice such love; where the American Way of Life disapproves, the great mass of Americans do not hesitate to confess that they do not practice it, and apparently feel very little guilt for their failure."[13]

The United States, Herberg was pointing out, was simultaneously professedly religious yet very secular. So, for instance, even of those Americans who said that religion was "very important" to them, well over half said that their religious beliefs had no real effect on their ideas or conduct in politics or business.[14] Catholics and Jews indeed had been largely absorbed into an essentially Protestant Anglo-Puritan tradition; but the resulting American cultural value system severely limited the functions of traditional religions.

One could read this as the outcome of liberal religionists' program of tolerance. The opinion was coming to prevail that religion, though valuable for personal fulfillment, should not interfere with being a good American. Hence, traditional religions were in danger of losing their identities in a blend of secular and religious humanitarian ideals. Though Americans spoke much of God, they often seemed to trust more in human abilities to solve humanity's problems.

From "Fundamentalist to Evangelicalist"

Not all of the religious revivals of the era were so broadly liberal. Some parts of it had strong traditionalist aspects. The Protestant versions of such traditionalism especially involved some strikingly paradoxical themes. On the one hand, in reasserting a distinct Christian

• • •

identity, they sharply challenged some of the values of the dominant culture. On the other hand, they too strongly affirmed aspects of the American way of life.

The best examples of such paradoxes are found among the heirs to fundamentalism. Fundamentalism of the 1920s, it should be recalled, already had this paradox deeply built into it. Fundamentalists, who were an antimodernist coalition of several Protestant traditions, were fighting a war on two fronts: they were trying to save the fundamental doctrinal purity of the churches and they were trying to save a much broader "Christian" American cultural heritage. Thus, they were seldom clear whether they were heirs to Roger Williams or John Winthrop. Was America a Babylon from which they should withdraw, or the new Israel, which they should rule? Were they a sect or America's church?

The rise of the "evangelical" movement surrounding Billy Graham best illustrates the tensions in this tradition.

Although defeated in the mainline Northern denominations, fundamentalists in the 1930s and 1940s were building their own institutions, especially evangelistically oriented local churches and other evangelistic agencies. Though they were not much noticed by the dominant media and power structures, they remained numerous. For instance, at some times during World War II, the radio program with apparently the largest audiences was not one of the popular comedy or entertainment programs, but Charles E. Fuller's "Old Fashioned Revival Hour." Fuller preached a simple, homey, but dignified old-time gospel of conversion. Despite his popularity, the three major networks, NBC, CBS, and ABC, would not carry Fuller. The only religious broadcasting these networks allowed was free Sunday morning time for Catholics and Protestants. The Protestant broadcasts were controlled by the Federal Council of Churches, anathema to the fundamentalists. Harry Emerson Fosdick, famed opponent of fundamentalism, was the principal, officially recognized Protestant radio preacher.

Despite such problems in gaining recognition (fundamentalists had similar difficulties in keeping the Federal Council from controlling the military chaplaincy), fundamentalists were sparking a wartime revival. In impressive youth rallies in many American cities they were filling famed sports arenas, such as Madison Square Garden, or Soldier's Field. A major outgrowth of such young people's revivalism was

• • •

the organization in 1945 of Youth for Christ. Billy Graham (b. 1918) was the national organization's first full-time evangelist.

In 1949 during a tent revival in Los Angeles, Graham gained the notice of the media establishment through support from newspaper publisher William Randolph Hearst (who told his editors to "puff Graham"). The young evangelist immediately hit the big time. Much of Graham's message sounded like America was more Babylon than Israel. He tied anxieties about the threat of nuclear destruction with Biblical warnings of judgment for sin. He preached for conversions and for traditional American values. Though he stayed away from public involvements in politics, he spoke often of the communist threat and the dangers to America of such atheistic and materialistic values.

Graham was part of a larger effort of many fundamentalist Protestants who, having found themselves now as cultural outsiders, were working to become insiders again. Their overriding motive was to convert people to Christ; but to do this they needed to regain respectability. Graham encouraged conservative scholars, seminaries, and publications to defend the integrity of biblical revelation and oppose liberal Protestant thought, but in intellectually sophisticated ways. He also used his immense popularity to cultivate the friendship of major political leaders and became a regular visitor to the White House through many administrations. At the same time Graham began moving toward the ecclesiastical center in his campaigns. Originally his revival crusades were sponsored exclusively by fundamentalists or other conservative Protestants who would not be associated with mainline churches. In 1957, however, at a major crusade in New York City Graham accepted the sponsorship of the local council of churches, which included Protestant liberals.

This move brought a sharp break between Graham and more militant fundamentalists, who now insisted on strict separation of fundamentalists from religious liberals. John R. Rice (1895–1980) (later a mentor of Jerry Falwell), whose weekly *Sword of the Lord* had a circulation of over 100,000, took the lead in breaking with Graham. So did Bob Jones, Sr., founder of the strictly separatist Bob Jones University. After 1957 "fundamentalism" as a self-designation meant those who totally separated from mainline churches. The larger group of conservative Protestants, who still held to the traditional fundamentals of the faith, but were trying to reenter or stay in the main-

· · ·

stream, came to be called "neo-evangelicals" or simply "evangelicals."[15] Though Graham himself could not be ignored, establishment Protestants and the secular media still did not pay much attention to this large group. Some people did, however, begin to speculate about "a third force" in Christendom of conservative Protestants.[16]

Pentecostal Healing

An important part of this third force was the pentecostal movement which was still small (its largest denominations still under half a million members) but growing. Paralleling the other revivals of the time there was a pentecostal revival, particularly in healing ministries. From 1947 to the early 1960s was the great age for a remarkable number of sawdust trial-healing tent evangelists. Oral Roberts (b. 1918) was the best known of these, but he was only one of many colorful figures, some more and some less reputable. Roberts himself was born into the home of an Oklahoma pentecostal preacher and grew up in the rural poverty of the depression. Before his birth, his mother later told him, she was informed by God that he was to have a special ministry. After a dramatic healing from tuberculosis when he was a teenager, he prepared to become a pentecostal preacher himself. After World War II, Roberts followed some others into healing tent evangelism and soon became its leading practitioner. Like other healers, he claimed miraculous powers, such as a "word of knowledge" about people's lives or their hidden illnesses. Like others of the early healing evangelists, Roberts also sent out anointed prayer clothes which reputedly had healing powers.

Popular responses to Roberts's crusades, especially among the poorer and less educated, were immense and his claims grew even larger. During a three-year period in the late 1950s he claimed to have won ten million converts, though perhaps a more accurate gauge of his following was the circulation of 600,000 copies of his magazine. Roberts also gained national fame with TV broadcasts during which he performed healings.

In addition to preaching for conversions and performing healings, Roberts's message promised success and prosperity. He developed a "seed-faith" principle, proclaiming that the more one gave to God, presumably via the Roberts ministry, the more one would get. In effect, Roberts's message amounted to a mix of revivalist Protestantism, pentecostalism, and a poor person's version of Norman Vincent

• • •

Peale's "power of positive thinking." Each proclaimed a gospel of success.

During the 1960s Roberts also began to move toward greater respectability. While not giving up pentecostal doctrine, he left the pentecostal denomination for the mainline Methodist church. He also started Oral Roberts University, including a medical center that would provide an unusual combination of advanced technology and openness to spiritual powers.[17]

The pentecostal movement in general was moving toward greater social respectability. After World War II, many of its constituents were freed from their desperate poverty of the depression years. At the same time some pentecostal leaders planned a major effort to reach into the American cultural establishment. In 1951 Demos Shakarian, a wealthy California businessman, supported initially by Oral Roberts, founded the Full Gospel Businessmen's Fellowship International in California. Partly through the efforts of this group and the leadership of David Du Plessis, a pentecostal minister, by the early 1960s pentecostal teachings began to make some inroads into mainline denominations. This was the beginning of the charismatic revival, which during the next decades had a tremendous impact in spreading pentecostal influence beyond the traditional, specifically pentecostal denominations.

THE MAINSTREAM WIDENS

Jewish Identity and the American Way

Though these resurgent evangelical movements signalled an important restructuring of American Protestantism, the religious revivals of the 1940s and 1950s nowhere had a greater impact than on American Judaism.

Between the world wars the central feature of American Judaism seemed to be its rapid secularization. Large numbers of the second generation of the massive Eastern European immigration turned from religious practice, often adopting overtly secular outlooks.

Nonetheless, during the time between the wars, most American Jews retained a strong sense of Jewish identity. This was a matter of

• • •

both choice and necessity. While the United States was more hospitable to Jews than most other nations, anti-Semitism was a constant fact of life. Between the wars, which were decades of international racism and fascism, some virulent anti-Semitism sprang up in America. Beginning in 1920 Henry Ford widely publicized the *Protocols of the Elders of Zion,* forged documents which claimed to expose an international Jewish conspiracy to rule the world. Populist preachers, such as Father Coughlin and a number of Protestant counterparts, also attempted to fan anti-Semite flames.

For most Jews, however, the most tangible effects of discrimination were those of everyday life suffered at the hands of the Anglo-Protestant establishment. Prestigious neighborhoods often had covenants that kept out Jews (as well as blacks), and most major country clubs routinely banned Jews.

In higher education Jews also often ran into major roadblocks. A much greater percentage of Jewish young people, compared with other ethnic groups, attended universities, but only a few schools, like City College of New York, were fully open to their presence. While Harvard, for instance, accepted Jewish students on the basis of merit before World War I, when after the war the number of Jewish students threatened to go over fifteen percent, the administration, despite some protests, maintained an informal quota. Most other schools had unpublicized quotas also. Some that were thoroughly secular in what they taught still talked about maintaining a "Christian" ethos.[18] In 1941 at Princeton, less than two percent of the students were Jewish. Prior to World War II, prejudice against Jews in most prestigious university faculties was strong enough to prevent Jewish appointments, except in rare instances.[19]

Jews were accepted in some areas of national life, including some significant government and court appointments, especially from Democrats, whom they now overwhelmingly supported as the party of assimilation. The best-known Jews in America, however, were on the stage and in comedy, fields that remained open to them. Comedians such as Jack Benny, George Burns, Fanny Brice, and the Marx brothers were loved across the nation; although it was significant that many of them dropped their Jewish names and were entirely secular in their styles. Secularized Jews, such as L. B. Mayer and the Warner brothers, created most of the Hollywood film industry and from it projected

• • •

an image of America both more glamorous and more secular than the WASP-dominated realities.[20]

World War II drastically changed the mood of Jews in America. Two events were overwhelmingly crucial. First was the ruthless slaughter of some six million Jews in Hitler's death camps. The total horror of this unforgettable genocide made the issue of survival central for Jews. The other world shaker was the establishment of the Jewish state of Israel in 1948. During the preceding seventy-five years American Jews were divided in opinion over Zionism, or the establishment of a Jewish state. With its actual establishment, however, Israel became a powerful religious symbol, eventually eliciting the support of the overwhelming majority of American Jews.

Their close identification with the state of Israel put the American Jewish community into a peculiar position regarding religion and culture. On the one hand, they had established a firm stance in the United States favoring the secularization of the culture. The residual Christian establishment often was discriminatory toward them; so it was in their interest to help dismantle it. Hence, Jews were often active with liberal Christians and secularists in the American Civil Liberties Union which, among other things, opposed all religious discrimination and religious observances and teaching in public schools. In the 1950s, for instance, some states still required reading from the Bible and recitation of the Lord's Prayer as part of their opening exercises. Not until 1962 did the Supreme Court of the United States strike down, in a symbolically important case, the use of a prayer composed by the Board of Regents for the New York state public schools.

At the same time that most Jews supported such secularization at home, much of their deepest commitment was to the state of Israel, which in addition to being a secular enterprise was a profound symbol of the Jewish religion. This loyalty to Israel became particularly intense during the Six Day War of 1967, when the continued existence of Israel seemed threatened. Such dedication to Israel meant that most American Jews saw the strong political implications of their faith, but only for a distant land. Jacob Neuser, one of the most astute and prolific internal observers, makes the point forcefully with some rhetorical overstatement: "How can American Jews focus their spiritual lives solely on a land in which they do not live?"[21] Such a question

· · ·

relates to a larger issue much discussed in the American Jewish community: "What does it mean to be Jewish?" To what extent does it mean ethnic identity, to what extent does it mean religious practice, and to what extent does it involve a political stance about Israel?

By no means was all of American Jewish religious energy directed toward the state of Israel. Following World War II there was a marked upsurge in Jewish religious observance and correspondingly wider inclusion of a religious component in people's definition of Jewishness. Weekly attendance at religious services remained relatively low (under twenty percent) in the 1950s and 1960s, but attendance at services celebrating high holy days was over fifty percent, comparable to regular observance in other major American religious groups.[22] Moreover, the size of the three major branches of Judaism was inversely proportional to their degree of liberalism and accommodation to the dominant American culture. The smallest, though not by a great deal, was the Reform; Conservative was next, and Orthodox the largest and the one that grew the most into the 1980s.[23]

At the same time, the Jewish community became proportionally more affluent than any other American religious-ethnic group and was moving to the suburbs. As with other religious groups, this move from close-knit urban centers took its toll. Ironically, so did the marked acceptance of Jews by other Americans and the virtual end of public discrimination by the 1960s. While as late as the 1950s only six percent of Jewish marriages were with persons of other faiths, by the early 1960s this figure rose to seventeen percent and by the late 1960s to thirty-two percent. Since Jewish identity was formed dually by ethnicity and religious practice, this secularizing trend was undermining one of the foundations of the community. The corresponding rise in Conservative and Orthodox observance was in part an effort by some in the community the reclaim identity that was otherwise eroding. So, probably, was the rise in distinctly Jewish education and day schools.

The American Jewish community, however, remained more deeply ambivalent toward the religious and the secular than any other major American group. Unlike the liberal Protestants, who are simultaneously religious and secular but at ease with the paradoxes, Jews more often see the problem. Both the Holocaust and the state of Israel reinforce the point that religion has profound implications. Moreover, despite the strong experiences of secularity which Jews have experienced with other urban-oriented Americans, most of them

• • •

"Sabbath studies."

have also been exposed to deep reverence for the tradition both in the family and in their religious education.

The tensions in the juxtaposition of the modern and the traditional are engagingly portrayed, for instance, in such novels by Chaim Potok as *The Chosen* (1967) and *The Promise* (1969), where modern sensibilities are contrasted with the strict observance and distinctive dress of the fervently orthodox Hasidic Jews.

Less reverently, one can see the ambivalence in the films and writings of Woody Allen. Unlike the Jewish comics of the thirties, Allen, who experienced eight years of Hebrew school, is constantly dealing with religious themes. He writes that at New York City College he was attracted to courses such as "Death 101," "Intermediate Truth," and "Introduction to God." In *Love and Death* (1975), set in Russia with mock Dostoevskian themes, the hero, Boris Grushenko (Woody Allen) suggests to Sonya (Diane Keaton) that there may be no God. Sonya replies, "But if there is no God, then life has no meaning. Why go on living? Why not just commit suicide?" Boris

• • •

quickly replies: "Well, let's not get hysterical. I could be wrong. I'd hate to blow my brains out and then read in the papers they found something." Later, an angel appears to Boris and tells him not to worry, he will be rescued from a firing squad. After he is not, the deceased Boris appears in an epilogue and says: "If it turns out that there is a God, I don't think he is evil. I think that the worst thing you can say about him is that he is an underachiever."[24]

Catholics Move into the Mainstream

At the end of World War II, both interreligious and interracial hostilities still ran high. One impact of the Holocaust, nevertheless, was that it alerted people to the dangers of such prejudices and strengthened the resolve of those who were working to bring about changes. The dramatic changes that eventually came, however, should not obscure our historical memory of how deep the antagonisms were until recently.

Particularly dramatic has been the revolution in the relationships between Protestants and Catholics. Immediately after World War II, Protestant spokespersons still often equated Catholicism with authoritarianism and hence with totalitarianism. One popular and influential book of the era was Paul Blanshard's *American Freedom and Catholic Power* (1949), which reiterated the old theme, commonplace in America since colonial times, that Catholics were threatening to take over and would bring an end to American freedoms.[25] The same year Bishop G. Bromley Oxnam, one of the most influential bishops in the Methodist church (America's largest Protestant denomination), spoke in a nationally distributed radio interview of

> the striking parallel between the organizational structure and method of the World-Wide Communist political party and the World-Wide Roman Catholic political party. Both are totalitarian. Both seek control of the minds of men everywhere. Both practice excommunication, character assassination, and economic reprisals. Neither Rome nor Moscow knows what tolerance means.[26]

For religious liberals such as Oxnam, who still looked for a world dominated by Christian principles, Catholic authoritarianism seemed to subvert their Protestant and democratic ideals. In 1951 President Truman attempted to appoint an ambassador to the Vatican; but a

. . .

public outcry, led by mainline Protestant churchmen, forced him to abandon the attempt.

Feelings ran deep. For instance, a Presbyterian magazine after the war warned against marrying Catholics, noting among other things that "it is Protestant theology, not Roman Catholic, which has provoked men to demand free government and the overthrow of tyrants."[27] The Episcopal church passed a strong resolution against mixed marriages in 1949.[28] The feelings, of course, were mutual; Catholic leaders discouraged mixed marriages at least as vigorously as did Protestants.

Catholicism, like other religious groups, was flourishing after World War II, although it was remaining fairly stable in size relative to Protestantism. In the early 1950s about twenty percent of Americans were Catholic, as compared to about thirty-five percent Protestant church members (plus many nominal Protestants).[29] Catholicism then had, however, vast and well-ordered organizations and educational systems.

Popular piety was also flourishing. Since Catholicism was a vast coalition, such piety was expressed in wide varieties that in Protestantism would have been manifest in denominational and social class division. Devotion to the Virgin Mary was particularly popular during this period. In the ten years from 1948 to 1957 ten thousand Marian titles were published. Devotion to Our Lady of Fátima, inspired by a Marian apparition in Fátima, Portugal in 1917, flourished in post-World War II America. Popular devotion also was often associated with anticommunism and prayers for the conversion of Russia.[30]

A somewhat different style of popular Catholicism was indicated by the vogue in the 1950s of Bishop Fulton J. Sheen's TV show, "Life is Worth Living." As the title intimates, Sheen (1895–1979) was the Catholic counterpart to Norman Vincent Peale. He skillfully provided Catholic commentary on contemporary society and offered an essentially upbeat message.

Perhaps most important was the growing sense within the Catholic community of being a full member of America's three-faith pluralism or "triple melting pot," as Will Herberg put it. Catholics were then, by and large, confident and comfortable with their status as one major faith in an essentially democratic and pluralistic society. Conservatism in Rome, as well as American Catholic ethnicities, had long

• • •

Bishop Fulton J. Sheen's "Life is Worth Living" drew large audiences in the 1950s.

kept most Catholics relatively isolated in America. However, there were glimmers of more openness in the church and certainly signs that Catholics were ready to assume a role as full partners in the American enterprise.

A number of devout Catholics were highly regarded cultural figures. Thomas Merton (1905–1968), who after his conversion in 1938 became a Trappist monk in Kentucky, was renowned for his inspirational and mystical piety, especially as expressed in *The Seven Storey Mountain* (1948), a best-seller of the 1950s. Another convert, Dorothy Day (1898–1980), founder of the Catholic Worker movement in the 1930s, although more controversial, was also one of the most respected religious writers and workers of the era. Publishing her views in her daily newspaper, *The Catholic Worker,* Day promoted a pacifist, non-Marxist, Christian socialism. She and her co-workers founded dozens of hospitality houses to help the poor throughout the country. She also nourished a small, politically radical wing within the church.

Of the mainline Catholic establishment, Father John Courtney Murray, S.J. (1904–1967), was the most effective and respected

• • •

spokesperson for Catholicism's full reconciliation with democratic pluralism. Murray faced squarely both Protestant and conservative Catholic critics and argued that the Catholic tradition itself included principles of democracy and religious freedom. Murray not only won Protestant respect, but his views eventually became the basis for the Vatican's redefinition of the relationships between the church and society.

Nothing, however, signalled the new status for Catholicism in America as the election in 1960 of John F. Kennedy as the first Catholic president. Although there was still some significant anti-Catholic opposition and the election was unusually close, the election of Kennedy showed that overt anti-Catholicism was eroding. His assurances that he would keep his faith and his politics in separate compartments and actually doing so while in office did much to allay any fears of influence on America by the foreign power of the Vatican. The oldest theme in American religious and political history—Protestant versus Catholic rivalries—was virtually at an end.

At almost the same time the Catholic church began its own revolution. The elderly Pope John XXIII, of whom little was expected when he assumed the papacy in 1958, convened the Second Vatican Council, which from 1962 to 1965 suddenly brought sweeping reforms to the church, including a much more open attitude toward Protestants and toward cultural pluralism. Differences between Protestants and Catholics and their virtual isolation from each other were suddenly and drastically diminished, thus reinforcing trends begun in the Kennedy years.

Though during his brief presidency John Kennedy freely used the symbolism of American civil religion on state occasions, his administration, like most Democratic administrations, set a slightly more secular tone for the nation. Kennedy's view of America resembled that of Reinhold Niebuhr, who indeed was much admired by many of Kennedy's "New Frontiersmen."[31] On the one hand, Kennedy could be critical of the United States and recognized some of its limits and imperfections; he was also a political realist who could play hardball. On the other hand, his firm opposition to international communism was also based on American idealism and he effectively preached a new vision of the American way of life built on justice for all peoples. The Peace Corps, which he initiated to send Americans overseas to aid third-world nations, was transparently a secularized version of the

. . .

Catholic President John F. Kennedy visited Pope Paul VI, but did not take orders from him.

American missionary movement. Enthusiasm for mainline Protestant missions, which long had been an important source for American presence and image abroad, had been declining since World War I. The Peace Corps, however, provided new opportunities for American young people to present the world with the tradition of service that was indeed part of the national heritage. Kennedy was no Woodrow Wilson Puritan, especially in his personal conduct, but there was in him a touch of national moral idealism as well as political realism.

In retrospect, Kennedy's administration had much more in common with the 1950s than with the later 1960s. He still represented the ideal of building a consensus America. Just as Protestants and Catholics were becoming more alike, so were the two political parties. The melting pot was still the ideal in which Americans would be brought together through the promotion of a consensus of American values. Despite lingering tensions, as over the race issue, WASP

• • •

America and other ethnic groups seemed to be successfully blending into a common meld.

Secularism

When Will Herberg talked about Protestants, Catholics, and Jews as representing three major faiths, he was pointing out that they were all to some degree secularized, in that they all supported the American way of life. Since the value system of the American way of life could function independently of the other three, some commentators of the era designated it as simply a fourth faith. John Courtney Murray, for instance, explicitly added "secularist" to "Protestant, Catholic, and Jew" to describe the dominant American religions.[32] Protestant Martin Marty followed Murray's lead in speaking of the fourth faith as "secular humanist" or "secular and humanistic."[33] This "religion of democracy," as Marty also called it, had "an 'established church' in the field of public education." Other commentators made the same point.[34] Such religious observers were observing that the actual situation in America was much like that which secularist John Dewey had earlier recommended.

Despite its support from the three traditional faiths, the consensus America, of which John Kennedy was the last great symbol, was based on a largely secular ideology. This did not mean that America was being overrun by avowed atheists and agnostics. Rather, it meant that most Americans held to two faiths, or some amalgam of the two; one traditional and one largely secular. In public life, however, it seemed that the secular style was triumphing. The absence of substantive religion, afterall, seemed to provide the best hope for bringing peoples of various faiths together.

The unanswered question was what such mutual tolerance might do to religion itself. Would it open the door for the ideological triumph of an aggressive relativism that would undermine all the traditional faiths? Would it drift into a bland relativism that would not long please anyone? Or would it provide an atmosphere in which distinctive faiths could flourish?

For the time being, however, the secular faith still provided the basis for a hopeful American idealism, even a secular millennialism. Secularism had indeed appropriated much of the rhetoric and the hope of the religious traditions.

• • •

Civil Rights

The United States, however, was not in fact nearly as secular as its public philosophy might indicate. All sorts of subgroups in the culture retained vital and distinctive religious traditions. Only rarely, however, did these impinge directly on public affairs. One place in which they did was the civil rights movement, where the inclusivism of the progressive American democratic faith converged with the millennial hopes of black Christianity.

The civil rights movement was also the best illustration that Puritan moral idealism was not dead in the Kennedy years. During the Roosevelt era, blacks shifted from their long-standing Republican allegiance to Democrats, who were doing more for the poor. Partly out of political self-interest, but just as certainly out of the religious and secular moral idealism of the traditions that supported them, liberal Democrats took over what had been the classic Republican reforming agenda—the cause of the black people. While liberal Democrats preached that it was the duty of all Americans to accede to the principles of elementary justice, conservative Republicans joined the old chorus of conservative Southerners that "morality cannot be legislated."

Morality was legislated, or at least in the 1950s and 1960s some behavior and attitudes were drastically changed largely through court and legal action. At the same time, however, as in the antislavery crusades, the churches played a significant role in providing the moral leverage necessary to change popular opinion. Liberal Protestant leadership, which had a basically Republican heritage, now shifted to the Democratic party in this moral campaign. The earlier social gospel had not made racial equality a prominent issue. Now liberal Protestants joined with secularists, progressive Catholics, civil rights-oriented Jews, and others for the new crusade.

The most important religious contribution to the cause, however, came from the black churches themselves. In the black communities, denied political power, clergy had remained the chief community spokespersons and organizers for political concerns. Even the formally secular civil rights organizations, such as the National Association for the Advancement of Colored People, founded in 1909, depended heavily on church support.

Clergy leadership in the black efforts to gain their civil rights meant

. . .

that black political thought retained an explicitly Christian prophetic tone that had disappeared in most other places in American politics since the mid-nineteenth century. In this respect blacks were responding to their outsider status in a way almost the opposite of Catholics. While successful Catholic politicians typically presented a secular public image, blacks could appeal to themes that were close to the heart of the dominant British-republican heritage, especially those who connected true Christianity with the spirit of political liberty.

Although the explicit appeal to Christianity was an anomaly in mid-twentieth century American politics, it was arguable that, for a group who had no political power or prospect of power, it was appropriate to appeal to a higher authority. One of the major dangers in mixing religion and politics is that, if it is routinely done, those who have power or who aspire to revolutionary violence will use religious rationales in combination with force to promote deadly, and often unjust, programs. The black civil rights movement, at least in its early stages, was hardly in danger of such an abuse of power.

Martin Luther King, Jr.

Martin Luther King, Jr. (1929–1968), one of the great religious thinkers of the twentieth century, not only understood such principles, but put them into practice. Graduating from Morehouse College at age nineteen, King went on to study at Northern liberal Protestant schools, Crozier Theological Seminary (for a divinity degree), and Boston University (for a Ph.D.). King's own thought reflected influences of liberal theology, Walter Rauschenbusch's social gospel, Reinhold Niebuhr, and the peaceful nonresistance of Mahatma Gandhi.

Nonetheless, central to King's synthesis of such traditions were themes drawn from the American black religious heritage, to which he was first of all committed. Rather than become a seminary professor, he chose to be a pastor of a Southern black Baptist church. He later wrote in *Ebony* magazine, "I am fundamentally a clergyman, a Baptist preacher. This is my being and my heritage, for I am also the son of a Baptist preacher, the grandson of a Baptist preacher, and the great-grandson of a Baptist preacher. The Church is my life and I have given my life to the Church."[35]

In 1955, early in his career as pastor in Montgomery, Alabama, King gained national prominence for his involvement in promoting

• • •

the Montgomery bus boycott. In January 1956 threats on his life and family brought him to a religious crisis and a spiritual experience that strengthened his resolve to renew the black church and community.[36] In 1957 he led the organizing of the Southern Christian Leadership Conference to mobilize forces for protest. Not all the clergy leadership in the black community, however, favored King's approach. Some opposed protests, felt that the church should be more purely spiritual in its activities, and that the black communities would do better to build their own strength and internal discipline than to engage in confrontational politics. Because of such objections, King and others felt it necessary in 1961 to secede from the largest black denomination, the National Baptist Convention, and form a smaller Progressive National Baptist Convention with about a half-million members.[37]

King, however, eventually won a wide following in the black communities, primarily by his abilities as an eloquent preacher to appeal to elements in their heritage as black American Christians. If the American black communities had a weakness in political outlook, as its more radical black critics said it did, it was that it often exemplified too well some of the cardinal Christian virtues. Black Christians had preserved better than most other twentieth-century Americans the nineteenth-century Christian teaching that one should expect suffering and should grow from the reality of suffering to find higher spiritual meanings to life. The American black communities had also been, on the whole, remarkable exemplars of the principles of the Sermon on the Mount. Despite much deep-seated resentment against their white oppressors, they often treated them with remarkable charity. Theories of violent revolution never found wide appeal in American black communities, despite the presence of all the economic and racial factors that were supposed, inevitably, to breed revolutionary attitudes.

Martin Luther King mobilized these long-standing Christian virtues in the black community, turning the power of love and the principles of the Sermon on the Mount into an active force. King hoped to bring social change by the power of love and nonviolence. One of the rare qualities of King's activism was that he made a clear distinction between the sin and the sinner. One should hate the sin, he repeatedly urged, but love the sinner. So he observed, early in his career, that most of the Southern white racists who thwarted and threatened him "are not bad men."[38] Rather, they were often up-

• • •

standing citizens in their community, but victims of that community's tradition of racist definitions of right and wrong.

All the elements of King's essential message are present in his famous, "I Have a Dream" speech, delivered at the Lincoln Memorial for the March on Washington, August 1963. King's words are today so often played almost as though they were background music for TV spots, that it has become difficult to hear their message. Nonetheless, King reiterated that the new black militancy must not degenerate into hatred of all white people or into violence. Rather, "we must rise to the majestic heights of meeting physical force with soul force."

Central to the speech, however, is the combination of American republican and biblical themes. The dream, he is not ashamed to say, is the "American dream." "We hold these truths to be self-evident, that all men are created equal." It is a dream, as the final, often heard, peroration elaborates, that "My country 'tis of thee, sweet land of liberty, of thee I sing. Land where my fathers died, land of the pilgrims' pride, from every mountainside, let freedom ring." Yet the appeal to the republican, and even the Puritan, themes, is interspersed with quotations from the Bible, which was always the heart of King's preaching:

> "I have a dream that one day every valley shall be exalted, every hill and mountain shall be made low. The rough places will be plain and the crooked places will be made straight, 'and the glory of the Lord shall be revealed, and all flesh shall see it together.' "[39]

The American dream was for King, ultimately, the dream of the millennial themes that inspired blacks and whites alike in the mid-nineteenth century. It was the dream to be "free at last." King was demanding that this tradition be faithful to its own claims.

King's ideal for the black people was integration into the mainstream of American society. He was calling on the mainstream to be true to itself, asking that blacks might be absorbed in the consensus. This consensus integrationist outlook, which was shared by the vast majority of the liberal leadership of the day, reflected trust in the American Christian and republican tradition, and an ultimately optimistic view of human nature and society.

• • •

Alternatives for Black Identity

Not all black activists, especially in King's later years, were happy with his approach. They appealed to another tradition that was represented by a minority in the black community over the years. This was the tradition of black nationalism. It was expressed early by Bishop Henry McNeal Turner (1834–1915) of the African Methodist Episcopal Church. With the collapse of Reconstruction and efforts for black civil equality, Turner promoted an African colonization movement, though he gained little following. More successful, but also more controversial, was the Back to Africa movement of Marcus Garvey (1887–1940) after World War I. Though his movement was not explicitly religious, Garvey was a flamboyant cult figure who attracted hundreds of thousands of followers before he was convicted for mail fraud in 1925 and deported to his native Jamaica in 1927.

Although not explicitly nationalist, a number of distinctly black alternatives to Christianity sprang up in the ghettos of the North between the wars. The best known of these were the movements founded by Father Divine and Sweet Daddy Grace, both messianic figures who followed long-standing American traditions of combining extravagant religious interests with creative free enterprise.

Of more lasting impact was the Black Muslim movement or the Nation of Islam, organized principally in Detroit by Wali Farad Muhammad (formerly Wallace D. Fard) in 1930. This highly disciplined black nationalist movement was strongly antiwhite and anti-Christian. Although because of its racial doctrines it was not recognized by other Muslims, it followed Islamic practices, and so demanded a puritanical ethic. The movement grew to some hundreds of thousands after World War II. Its best known proponent was Malcolm X, who after experiencing interracial Muslim brotherhood during a pilgrimage to Mecca, broke with Elija Muhammad (1897–1975), leader of the Nation of Islam. He was assassinated in 1965, shortly before the appearance of *The Autobiography of Malcolm X*, which became a leading work promoting a sense of black identity, based on the rejection of Christianity as the white man's religion. A number of leading sports figures, including heavyweight boxing champion Mohammad Ali, helped give the movement continued prominence.

By the mid-1960s the situation in America was changing drasti-

. . .

cally. During the summer of 1964 major riots broke out in black ghettos, leading to widespread burning and lootings. This was the summer after President Kennedy was assassinated and America's deepening commitments in Vietnam were beginning to raise additional questions about the American dream.

Some of the most vocal of black leadership turned from the nonviolence of Martin Luther King toward emphases on black power, black pride, and black liberation. Parts of the movement reflected the secular radicalism of the day. But as always, the dominant black leadership was Christian. By 1966 black theologians such as James H. Cone were developing a theology of black power. Rejecting integration as a goal, they turned to the liberation themes of Christianity as normative in defining its essence. They rejected white theologies which they saw as defining Christianity in such a way as to make it a justification of oppression. Nonetheless, in affirming a black theology, they were also retaining continuity with the black American Christian heritage.[40]

Even before the assassination of Martin Luther King in 1968, then, the black community was deeply divided on goals and strategies. Black consolidation and organization of effective black institutions was essential for black power; but, ironically, massive gains for integration during the Lyndon B. Johnson years were undermining those very separate institutions. Black churches remained separate, but they were divided into several camps, ranging from those who found King too radical to those who found him too conservative. The inability to resolve this impasse of integrationism versus separatism, as well as continuing white racism, left the black community with important gains in legal civil rights, but limited means to improve their economic, social, and educational situation.

The civil rights era coincided with the ongoing secularization of the black communities, especially in urban centers. Black culture involved striking contrasts between intense religion and intensely secular lifestyles. The continuing twentieth-century migrations to the cities strengthened these contrasts, fostering the growth of the secular aspects of the community, even while the churches remained as significant, if relatively diminished, counterforces. In the years after the gains in civil rights, the roles of the churches became more ambiguous as the community became increasingly dependent on government ac-

• • •

tion. Though the community welcomed the government support it received, one side consequence was that it looked relatively more toward secular agencies to help resolve its problems.

As with other ethnic and racial groups in America, the central question for the black community was whether it would be a gain or a loss to give up its distinctive cultural religious heritages, to be absorbed into a wider American culture. For the blacks this was an especially poignant question since they were as fully "American" as any of the Europeans who settled here and had long been among the chief proponents of the nation's dominant religious heritages and political ideals. Yet those very ideals were contradicted by forces which kept most blacks from sharing in material promises that seemed so central to the American dream itself.

• • •

CHAPTER SEVEN

Fragmented America—A Nation in Search of a Soul: 1960s to 1980s

---

". . .a nation with the soul of a church. . . ."

G. K. Chesterton, *What I Saw in America* (1922)

The Great Divide

During the second half of the twentieth century, a long-standing ideological fault line significantly widened, cutting across the traditional patterns of American religious and cultural life. Insider versus outsider issues receded in relative importance, while differences regarding basic values between conservatives and liberals gained in prominence. As in the earlier conflicts among ethnic groups, religion played a significant role in defining the outlooks of the contending parties.

Traditional ethnic and religious differences, although still significant, were declining in intensity. Especially dramatic was the near disappearance of the longest-standing religious barrier dividing the American population, that between Protestants and Catholics. Although the divisions between blacks and whites were far more persistent, major changes did occur in those relationships over the period, as blacks gained at least formal representation in most areas of American life. Jewish and Christian differences persisted as well, but with considerably less antagonism than at mid-century. New outsiders were present in rapidly growing Hispanic and Asian populations; but, even so, most of the nation seemed more solidly committed to a cultural pluralism that was accepting of greater diversity with less antagonisms along ethnoreligious lines.

In the meantime, the gulf between liberal and conservative views on some basic principles of morality was widening to an extent that made many of the traditional divisions seem even less relevant. Among most Protestants, the reasons for old denominational rivalries were now largely forgotten, so that liberals from denominations such as Methodist, Baptist, Presbyterian, Disciples of Christ, or Episcopalian clearly had more in common with each other than they did with conservatives in their own denominations. Protestant versus Catholic differences, while more considerable, were likewise overshadowed by the growing ideological division. Similar lines of division were found within most American subcommunities, even in those, such as the Jewish or Eastern Orthodox, who retained a strong sense of identity.

On the liberal side of the divide were those Americans who placed their strongest emphasis on the values of openness, pluralism, diversity, and mutual tolerance of differences. If they were religious, they typically subordinated theology to ethical concerns. Their typical eth-

· · ·

ics emphasized love, relationships, peace, justice, inclusiveness, tolerance of minorities, and acceptance of varieties of lifestyles and expressions of sexuality.

Various resurgent conservatives, on the other hand, tended to talk more of finding ethical absolutes, which reflected long-standing Christian and Jewish teachings concerning family, sexuality, discipline, and the importance of moral law. Often they saw these as implications of more-or-less traditional theological beliefs. They also tended to be patriotic toward America, firmly anticommunist, for a strong military, and for law and order.

These two tendencies (here roughly characterized though actually coming in many varieties and variations) could be seen as the opposed efforts of two groups who, as the old lines between insiders and outsiders blurred, each sought to establish themselves as the new cultural insiders and to define the nature of an American consensus.

Of course, divisions between liberals and conservatives in American religion were nothing new. We can see similar tensions, for instance, in eighteenth-century divisions between pietists of the Great Awakening and liberals influenced by the secular dimensions of the Enlightenment. The common cause of the American Revolution helped avert a deeper split and in the nineteenth century evangelical religion and liberal politics cooperated in building something of a dominant cultural consensus. During the first half of the twentieth century liberal politics, supported by tolerant liberal Protestantism, sustained an increasingly secularized and tolerant version of this consensus. Now, however, avowed cultural conservatism with pietist and other conservative religious support was sharply challenging the directions that the unchecked principles of tolerance seemed to be leading.

In this chapter we shall look at the religious dimensions of how these tensions have developed, considering first those groups and forces that moved in the more liberal directions and then the counterforces on the more conservative side.

The Counterculture as a Moral-Religious Quest

The assassination of President Kennedy on November 22, 1963 was a critical psychological turning point in the history of the nation. Although Kennedy was deeply disliked by many political conservatives, his administration seemed to others to be a triumph of the liberal consensus that had been developing since the New Deal. The

• • •

dominant mood of optimism and progress, which had characterized the Eisenhower years, still prevailed. Within a year or two of the assassination, however, the dominant national mood changed toward frustration and suspicion and a new "counterculture" with radically unconventional values was beginning to emerge.

Although the appearance of the counterculture was not a solely American phenomenon, American developments contributed substantially to it. Among the early signs were the urban riots and fires of the summer of 1964, reflecting black frustrations and suspicions of the New Deal culture's true commitment to civil rights and equality of opportunity. But the primary contributor to the growing mood of disillusion with the old establishment was America's deepening involvement after 1964 in the Vietnam morass.

This widespread reaction in the youth culture was accentuated by its sudden expansion with the emergence of the baby boom generation, which, in turn, coincided with the rise in the 1960s of mass higher education. This created large self-contained youth communities at universities. Moreover, the war directly threatened the self-interests of most males in the group, who had to face the draft and risk of killing or being killed for a cause they did not accept. Self-interest thus became a way of clarifying moral values.

The countercultural critique of the establishment also cut much deeper, however. It said that there was something fundamentally wrong with American culture itself. Part of the critique focused on the technocratic aspects of the society. The new generation of protesters saw science and technology as the gods of the culture and the technical experts as the high priests.[1] They saw a culture that had systematically enthroned what Theodore Roszak called the "myth of objective consciousness." That is, the structures of business, technology, and government favored dealing with problems by means of detached "objective" observers or experts. Subjective human values were sacrificed to the mythologically neutral objective. In fact, the counterculture pointed out, American technical and scientific expertise was not objective at all. It was in the service of other, even higher, religions of the culture—business profit and self-interested nationalism. If anyone stood in its way, whether it be the black laborer or Vietnamese peasants, technical solutions would dehumanize or destroy them.[2] Hence, the vaunted professions of American ideals, of liberty and justice for all, were riddled with deep hypocrisy.

• • •

The counterculture drew on a number of American heritages in its spontaneous and informal critique of the dominant culture. For one thing, it drew indirectly on the biblical heritage of moral imperatives, since its indignation was built upon an outrage that the American establishment served its own interests rather than those of the poor or non-Americans. In addition, the counterculture drew on the romantic tradition which had long provided a subjectivist counterbalance to scientific-technological objectivist trends. In some striking ways, in fact, the counterculture resembled the romantic radicalism in the decades before the Civil War. Each emphasized being true to self and finding truth intuitively. Each also emphasized finding the divine in nature rather than civilization. Each built radical communes, and went back to nature. Each was influenced by Eastern religions. There were many differences, of course, but also these striking similarities.

The counterculture of the 1960s had many sides and no fixed or unified ideology (another American trait). On the one hand it championed radical politics, largely hopeful until 1968, and then developed increasingly violent and revolutionary rhetoric. At the same time, the same people often advocated "dropping out" of society and pursuing purely experiential solutions to the world's problems. The ubiquitous slogan "Make love, not war" suggested two of the sides of the movement—personal freedom and political concern. The drug culture, often mixed with Eastern and mystical religion and the occult, set up a value system at a polar opposite to the dominant technological culture and its conventional morality.

To the extent that we can generalize, we can see the counterculture as the emergence of a new religious worldview and value system. This millennial philosophy of a new age or the "age of Aquarius" was built around "the monistic assumption that all life is united and all existence is one." Its truth system was built on trusting immediate intuitions. And, while its expressions of public morality were almost biblically prophetic, its private morality was built around individual expression and fulfillment. "Do your own thing," "let it all hang out," "express love and awareness for all beings" or "get the most good vibes" were typical moral maxims.[3]

While the counterculture was a major force on the liberal side of the cultural trends, it was also a radical critique of the old-style New Deal liberalism. To the protesters, Lyndon B. Johnson and Hubert H. Humphrey did not look much different from Richard M. Nixon.

• • •

All seemed part of a corrupt, self-serving establishment. The critique thus opened the door for other doubts about the old liberal consensus that dominated American life from the 1940s through the early 1960s.

The Mainline Churches

Religious liberals in the mainline churches, still mostly Protestant, but now including some newly liberated Catholics, were caught in an awkward position by the emergence of an ever-more-radical counter-culture of the 1960s.

At the outset of the era, mainline denominations had been flourishing near the progressive forefront of American life. Their leadership were usually Kennedy liberals whose major concern was still integrative unification of American life. Central on the agenda of mainline denominations was the ecumenical movement, represented primarily by the National Council of Churches, but also hopeful for mergers that would bring most of the Protestant sects into one group.

Essentially, they were affirming American life. One of the best-selling books of the hopeful half of the 1960s was Harvey Cox's *The Secular City* (1965). Rather than deplore the secularization of urban civilization, Cox celebrated it. "Urbanization," he wrote, "means a structure of common life in which the diversity and the disintegration of tradition are paramount."[4] To the liberal, disintegration of tradition meant opportunity for unity or, as Cox put it in biblical language, the transformation of 'strangers and outsiders' into 'fellow citizens and members of one another.' "[5] In this view, there was no distinction between the nation and the church. In fact, as a popular slogan of the time put it, "the world should set the agenda for the church." Or as Cox said, "Theology . . . is concerned *first* with finding out where the action is. . . ."[6]

Even though portions of some of America's cities burned in the summer of 1964 before Cox's words were published, old-style liberals plausibly saw themselves as staying in leadership by keeping up with the secular trends and bringing out their redemptive meanings. One constantly had to be freeing oneself of the traditional and the outdated. A few theologians went so far as to say that God-language was no longer meaningful or relevant to "modern man." In 1966 this view got startlingly wide publicity when a *Time* magazine cover appeared with only the three giant words on it: "IS GOD DEAD?" In fact, it

• • •

turned out to be an obituary for theology in public life; no longer would there be theologians, such as the Niebuhrs, who could command national attention.

At the time, however, it seemed plausible to see that the future of the church depended primarily on maintaining relevance to the culture. Some of the mainline church leaders, after all, were in the forefront of the civil rights movement and were among the most outspoken critics of the Vietnam War. They shared with the counterculture some of its critique of the materialism and nationalism of modern America. The strategy seemed to be to stay "where the action is." Campus ministers put on bluejeans, handcrafted shirts, and beads. They brought guitars and balloons into their services, hugged and shared, and talked of "love." Playing down the exclusivism of any particular tradition or its practices, they hoped to include all.

As historian Leonard Sweet has observed, "The wildest miscalculation of many churches in the 1960s was their belief in the basic inhospitality of the 'modern mind' to traditional religious symbols and doctrines."[7] Just as segments of the counterculture were seeking more distinctive religious expression, some of the liberal church leadership was still trying to be relevant by being less distinctive. Eastern, cultic, and exotic religions began to flourish and campuses became far more open to overt spiritual expression than they had been in the 1950s. By the end of the 1960s many counterculture young people were being swept into the "Jesus people" movement, which had many radical countercultural traits, such as close communal living and simple lifestyles, but was based on a strict discipline and reverence for the Bible. Many more, both young and older adults, and Catholics as well as Protestants, were turning to the new charismatic movement, which likewise emphasized some traditional theology as well as ecstatic spiritual experience. Meanwhile, young people were beginning to stay away from liberal churches in droves. By the 1970s liberal campus ministries had declined drastically. For many in a generation seeking authenticity, relevance to prevailing cultural standards, even progressive ones, held little attraction.

Of course, not all in the mainline churches followed the most liberal trends. Since these denominations were always a mix of conservative, moderate, and liberal elements, it is hazardous to generalize about their messages, which were always partly traditional and moderate. Nonetheless, particularly conspicuous in the era, in almost all major

• • •

groups, was the triumph of "therapeutic" religion, a development that reflected a synthesis of some traditional and countercultural themes. Therapeutic religion was, of course, not new to America and had flourished in the 1950s in the positive thinking of Norman Vincent Peale and others. During the 1960s psychological solutions to human problems became increasingly popular, and many churches followed suit.

From a therapeutic outlook, questions of morality were no longer considered in terms of rules of right and wrong, but rather in terms of relationships. Protestant ethicist Joseph Fletcher caused a stir with the publication in 1966 of his *Situation Ethics* which argued that personal consequences were more important than rules. But the triumph of psychological-relational definitions of values was so widely based that it was not usually considered a matter for debate. In the churches it combined Christian teachings of loving one's neighbor with utilitarian ethics ("what promotes the greatest happiness") and a middle-class version of expressive individualism ("feeling happy is a highest goal"). Such an outlook was the counterbalance to a technological society of managers and experts who depersonalized life for technical efficiency. Personal relationships and feelings were put at the center. Sermons of the era thus often offered advice on promoting better personal relationships.[8] As one mainline critic of the trend later put it, "Our main message has been 'God is nice and we should be too.' "[9]

Perhaps the most serious problem facing the old-line liberal denominations was that of identity. Very few people knew or cared what the difference was between a mainline Baptist, Methodist, Presbyterian, or Disciple of Christ. The traditions that once defined these differences had been largely jettisoned. Therapeutic religion, which often tended in an "I'm OK, you're OK" direction further blurred differences. Evangelism, which would presume authority and the need for people to change, was considered an embarrassment. Mainline foreign mission programs, which early in the century were the pride and joy of their denominations, were mere shadows of their former magnitude. Mainline leaders often believed that it was imperialistic to present their religion as superior to other traditions. This may or may not have helped America's image abroad as the nation proceeded to unprecedented heights of imperialism without the benefit of mainline missions. The broader issue at home, however, was identity. If there was little reason to invite others to change to one's religion, there was

• • •

little reason to remain with that religion if an alternative presented itself.

The Catholic Revolution

The revolution for America's fifty million Catholics in the decades following 1960 was far more dramatic than that for most mainline Protestants.[10] Catholicism of the 1950s had been, by and large, far more conservative than mainline Protestantism and far more insulated from the mainstream culture. The changes of the next decades accordingly were not necessarily in the direction of embracing liberalism. More essentially, the revolution involved a new openness within the church. At the same time many Catholics were moving from old ethnic neighborhoods to the suburbs. The result was that growing up Catholic in the 1980s was far different from growing up Catholic in the 1950s. A whole way of life had almost disappeared.

By the 1950s the American Catholic church had, despite its ethnic diversity, developed a clear identity. This identity developed within and among relatively isolated, self-contained communities that included their own educational systems, relative uniformity in religious

• • •

practice based on acceptance of church authority, and a strong patriotism. During the 1960s, all three of these supporting elements were removed simultaneously, creating a massive crisis in Catholic identity.

Like other urban Americans who were prospering in the 1950s, Catholics were moving to the suburbs. This move in itself might not have been so disruptive had it not coincided with the religious and cultural revolutions of the 1960s.

For Catholics, the religious revolution came suddenly and from the top. The Second Vatican Council, inaugurated by Pope John XXIII in 1962, had by its completion in 1965 drastically changed Catholic doctrine and practice. The reforms, called *aggiornamento*, were essentially efforts to bring the church up to date.[11] In effect, they instituted many of the ideas which "Americanist" Catholics advocated in the late nineteenth century before they were suppressed. For instance, the council followed American John Courtney Murray in declaring that religious freedom, rather than the universal establishment of Catholicism by law, was a desirable state of affairs. Furthermore, the Catholic church now recognized Protestants as "separated brethren" and encouraged dialogue with them, which was rare until that time. Vatican II also redefined the nature of the church. Rather than seeing the church primarily as an institutional hierarchy which dispensed justice and grace, they emphasized that the church is the body of Christ at the service of humanity.

But of greatest practical consequence for most Catholics were the remarkable changes in the liturgy. Consistent with the principle that the church was not simply an institutional hierarchy, but the body of Christ including the laity, the reformers tried to relate the service more directly to the people. No longer was the mass said only in Latin by the priest facing the wall, while the people listened in silence. The reforms called for active participation of the congregation, with the mass and prayers in English, singing hymns, and more emphasis on sermons.[12]

Most Catholics welcomed these changes, which were introduced gradually. At the same time, however, the liturgical reform cut off the sense of continuity with the past, which is important to religious identity. Practices that seemed essential to Catholicism, such as when to say the rosary, were changed. Familiar saints whose historicity proved dubious were declared no longer saints. So, for instance, Saint Christopher, who was supposed to keep one safe in travel and was often

• • •

Pope John XXIII inaugurated an era of reform within Catholicism.

seen on Catholic car dashboards, disappeared. So did other symbols of Catholic identity. Pious Catholics were always identifiable by their practice of eating fish instead of red meat on Fridays. Now that mark of identity suddenly disappeared also.

For whatever reasons, Catholic practice dropped off sharply after the revolution. In 1974 only fifty percent of Catholics were attending church regularly as opposed to seventy-one percent in 1963 and the rate of those not going at all doubled. Only seventeen percent were now going to confession regularly, as opposed to thirty-seven percent in 1963. An estimated 10,000 priests left the ministry between 1966 and 1978, and by 1984 the number of seminarians studying for the priesthood dropped to 12,000, only one-fourth of what it was in 1964.

Just as remarkable was the widespread dissent among the laity

• • •

from official church teaching, especially regarding sexuality. Here the leading issue, especially during the 1960s, was artificial methods of birth control, which the church continued to ban. In 1955 an estimated thirty percent of Catholic women defied the church and used such birth control. By 1970 the number defying the church had risen to two-thirds and about nine of ten Catholics disagreed with the church's stand on birth control.[13]

Other changes were just as momentous. Attitudes toward divorce, on which the church took an officially strict stand, were changing also. On the other hand, most Catholics agreed with the church's stand in opposing abortion and homosexual practice; although some dissenting voices were heard. The church, which was controlled by a male hierarchy, allowed little for the women's movement, another source of discontent for many Catholics.[14] Religious orders for nuns declined dramatically along with almost everything else in this era. The Catholic school system, which long depended on the sacrificial services of nuns, lost much of its distinctiveness and the teaching was taken over by laypeople, and their constituencies ceased to be so exclusively Catholic.[15]

In addition to the changes of moving from city neighborhoods to suburbs, and the reforms from Rome, the cultural changes of the 1960s intensified this upheaval in American Catholicism. As in other subgroups, Catholics divided sharply on controversial cultural political issues. Integral division and dissent thus further undermined a sense of identity.

One of the factors that bound most American Catholics together until the 1960s was their common patriotism. With the Vietnam era, that suddenly came into question also. A number of leading Catholics were among the best-known opponents of the war. Dorothy Day of the Catholic Worker movement in the 1930s was still an outspoken anti-war advocate. So was the renowned Trappist monk Thomas Merton. As the national crisis of the 1960s mounted, other Catholic anti-war activists gained prominence. Two of the best known were the brother Catholic priests, Fathers Daniel and Philip Berrigan, famed and notorious for draft card burnings and raids on draft board records. More in the mainstream, two of the most effective spokespersons against American Vietnam policy were two Catholic laymen, 1968 presidential contenders Eugene McCarthy and Robert F. Kennedy (assassinated during the campaign). Catholics were in fact somewhat

. . .

more likely than Protestants to oppose the war; although the majority in both groups supported it.

The breakdown in trust in America among some Catholics during the Vietnam era together with the defection of many Catholics from traditional church teachings and practices signalled a deep division that was developing within the Catholic communities. This division fell essentially across the same faultline that was dividing Protestants from the 1960s to the 1980s. By the 1980s, no longer were the most prominent divisions between Protestants and Catholics. Rather, they were between liberals and conservatives.

The dominance of progressive trends in the church hierarchy was reflected in two significant pastoral letters issued in the 1980s from the Council of Catholic Bishops. One on nuclear war carefully questioned whether nuclear war could be consistent with a "just war" tradition. The other, on the economy, questioned whether Americans were doing enough to support the poor at home and abroad. Both of these documents received severe criticisms from Catholic conservatives.

In theology and biblical criticism Catholics by the 1970s and 1980s were also divided on most of the same questions that divided Protestants for many years. In the Catholic case, expressions of some of the most liberal views were still limited by the presence of a conservative pope, John Paul II, elected in 1978.

Catholics also differed sharply with each other over liberation theology. Liberation theologies typically fused Christian principles of concern for the poor with Marxist economic analysis. In predominantly Catholic Latin America, such theologies were influential in demands for political reform or revolution. Catholics (as well as Protestants) in both North and South America were divided on the issue. In the United States, the question was closely related to American foreign policy in deciding which regimes it would support in Latin America. Moreover, the rapidly growing Hispanic population of the United States was overwhelmingly Catholic. Some of these came in reaction to communism and were aligned with the political right. Others inclined to the political left or, more often, were politically neutral. Correspondingly, among longer established American Catholics, liberals typically supported the liberation cause while conservatives favored militant anticommunism.

Though such divisions were deep, Catholicism still differed from

• • •

Protestantism in at least one very important respect. Catholics still all belonged to one institutional church. Even though much of the traditional Catholic identity was lost, the church survived intact, and the opening up of the heritage provided some hopeful prospects for relating tradition to contemporary trends. Trying to relate the best of the two, however, was a massive challenge.

The Women's Movement

The major transformations of old-line American churches came not only as changes from within that helped direct cultural change, but also were responses to massive changes in the broader culture. Of these changes, none promised to have wider and more lasting effects than the women's movement.

While women reformers for over a century had been campaigning to end discrimination in American life, the cultural upheaval of the 1960s opened the door for a more popular feminism directed toward full equality. They demanded, and often got, formally equal opportunities and affirmative action in the workplace. They also widely promoted the ideal of the independent career woman, freed from subordinating roles to spouse or children, or at least from any obligations beyond what would be expected of males also. These ideals raised questions about the structure of the family. The traditional view that the man was the head of the household came under heavy and often successful attack. But even more fundamental was the question of whether the family was based on a temporary contract among equal individuals, or whether its structure reflected a divinely sanctioned order, as Christians and Jews traditionally said. If essentially a voluntary contract, was it not then subordinate to the individuals who made the agreement and could therefore dissolve it at will? The prevailing trends in individualistic America were toward the latter view.

Churches not only had to face sharply divided opinions on these issues, but they also had to face the practical question of whether women would be granted fully equal roles in the churches themselves. In the Judeo-Christian tradition, churches and synagogues were almost exclusively governed by men. For Orthodox Jews, Catholics, and Eastern Orthodox Christians, groups who depended largely on the authority of tradition, the whole structure of authority would be threatened by ignoring ancient precedents. For Bible-believing evan-

· · ·

gelicals and fundamentalists the Apostle Paul's apparent ban on women in leadership roles in the New Testament church was seen as still applying to the church today.

Liberal and moderate Protestants, and Reform and Conservative Jews, who long had been frankly open to interpreting Scripture in the light of current trends, were largely accepting of new roles for women. Mainline Protestant constituency overlapped with the largest social group in which the women's movement took place—among the old-line white middle class. In the late nineteenth and early twentieth centuries, in fact, mainline churches were the principal place where independent women's organizations were formed. Missionary and educational societies, run by women, played major roles in denominational life. With greater pressures for women's equality by the 1920s, mainline denominations typically integrated men and women in such societies and began opening up positions for women in denominational bureaucracies. Although some women were ordained in mainline groups, the practice was still rare. Typically, by the 1920s subordinate church offices, such as deacon, were opened to women and by the 1950s ministerial ordination was allowed.[16]

Women clergy, however, were still a rarity until the feminist uprising of the 1960s. By the end of the 1970s all mainline Protestant denominations were ordaining women. Women also began attending mainline theological seminaries in large numbers. By the early 1980s they constituted over twenty percent of all seminarians, and over fifty percent in some mainline seminaries. Their presence took up the slack created by a decline in numbers of male seminarians which was part of the wider attrition of young people from mainline denominations. Nonetheless, even though increasing percentages of women were among the graduates of seminaries, they still often found difficulty in winning acceptance by congregations as equals with male clergy. People in the pews tended to be more traditional than the seminaries and the denominational leadership.

Women also developed feminist theologies to promote their cause. Such theologies were typically built around the themes of liberation for the oppressed and around attacks on theologies formulated by male oppressors.

Particularly important in forcing denominations to face the question of feminism was the practical revolution in religious language promoted by feminists. Both the Bible and its traditional English

• • •

Barbara Harris, the first woman bishop of the Protestant Episcopal Church.

translations used male pronouns for references to both man and woman. By the 1970s American feminists had already won the battle in much of the wider culture to use explicitly inclusive language when referring to male and female. They now pressed to have translations of the Bible do the same and asked for new renderings of church hymns. Especially controversial was the insistence that God not be referred to only by male pronouns but rather that God be spoken of as female as well as male. Such practice had both liturgical and theological implications, since reference to God as "father" was prominent in the Lord's Prayer, and in formulations concerning the Trinity as "Father, Son, and Holy Spirit." Once again, progressive church leaders pressed for the changes, while many mainline laypeople resisted.

• • •

The Gay and Lesbian Movement

Paralleling the women's movement was the remarkable advance of avowed homosexuals in American life after the 1960s. At the beginning of the period practicing homosexuals were considered pariahs in most of American society. By the 1980s they gained wide recognition as a minority group and significant legal protection against discrimination.

The most liberal wings of religious groups supported this revolutionary sexuality. Tolerance of homosexuals fit their ethic of personal fulfillment and love. Liberal Christians saw acceptance of the formerly outcast as an expression of the ethic of Jesus. They celebrated human difference and formed support groups. Some liberal Protestants ordained avowedly practicing homosexuals into the ministry; but the issue remained deeply divisive.

New Age

Although a division between liberals and conservatives was the major motif in American culture and religion from the 1960s to the 1980s, the situation was more complex. One of the major manifestations of the complexity was the presence of a bewildering myriad of new religions that blossomed especially in the 1960s and 1970s and were a major established feature of the American scene by the 1980s. Growing largely out of the new spiritual openness of the counterculture era, they provided continuing alternatives to the dominant trends.

The United States has always included many alternative religions and religious practices. For one thing, it long included subcommunities in which non-Western ancient religions, such as Buddhism, Shinto, Hinduism, and Islam, have been practiced. Such communities grew as the American population became ethnically more diverse. By the 1980s adherents of these ancient religions totaled over one percent of the population.[17]

Americans also have long engaged in many ancient forms of occult and folk religions. Among them have been the ancient practices of witchcraft, which drew on some pre-Christian traditions. Symptomatic of the new era were the revival of such practices.

In addition to these imported religions and practices, America has always added many homegrown varieties, and never more than recently. In part, this reflects apparently innate human religious procliv-

· · ·

ities; but also, it reflects remarkable qualities of the American environment, which might be thought of as analogous to a fertile bank described in a famous passage of Darwin's *Origin of Species*. There in a small area grew almost every imaginable variety of natural life. So the United States of the late twentieth century was especially fertile for the growth of countless religions. Freedom of religion, a strong religious heritage, free enterprise and opportunity for any individual to succeed, and the openness to new expressions cultivated by the counterculture were all conducive to exotic religious varieties.

To the extent that one can classify these, the non-Christian types fall into two major categories, each with a considerable American heritage. On the one hand there were groups, often called cults, that were variations on a Judeo-Christian heritage or worldview, but yet were distinct new religions. Probably the best-known example is the Unification church founded by the Reverend Sun Myung Moon, a Korean with a Christian heritage. Moon intimated that he was the latest prophet of God, going beyond the work of Jesus and promising a coming millennial kingdom. Although the numbers of his strictly disciplined American followers were never large, they were conspicuous. Mammoth international business enterprises, publishing, and political campaigns gave the religion prominence.[18] The Unification church had similarities to Mormonism with its prophet, new revelations, and millennial promises of eventual worldwide dominance.

Most notorious of the religions of this Judeo-Christian type was the People's Temple community of the Reverend Jim Jones. Though he began his movement as a Christian sect, Jones soon proclaimed himself a prophet of a new religion. Accentuating authoritarian leadership even more than in most such groups, Jones moved his community to Guyana in South America. There, in November 1978, in a remarkable demonstration of cultic power, he led nine hundred people into a voluntary mass suicide.

Other groups, of course, did not go to such extremes and generalization should not be based on the most unusual cases.

The other type of new religion, or variation on old religions, to flourish in America at this time, typically turned to the East for alternatives to Christianity. These religions came in many varieties, including American Zen, Hare Krishna, the followers of the Indian Guru Maharaj Ji (who briefly gathered a wide American following when he was an enterprising teenager in the early 1970s), the community of

• • •

Bhagwan Shree Rajneesh (which took over a town in Oregon for a time in the 1980s), and followers of a number of other Indian gurus. Occult or secret practices, including those of older groups such as Spiritualists, Theosophists, and Rosicrucians, were also popular. More a mix of Eastern and Western ideals than formal religions were groups that promised success through mind discipline, such as Transcendental Meditation, EST (Erhard Seminars Training), and the Scientology of L. Ron Hubbard.[19]

With so many varieties—and there are more—generalizations will not do justice to all. Nonetheless, Robert S. Ellwood, Jr., offers some helpful characterizations of such religions. They typically look to a distant Eastern culture for inspiration, they sometimes involve feminine spiritual leadership, they usually advocate meditation or some sort of mind control that allows the spiritual to overcome the material, and they are monistic. By monism (which is a central characteristic) is meant that, unlike Judeo-Christian religions premised on the distinction between the Creator and the creatures, these religions are premised on the unity of all life, which is essentially spiritual. They are—again in contrast to Judeo-Christian religions—nonhistorical; that is, not based on historical claims, but on methods by which the individual transcends history by entering into harmony with a spiritual realm.[20]

As a group, these religions may be seen as part of a general "new age" culture that has gained millions of adherents in the United States since the 1960s. Although involvement in new age cultic communities, such as Hare Krishna, demands total commitment, many middle-class Americans' contacts with new age or occult practices have been temporary and often have been supplemental to continuing Christian practice.[21] Nonetheless, a significant new outlook, promoted by networks of publications and bookstores, was apparent. The popularity of spiritualist contact with persons from other times, as popularized by actress Shirley MacLaine in the 1980s, was one manifestation. One significant cultural trait of the new age movement is its inherently pluralistic and hence often ethically relativist nature. Whereas Judeo-Christian religions have been traditionally rule-oriented regarding morality, new age practices, which open one up to the wisdom of many cultures and times, are experiential and expressive in their orientations.[22]

Such beliefs have not been new to America just since the 1960s.

• • •

They had substantial precedents, especially among mid-nineteenth century refugees from New England Protestantism. Many such people learned of Eastern wisdom through the writings of Emanuel Swedenborg, an eighteenth-century Swedish sage. Ralph Waldo Emerson turned to Swedenborg and to Eastern religions for alternatives to Christianity, and in the later nineteenth century spiritualist practices such as contacting the dead were popular. Perhaps the most "respectable" of American occult religions has been Free Masonry, practiced by a number of American founding fathers and by many other leading citizens since. While membership in Masonic lodges is not regarded as an alternative to Christianity, its secret mystical rituals and affirmations of universal brotherhood expressed some of the traits of later new age religions. In each case the appeal has been primarily to the American middle classes.

The new age culture of the late twentieth century was in many respects thoroughly American, at least as American as Ralph Waldo Emerson. For one thing, it accentuated the pluralist and inclusivist impulses which have long been strong in American life. Moreover, it included long-standing antitechnological sentiments, reinforced by the counterculture. Dominant American cultural values have often oscillated between two poles: one of immense trust in technologies and the other of extravagant assertions about the value of the individual and subjective experience. New age religion, like much of American culture, ultimately asserts total trust in humanity. Within each individual are the resources to find the divine.

Habits of the Heart

Such beliefs were not so far either from what many ordinary Americans already believed. During the 1980s a team headed by Robert Bellah of the University of California at Berkeley took an in-depth look at the beliefs and values that are typical of the dominant American middle classes. Their findings and analysis were published in *Habits of the Heart* (1985), one of the influential books of the 1980s. Among the most important factors that have shaped twentieth-century American life, the authors observed, was the increasing compartmentalization of life. In a technological society private life is typically sharply separated from work and work itself is divided into separate sectors that require expert managers. The two major definers of American life, accordingly, are the managers and the therapists. The

• • •

managers oversee the technological aspects of the society that tend to depersonalize life and treat individuals as interchangeable parts. In their work, Americans have often been driven by the ideals of "utilitarian individualism," which makes success paramount. This also can be dehumanizing. The therapists (whose ideals pervade mass media) counter with expressive individualistic ideologies that emphasize fulfillment of the self as a unique individual.[23]

Whether Americans are dominated by the success orientation of utilitarian individualism or by the fulfillment of expressive individualism, the society is remarkably individualistic and privatistic in its most modern style. Beliefs are considered to be private affairs, and most modern Americans have considerably less concern for the community at large than their small town forebears. The modern Americans, rather, seek people of their own kind in "lifestyle enclaves."[24]

These features of modern American life have important implications for religion. In the modern popular view, dominant in the mass media, values are determined subjectively on the basis of how they promote the fulfillment of the self. Religion, accordingly, is seen as an entirely private affair. One poll revealed that eighty percent of Americans would agree that "an individual should arrive at his or her own religious beliefs independent of any churches or synagogues."[25] In *Habits of the Heart*, the authors reported an interview they believed epitomizes much of American religion. The interviewee, named Sheila, said frankly that her religion was "Sheilaism." "I believe in God. I'm not a religious fanatic. I can't remember the last time I went to church. My faith has carried me a long way. It's Sheilaism. Just my own little voice."[26]

EVANGELICAL RESURGENCE

While conflicts between conservatives and liberals are nothing new, in the late twentieth century they seemed to signal a realignment that cut across older ethnic and religious divisions. On the conservative side one of the most remarkable developments of the 1960s to the 1980s was the resurgence of evangelicalism.

Evangelicalism was a very diverse movement. It was at most a

• • •

loose coalition of Christians who had in common a traditional "Gospel" message (evangelical means "Gospel") of salvation (often called being "born again"), based on the historical work of Christ as revealed in the authoritative Scriptures. This designation would include most Protestants who were more or less traditional theologically. Some groups were organized into tighter coalitions or networks and were very conscious of being "evangelical." Some, such as most black Protestants, some ethnic Protestant conservatives, and many smaller groups, would have primarily denominational loyalties, and would not ordinarily call themselves "evangelical," even though they might be classified as such.

In 1960, despite the popularity of Billy Graham and Oral Roberts, most analysts continued to write-off evangelical Christianity as a leftover from an earlier era, rather than as a major force for the future. For the past century sociologists and other informed observers had been saying that as modern industrial societies advance and modern scientific education becomes universal, traditional religion will fade away.

Some of the evidence said otherwise. Conservative churches had long been growing, but as long as the mainline establishment was dominant, few observers paid much attention. From 1940 to 1960, for instance, the Southern Baptist Convention, a conservative (and overwhelmingly white) evangelical group that did not belong to the National Council of Churches, doubled in membership, from five to ten million. The fact, however, was not much remarked on. From the mid-1960s to the mid-1980s, however, conservative membership growth was accompanied by declines in the old mainline. By 1965 the Southern Baptists virtually equalled the United Methodist church as the largest Protestant bodies, with about eleven million members each. By 1985, the Southern Baptists were still growing in all regions of the country and had reached fourteen and a half million members. The United Methodist church, which was controlled by liberal and moderate leadership, in the meantime declined to nine million. Just a hundred years after Methodist Church Extension Society spokesman Charles McCabe triumphantly proclaimed that the Methodists were starting a church per day, the Methodists were losing well over a hundred members per day.[27]

Meanwhile, almost all conservative churches were growing. Pentecostalism was probably growing the fastest. For instance, the As-

• • •

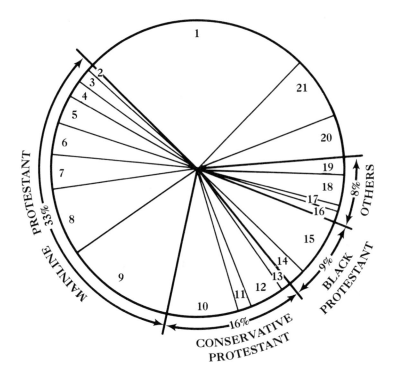

1. Roman Catholics 25%
2. Reformed 0.5%
3. Christians or
   Disciples of Christ
   1.5%
4. United Church of
   Christ 1.5%
5. Episcopal 2.5%
6. Northern Baptist 4.5%
7. Presbyterian 4.5%
8. Lutheran 8%
9. Methodist 10%
10. Southern Baptist 9%
11. Churches of Christ 1%
12. Holiness-Pentecostal
    4.5%
13. Other
    (Conservatives) 1%
14. Black Methodist 1.5%
15. Black Baptist 7.5%
16. Mormon 1%
17. Jehovah's Witness
    0.5%
18. Miscellaneous 4%
19. Eastern Orthodox 2%
20. Jewish 2.5%
21. No religious
    preference 7%

These figures are based on eleven surveys conducted between 1972 and 1984, in which English-speaking Americans were asked their religious preference. Since only "preference" is asked for, the resulting figures are larger than those of actual memberships in religious groups.

The figures have been rounded to the nearest half percent. The figure for Eastern Orthodoxy (not reported in the survey) is an estimate based on other sources.
Source: The General Social Survey as tabulated in Wade Clark Roof and William McKinney, American Mainline Religion: Its Changing Shape and Future *(New Brunswick: Rutgers University Press, 1987).*

• • •

Drawing by Ed Fisher; © 1989 The New Yorker Magazine, Inc.

semblies of God, the largest of the many pentecostal denominations, grew from a little over a half-million in 1965 to over two million by 1985.[28] A number of fundamentalist and pentecostal individual congregations had also grown to memberships of 5,000 to 15,000.[29] Many conservative congregations within mainline churches were gaining members as well. Most of these denominations also included vigorous evangelical renewal movements which were combatting liberal trends. By the 1970s and 1980s pollsters were estimating that some thirty to fifty million Americans could be classified as "evangelical," the general term that now came to be used for conservative Protestant groups.[30]

A major source of the growth within mainline churches was the wildfire spread of the charismatic movement. Charismatics differed from pentecostals mainly in that they did not form separate denominations but, rather, worked within established congregations. Typically, the charismatic movement grew by means of networks of small-group Bible studies and personal contacts. Developing from the efforts of the Full Gospel Businessmen's Fellowship, the charismatic movement gained its first firm foothold in a mainline denomination when its teachings spread widely in an Episcopal congregation in Van

• • •

Nuys, California, in 1960. From there it spread to other mainline and evangelical groups and by the end of the decade was reaching many Catholics as well as Protestants. By the early 1980s some twenty-nine million Americans identified themselves as charismatic Christians. Since the movement operated mainly through small groups, and since many people who spent some time in the movement later became inactive in it, its impact is difficult to measure, yet the number of Catholics and Protestants it appears to have touched is immense.

Reasons for Growth

A number of forces contributed to the remarkable spread of evangelical and conservative Protestant movements. One cultural factor was that, as in the counterculture, beginning in the 1960s Americans were becoming increasingly dissatisfied with the materialistic and rationalistic definitions of reality that had been growing since the Enlightenment and were now dominating education and the media. Contrary to prevailing academic opinion, Americans, whether charismatic, evangelical, or new age, were increasingly open to the spiritual dimensions of reality.

Also, as with the counterculture attacks on the establishment, traditional religion provided many Americans with a simple critique of the perceived failures of liberal American culture. It proclaimed certainty in a world of uncertainty. It offered fixed moral standards in place of confusing moral relativism. It made demands on people who did not find full satisfaction in an indulgent culture.[31]

Another factor was effective mobilization, as the small-group strategy of the charismatics and others illustrated. Moreover, especially since World War II, evangelicals had been building independent organizations to channel their energies outside of the major denominations. The network of organizations that were friendly to Billy Graham were especially significant in this renewal. These included several fast-growing theological seminaries, publications, and campus and youth ministries. Evangelicals, including Southern Baptists, also continued to expand their overseas missionary efforts while mainline groups were curtailing theirs, giving evangelicals a near-monopoly on traditional missions. With the continued spread of Christianity worldwide, most missionaries worked more cooperatively with overseas national churches than did the imperial missions a century earlier.

Another aspect of evangelical and conservative evangelical growth

. . .

was the reemergence of the South as a full participant in national life. Until World War II much of the South remained relatively isolated. It also was largely conservative and evangelical religiously. With greater mobility and affluence coming to the South, contacts with the North increased. Evangelicals from the two regions made alliances, and while Northern evangelicalism was still influential, evangelicalism often had a Southern accent.

"Born-Again" Politics

With the emergence of evangelicalism as a recognized cultural force in the 1970s, politics was initially not much of a factor. One reason was that evangelicalism was so diverse. White evangelicals stood on the opposite side of most political issues from black Bible believers. White evangelicals also had been divided among themselves, as between southern Democrats and northern Republicans. Most white evangelicals were conservative in their politics and at least in the South had favored segregation; but partly in reaction to liberal Protestants emphasizing politics so heavily, most evangelicals did not have overt national political agendas.

The spark that touched off organized evangelical politics was the election of Jimmy Carter to the presidency in 1976. During the campaign, Carter avowed that he was a "born-again" evangelical Christian. This sent secular reporters—who often lived in communities that long refused to take the evangelical part of America seriously—scurrying to find out what "born-again" meant and whether it was a subversive opinion. Carter, in fact, was a moderate Southern Baptist, a tradition that included strong views on the separation of church and state. The public was satisfied that his religious views would not intrude unduly into his office. Carter received strong support from voters who would also identify themselves as "born-again" and his election led *Newsweek* to dub 1976 "the year of the evangelical."

Despite his evangelical credentials, Carter's liberal Democratic politics soon proved unpopular with many white evangelicals. Sociologically, many of them came from groups who had deep reactions against the liberalization and especially against the permissiveness that was prominent during the counterculture years. They were part of the backlash that Richard Nixon's vice president, Spiro Agnew, cultivated as the "silent majority." During the Vietnam war, they deeply re-

• • •

President Jimmy Carter helped make it respectable to be "born again."

sented attacks on patriotism and they feared that liberals and radicals were naively generous toward international communism.

The Nixon-Agnew administration also gave some lip service to the idea that America needed moral renewal; but when it turned out that the administration itself was deeply deceitful and scandal-ridden, and that the president's profane and vulgar private language seemed to belie his public intimations of piety, conservative religious people felt they were co-opted by secular political forces.

· · ·

*Belief that abortion kills humans brought many religious
conservatives into politics.*

One impact of the Nixon Watergate scandal, however, was that it
convinced many Americans that morality and politics should not be
separate. Religion and morality were obviously related already. So
conservative church leaders who might have been reluctant to become
involved in politics now felt more free to actively campaign on moral
questions that had political implications.[32]

Particularly important in generating this sense was the *Roe v. Wade*

• • •

Supreme Court decision of 1973 legalizing abortion on demand. At first the principal reactions against this decision came from conservative Catholics. But soon conservative Protestants, Mormons, and others joined in the outcry. In their view, the unborn were still humans, so that killing millions of them amounted to mass murder on the scale of the Holocaust. Religious liberals and secularists, on the other hand, took the view that a fetus, at least in its early stages, is simply a part of a woman's body and so is not to be treated like an independent person. Basic concepts of the family were also involved. In the conservative view, the unborn child was part of the family and so the concern of both father and mother. In the liberal view it belonged to the individual woman alone.

Mounting reactions against the Equal Rights Amendment forbidding discrimination against women, first sent to the states from Congress in 1972 and debated until its close failure of ratification in 1979, also helped mobilize conservative religious opposition about family issues. Also, as pressures rose for full acceptance of gay and lesbian lifestyles in American life, so did religiously based opposition, both Catholic and Protestant. Again, basic systems of morality clashed. Conservatives based their opposition to homosexual practice on biblical condemnations and church tradition, which called it a sin.

Evangelical and conservative groups, true to their diverse characters, were often divided within themselves, especially on the women's issues. Particularly divisive were women's ordination to the ministry, a practice resisted in many conservative and fundamentalist groups, although approved in many holiness and pentecostal traditions and among moderate evangelicals, especially those who remained in mainline denominations.

Fundamentalist and conservative evangelical antifeminism was usually tied to the doctrine of the inerrancy of the Bible. Affirmations of biblical inerrancy had, during the past century, become increasingly important as tests of the faith when fundamentalists and related groups were battling theological modernism and higher criticism of the Bible. In the Southern Baptist Convention, for instance, conservatives were mobilizing around the doctrine of inerrancy since at least the early 1960s. By the late 1970s their conservative theological concerns coalesced with growing conservative political interests, including antifeminism, other issues of family and sexuality, conservative economics, militant patriotism, and a number of other issues.

• • •

BLOOM COUNTY  **by Berke Breathed**

A *liberal press view of fundamentalist politics.*

Promoters of this package of ideals were gradually taking control of the denomination away from moderates.

The "Moral Majority"

By 1980 alarm among conservatives in all sorts of religious groups was generating a notable new political coalition. Most significant was that these concerns brought large numbers of conservatives Protestants and Catholics together, who united on issues of family and sexuality, and on militant patriotism and anticommunism. These issues drew others who were rivals religiously into the coalition. Mormons, for instance, shared these concerns. So did some conservative Jews. Also, capitalizing on many of the same political and social resentments was the Reverend Sun Myung Moon, who raised remarkable amounts of money to help finance conservative political efforts. Politically conservative evangelical Protestants and Catholics, who in another era would have had nothing but disdain for Moon's claims to improve on the work of Jesus, now joined in a common political effort.

One conspicuous issue that brought such people together was a widespread sense of outrage at the sexual permissiveness that had become characteristic of American life. Popular music, movies, pornography, and advertising all flaunted open sexuality, observing varying minimal standards of discretion. TV shows now routinely made fun of anyone with antiquated ideas about sexuality, and presented sexual permissiveness as a normal lifestyle. Such campaigns to some degree reflected a broadly-based upheaval in attitudes toward sexual-

• • •

Fundamentalist evangelist Jerry Falwell organized the "Moral Majority" in 1979.

ity. The percentage of Americans who said that premarital sex, for instance, was morally wrong dropped from nearly eighty percent in 1959 to less than fifty percent by 1973. Disapproval of divorce, according to one study, dropped from forty-three to eighteen percent.[33]

Most effective of a number of organizations bringing together the emerging politically conservative religious coalition was the Moral Majority, founded by Jerry Falwell in 1979. Falwell, pastor of a Baptist megachurch in Lynchburg, Virginia, was an avowed fundamental-

. . .

ist. Fundamentalists, who formed the militant right wing of evangelicalism, since the 1950s typically insisted on separation from mainline denominations and usually from other evangelicals. Falwell and many other fundamentalists also opposed church political involvement during the civil rights era. Now, however, Falwell took the lead in bringing large numbers of fundamentalists, as well as related evangelicals and some other conservatives, back into the political arena.

The fundamentalist tradition long supported some avid anticommunist crusaders, but the addition of the family issues brought it back to political prominence for the first time since the 1920s. Actually, the fundamentalist heritage contained two contradictory traditions regarding the church and politics. On the one hand, their dispensational premillennialist teaching that Jesus would return any day and set up his kingdom would seem to undermine political interest. In this view, America would be regarded as Babylon and believers should simply be spiritual and wait for the coming kingdom. On the other hand, fundamentalists, like most white Protestants, shared in the Puritan heritage that America was a new Israel. So Falwell and other new religious right leaders typically talked about a covenant between God and the American people, and advocated a return to a "Christian America." So, despite their sectarian proclamations of the importance of Christians separating from the world, they were often avid patriots.

In 1980 the Moral Majority claimed some credit in helping to elect Ronald Reagan, although its influence likely was not decisive. The religious factor in shaping the political right was also larger than the Moral Majority and its fundamentalist leadership. It included, for instance, Catholic and some mainline Protestant neoconservatives who were uncomfortable with fundamentalism's simplistic approaches.

Ronald Reagan himself was an ardent anticommunist and professed sympathy for the concerns regarding the family questions and other symbolic issues favored by the religious right, such as allowing organized prayers in public schools. At one time Reagan was influenced by conservative evangelical teachings, including dispensationalist interpretations of biblical prophecy, in a church in California. However, during his presidency he was not a church goer and gave little more than rhetorical attention to most of the new Christian right concerns.

One politically significant aspect of the new religious right agenda

• • •

Revivalism and patriotism often go hand in hand.

was its unswerving support for the state of Israel. Because of the importance of Israel in dispensationalist interpretations of biblical prophecy, fundamentalist leaders were particularly concerned for the continued existence of Israel as an independent state. This added some political backing for the already established U.S. policy of massive support for Israel. It also created some ambivalence in the attitude of the Jewish community toward fundamentalists. On the one hand, Jews generally were strongly opposed to any suggestions of a return to a "Christian America," and saw political fundamentalism as potentially a new American fascism. Moreover, they deeply resented fundamentalist efforts to convert Jews. On the other hand, funda-

• • •

mentalist beliefs in the importance of Jews and of Israel to the fulfillment of prophecy gave Jews and fundamentalists an uneasy
commonality on an important religious point.

Commercial Conservatism

The impact of the religious right in the 1970s and the 1980s was
amplified by the emergence of extensive TV ministries. How widespread was their influence is a matter of dispute. In the 1980s the
most modest estimate is that about thirteen million Americans watched
such shows regularly; but other estimates claimed that up to sixty
million Americans were at least occasional viewers. These audiences
were disproportionately from the South and the Midwest and overwhelmingly from people of modest to poor means. Several of the largest ministries, nonetheless, raised well over a million dollars from their
audiences every week.[34]

Most of the largest of these ministries, such as Oral Roberts, Pat
Robertson of the 700 Club, and Jim and Tammy Bakker of the PTL
Club, represented pentecostal-charismatic traditions. They typically
provided healings for innumerable small ailments among the viewing
audiences, were upbeat and promised health, wealth, and success to
their supporters. Robert Schuller, of the Crystal Cathedral in southern
California, provided a similar success-oriented message for middle-
class audiences. Schuller, from the mainline Reformed Church of
America, stood in the tradition of Norman Vincent Peale, stressing
the spiritual potential within everyone, rather than claiming special
pentecostal healing gifts. Jimmy Swaggart, the most popular of the
TV evangelists through much of the 1980s, though a pentecostal,
preached a simple fire-and-brimstone gospel of moral purity. Jerry
Falwell, like most strict fundamentalists, did not believe in pentecostal gifts and also preached a more traditional gospel as well as conservative politics. Falwell's, however, was the most politically oriented
of the ministries, though during the 1980s Robertson also moved in
that direction. Ignoring the complexities and ambiguities of the role
of Christianity in American history, fundamentalists and others longed
for a time when the rule of God would prevail.

In 1987 and 1988 Robertson surpassed Falwell as the leading religious TV figure in politics when he ran in the Republican presidential primaries. He gained considerable early attention by his ability to
mobilize about ten percent of the Republican vote in most states where

• • •

Charismatic TV evangelist Pat Robertson yoked pulpit and presidential platform.

he ran. Nonetheless, he also proved unable to move beyond that solid core of support and eventually dropped from the race.

In 1987 and 1988 the character of some of these ministries was revealed in a series of scandals that could make a soap opera writer envious. Early in 1987 Oral Roberts claimed that he had a message

BLOOM COUNTY   **by Berke Breathed**

Bloom County commented on scandals involving evangelicalists.

• • •

After a scandalous exposé, Jimmy Swaggart preached more on forgiveness.

from God that God would kill him if Roberts's supporters did not raise enough money by a specified date. About the same time, a scandal broke around Jim Bakker, alleged to have carried on illicit sexual relationships. Early in 1988 Jimmy Swaggart, who was particularly critical of Bakker, was forced to step down from his ministry because of sexual improprieties. Defying his denomination, the Assemblies of God, Swaggart soon returned to the air, now preaching more about forgiveness.

The personal foibles of the evangelists, however, were perhaps not as revealing as their everyday public performances which evi-

• • •

denced the power of commercialism in a technological civilization. Although there were exceptions and often good intentions, the commercial pressures were high to do whatever worked and to give people what they wanted. Fundraising appeals, not regulated like commercial advertising, sometimes stretched the truth, used high-pressure scare techniques, or implied extravagant benefits to donors. Some of the ministries constantly celebrated self and success. So, although these ministries offered affirmations of many aspects of traditional Christianity and were valued for that by wide audiences, these commercial ministries also vividly illustrated some of the paradoxes found throughout American culture and religion.

RELIGION AND AMERICAN CULTURE: THE OUTLOOK

Two Poles of a Common Culture

Despite the diametrically opposed stances on many issues, commonalities could often be found between the ideological left and the ideological right. Both sides, for instance, were remarkably individualistic. Americans typically insisted on believing what they wanted and had a low view of the authority of institutions. Many people on both sides talked of personal fulfillment and favored expressive individualism which valued intense personal experience. Both sides, despite professions to the contrary, tended toward materialism, often defining values in terms of availability of material comforts and security. Both sides were largely comfortable with the benefits and many of the pleasures of technological society, although ironically the religious right was often less critical of relying on technology than the left. Both sides were in their own ways moralistic, insisting that certain sorts of beliefs and behavior were unacceptable, hoping to legislate their standards for the whole society.

These outlooks, shared by wide varieties of Americans, point to a vast and often unrecognized revolution in what modern Americans expect from life. Whereas their forebears in the nineteenth century and throughout the Judeo-Christian era saw life and religion largely as learning to live with and accept adversity, contemporary Americans more typically presumed that the world owed them a living and that

. . .

religion should be (at least in part) a means to self-fulfillment. Though there are many exceptions, the American characteristics which the Robert Bellah team identified in *Habits of the Heart* have influenced almost the whole spectrum of American religion.

The Fields of Conflict

Such commonalities pointed to a common American culture and heritage and also provided some potential alleviation of possible conflicts between right and left. Despite differences on some basic issues, Americans usually had much in common on others.

Moreover, it is important to keep in mind that this cultural conflict was relatively mild and that most Americans did not stand with either of the extremes, but somewhere in the middle. The extremes, which are easier to talk about than all the combinations of positions in between, were simply the poles toward which people on two sides tended. In between the extremes were much variation, vagueness, and indifference.

Nonetheless, a continental drift toward a cultural divide between two ideological camps posed some problems difficult to resolve.

In part, this potential for conflict may have been fostered by the vast expansion of government in the past half-century. Whereas in earlier times the dominance of one relatively unified religious, moral, and cultural heritage provided the national cohesiveness that could be taken for granted, in a more radically pluralistic situation that cohesiveness was beginning to give way. One way to compensate was through expanding government attempts to fill the vacuum with public agencies to hold things together. Activities that in a time of an informal religious establishment were performed by the churches, or by churches in cooperation with the government, were now increasingly performed by government alone. This was particularly true of education and public services to the needy.

Not surprisingly, most areas of conflict have to do with religiously or morally based resistance to, or advocacy of, expansion of the government. Although the political and religious right resists most expansion of the welfare state, the left resists expansion of the military, especially nuclear arms. Other conflicts have to do with campaigns to further expand government activities, such as regulating abortions or pornography on the one hand, or ending discrimination against minorities on the other.[35]

• • •

The Unsolved Problem of Education and Religion

Probably the best illustration is found in contemporary education. The shift from church to government control has been no small revolution, since education is one of the chief conveyers of cultural values. Though governmental support for education is not new, its implications for religion were hidden for a long time, as long as most of the schools had a quasi-Protestant character or at least retained vestiges of church-state cooperation in education, such as required prayers and Bible reading. But by the 1960s, when it became clear that the United States was a more truly pluralistic society, it seemed increasingly inappropriate for the government to take sides on disputed religious issues. So, during the past generation the courts have been ruling against efforts to retain or introduce, directly, religious teachings into public schools. Public education is now almost purely a governmental domain.

In college and university education the role of government has likewise expanded, especially since about World War II. Even most private and church-related institutions receive so much federal aid and are seen so much as responsible to the public that it is widely believed religion can have no place, except perhaps in ceremonial ways and private campus organizations.

Nowhere is the problem created by these developments better illustrated than in the very reason that this book has been written and published. One of the ways of dealing with the delicate issues of religion in the public sphere has been to ignore it altogether. This has been especially conspicuous in American history textbooks, where the absence of reasonable attention to religion actually distorts the facts about the character of American culture. Hence the need for supplemental works.

While the religious right has sounded the alarm about such issues, many of their proposals seemed to most other observers so heavy-handed that they are counterproductive. Fundamentalist writer Tim LaHaye, for instance, argued in 1980 that a few hundred thousand atheists or "secular humanists" had taken over and controlled media and education, and that such people should be excluded from public schools.[36] Others proposed curricular reforms such as countering evolutionary theories of origins with "creation science," which teaches that the earth is only some thousands of years old and that the geo-

• • •

logical columns are explained by a worldwide flood. In 1981 both the Arkansas and Louisiana state legislatures adopted such legislation. Eventually, the federal courts ruled that they were thinly veiled attempts to teach fundamentalist interpretations of the Bible. Parents in other schools in the 1980s sued against texts and teachings in public schools that conflicted with their religious beliefs; but they also received little help from the courts. Many conservative religious groups turned to founding their own schools.

Despite the lack of sympathy generated for fundamentalists by some of their more extreme demands for public education, they were pointing to an unresolved dilemma and an area for potential conflict in American religion and culture. Education is presented always from a point of view and hence cannot be neutral. Since in efforts to be neutral governments recently have simply excluded religion, and even the discussion of religion, from education, they have in effect favored the point of view of secularity in education. Such secularity, introduced for reasons of equity, in practice (and often inadvertently) favors those who advocate nontheistic secular worldviews. These worldviews are almost exclusively on the liberal side of the great moral divide in American life and tend to promote relativistic positions that would undermine traditional religions.

One of the serious problems facing the United States at the end of the twentieth century, then, is that many Americans are strongly committed to traditional or semitraditional religious and moral values; yet in an era of the vast expansion of government control and regulation, the necessities of public neutrality toward religion seem increasingly to limit areas where distinctive religious views can be freely exercised.

Free Exercise of Religion in a Pluralistic Society

Probably the key issue is whether governmental neutrality toward religion will be essentially hostile to all religion by attempting to exclude as much of it as possible from the public sphere, or whether the neutrality will take the form of truly encouraging religious pluralism whenever that is compatible with equity. This is an old issue in American life, but in the twentieth century some roles have been reversed. In early American history it used to be religious groups who wished to impose their outlooks on the whole nation, hoping to absorb everyone into a Protestant or quasi-Protestant melting pot. In the

• • •

twentieth century, however, with the vast technological and governmental expansions of secularity, secularism or nontheism is the only point of view that has any prospect of becoming the semi-official philosophy for the nation. During the middle decades of the century such views gained almost establishment status. Since the 1970s, however, conservative religious groups have had some success in pointing out that such a triumph of the nonreligious would be destructive of pluralism.

What is needed in America today is recognition by both religious and nonreligious peoples that the days are past when any one group, whether religious or nonreligious, can dictate a comprehensive public philosophy that will prevail for the whole of the people. The moral divide in the nation is too deep for that. So are some of the traditional religious, ethnic, and political differences.

Nonetheless, in a pluralistic setting there may be enough common experience of tolerance and intolerance for there to be hope for wide acceptance of a more limited public philosophy that involves mutual consent to play by the same rules for others as one would want for oneself.

With respect to religion, the formula most likely to gain wide assent is probably that stated in the First Amendment to the Constitution, which guarantees the free exercise of religion as well as its nonestablishment. Every group, whether religious or secular, should recognize that this is a two-sided rule. If groups are to have the free exercise of their own views guaranteed, they must not demand a monopoly on public opinion, but rather protect the free exercise of all religious views.[37]

At the same time, they should also recognize that religion has always been a source of human conflict. Hence, it is appropriate, as has long been customary in America, to distance explicit religious affirmations from many public and governmental activities. Theological debates are not appropriate in courtrooms or on the floors of legislatures. Public officials should not claim divine sanction for their policies. Nonetheless, such desirable restrictions on religion in public life need not lead to inhibiting legitimate expressions of religion in both the public and the private spheres.

Though such a two-sided rule does not solve all the problems, it would provide some guidelines that would help guarantee that religion as well as nonreligion will flourish. One of the remarkable as-

• • •

pects of the history of American religion and culture has been that so many strongly held religious views have been able, by and large, to co-exist peacefully. The two-sided constitutional principle, even if not always applied consistently, has been an important contributor to this remarkable achievement.

Religion is going to continue as a major force in American life. Its resiliency even in the public sphere is illustrated by the role it has played in shaping the moral stances that have divided Americans in the late twentieth century. Even if in a pluralistic society public debate can no longer be conducted in terms of a supposedly common religious heritage, the teachings of many heritages will inevitably filter into all dimensions of national life.

Yet in studying about religion and culture it is also important to remember that, while religion often has immense impact on culture, for religious people themselves that is not usually its primary function. For countless individuals and groups in late twentieth century America, their religion is of primary value as a means by which they seek and sometimes find allegiances higher than simply to the nation and meanings deeper than those defined by a cultural consensus.

• • •

Notes to the Text

Preface

[1] Paul C. Vitz, *Censorship: Evidence of Bias in our Children's Textbooks* (Ann Arbor: Servant, 1966).

Introduction

[1] "Appendix: Facts and Figures on Unsecular America," in *Unsecular America*, ed. John Richard Neuhaus (Grand Rapids: Eerdmans, 1986), pp. 21, 115–45. "Evangelical Christianity in the United States—National Parallel Surveys of General Public and Clergy," in *George Gallup Polls America on Religion* (Wheaton: Christianity Today, 1980), p. 45.

[2] Steven M. Tipton, *Getting Saved from the Sixties* (Berkeley: University of California Press, 1982), p. xiv.

[3] Clifford Geertz, "Religion as a Culture System," in *Anthropological Approaches to the Study of Religion*, ed. Michael P. Banton (New York: F. A. Praeger, 1966), p. 3.

[4] Peter L. Berger, *The Sacred Canopy: Elements of a Sociological Theory of Religion* (Garden City, NY: Doubleday and Company, 1967), p. 21.

Prologue

[1] Robert R. Mathisen, *The Role of Religion in American Life: An Interpretive Historical Anthology* (Washington, D.C.: University Press of America, 1982), pp. 166–67.

[2] James H. Morehead, *American Apocalypse: Yankee Protestants and the Civil War, 1860–1869* (New Haven: Yale University Press, 1978).

Chapter One

[1] John Rolfe, *A Relation of the State of Virginia* (1616), p. 113, quoted in Perry Miller, "Religion and Society in the Early Literature of Virginia," *Errand into the Wilderness* (New York: Harper and Row, 1956), p. 119.

[2] Perry Miller, *The New England Mind: From Colony to Province* (Boston: Beacon Press, 1953); Sacvan Bercovitch, *The American Jeremiad* (Madison: University of Wisconsin Press, 1978).

[3] Sydney E. Ahlstrom, "Thomas Hooker—Puritanism and Democratic Citizenship," *Church History* 32 (December 1963): 415–31.

[4] Reinhold Niebuhr, *The Irony of American History* (New York: Charles Scribner's Sons, 1962).

• • •

[5] Early Maryland, first settled in 1634, had genuine religious freedom at times, though clearly this was in the interest of the Catholic proprietors and settlers, rather than a matter of principle. During most of Maryland's colonial history, however, Protestants dominated and Catholic practice was officially outlawed, though it survived.

[6] Harry S. Stout, *The New England Soul: Preaching and Religious Culture in Colonial New England* (New York: Oxford University Press, 1986).

[7] Donald G. Mathews, *Religion in the Old South* (Chicago: University of Chicago Press, 1977); Albert J. Raboteau, *Slave Religion: The "Invisible Institution" in the Antebellum South* (New York: Oxford University Press, 1978).

[8] Mathews, *Religion in the Old South*, pp. 101–24.

[9] Mark A. Noll, *Christians in the American Revolution* (Grand Rapids: Christian University Press and Eerdmans, 1977).

[10] Robert Kelley, *The Cultural Pattern of American Politics* (New York: Alfred A. Knopf, 1979), pp. 71–72.

[11] Jon Butler, "Magic, Astrology, and the Early American Religious Heritage," *American Historical Review* 84 (April 1979):317–46.

[12] Rhys Isaac, *The Transformation of Virginia, 1740–1790* (Chapel Hill: University of North Carolina Press, 1982), pp. 120–21. Isaac's book is valuable in drawing contrasts between the religious and irreligious of the day.

[13] For instance, Gary Wills, *Inventing America: Jefferson's Declaration of Independence* (Garden City, NY: Doubleday and Company, 1978) helpfully emphasizes the contributions of the Scottish Enlightenment to Jefferson's moral thought; but the parallels to Locke are nonetheless striking.

[14] Bernard Bailyn, *The Ideological Origins of the American Revolution* (Cambridge: Harvard University Press, 1967).

[15] Bailyn, *Ideological Origins*, p. 43.

[16] Carl Bridenbaugh, *Mitre and Sceptre: Transatlantic Faiths, Ideas, Personalities, and Politics, 1689–1775* (New York: Oxford University Press, 1962).

[17] Bridenbaugh, *Mitre and Sceptre*.

[18] John Adams, "On the Canon and the Feudal Law" (1765), quoted in *Sources of the American Mind*, Loren Baritz, ed., 2 vols. (New York: John Wiley and Sons, 1966), 1:114.

[19] Gordon S. Woods, *The Creation of the American Republic, 1776–1787* (New York: W. W. Norton and Company, 1969).

[20] Nathan O. Hatch, *The Sacred Cause of Liberty: Republican Thought and the Millennium in Revolutionary New England* (New Haven: Yale University Press, 1977), p. 87.

[21] Samuel Davies, "The Crisis," in *Sermons on Important Subjects* (Phila-

• • •

delphia, 1818), 5:257, 258, quoted in Mark A. Noll, Nathan O. Hatch, and George M. Marsden, *The Search for Christian America* (Westchester, IL: Crossway Books, 1983), p. 62.

²² Noll, Hatch, and Marsden, *Search for Christian America*, p. 64.

²³ Reinhold Niebuhr, *Moral Man and Immoral Society* (New York: Charles Scribner's Sons, 1932); Reinhold Niebuhr, *The Irony of American History*.

²⁴ Cf. Robert Bellah, "Civil Religion in America," *Daedalus* 96 (Winter 1967):1–21.

²⁵ Noll, *Christians in the American Revolution*, p. 134.

²⁶ John F. Wilson, "Religion, Government, and Power in the New American Nation." Paper presented at a conference on "Religion and American Politics," Institute for the Study of American Evangelicalism, Wheaton, Illinois, March 1988.

²⁷ William Lee Miller, "Religion and the Constitution." Paper delivered at Christ Church, Philadelphia, October 4, 1987.

Chapter Two

¹ Lyman Beecher, *The Autobiography of Lyman Beecher*, ed. Barbara M. Cross, 2 vols. (Cambridge, MA: Harvard University Press, 1961), 1:252–3.

² Richard Hofstadter, *Anti-Intellectualism in American Life* (New York: Vintage, 1966), pp. 89–90. These are estimates. Another earlier estimate is from Allan Nevis cited in C. C. Goen, *Broken Churches, Broken Nation* (Macon: Mercer University Press, 1985), p. 55, who suggests there was seating for three-fifths of the population in 1860.

³ Alexis de Tocqueville, *Democracy in America*, trans. H. Reeve, vol. 1 (New York, 1955), p. 316, cited in John F. Wilson, *Public Religion in American Culture* (Philadelphia: Temple University Press, 1979), p. 11. Cf. Goen, *Broken Churches*, pp. 28–32.

⁴ Perry Miller, *The Life of the Mind in America: From the Revolution to the Civil War* (New York: Harcourt, Brace, and World, 1965), p. 7.

⁵ Miller, *Life of the Mind in America*, p. 6.

⁶ William G. McLoughlin, ed., *The American Evangelicals, 1800–1900* (New York: Harper Torchbooks, 1968), p. 1.

⁷ Edmund S. Morgan, "The American Revolution Considered as an Intellectual Movement," in *Paths of American Thought*, Morton White and Arthur M. Schlesinger, Jr., eds. (Boston: Houghton Mifflin, 1963), p. 11.

⁸ Samuel S. Hill, *The South and the North in American Religion* (Athens: University of Georgia Press, 1980).

⁹ Bruce Kuklick, *Churchmen and Philosophers: From Jonathan Edwards to John Dewey* (New Haven: Yale University Press, 1985).

• • •

[10] Nathan O. Hatch, *The Democratization of American Christianity* (New Haven: Yale University Press, 1989).

[11] Erastus O. Haven, quoted in Kent Sagedorph, *Michigan: The Story of the University* (New York: E. P. Dutton, 1948), p. 115.

[12] John H. Westerhoff, III, *McGuffey and His Readers: Piety, Morality, and Education in Nineteenth-Century America* (Nashville: Abingdon, 1978), pp. 19, 75.

[13] Quote from *Second Reader*, 1836 ed., p. 136, in Westerhoff, *McGuffey and His Readers*, p. 78.

[14] Lewis W. Green, *Lectures on the Evidence of Christianity* (New York: Richard Carter, 1854), pp. 463, 464.

[15] Francis Wayland, *Elements of Moral Science*, Joseph Angus, ed. (London, c. 1860 [1835]), pp. 219–20.

[16] Theodore Dwight Bozeman, *Protestants in an Age of Science: The Baconian Ideal and Antebellum American Religious Thought* (Chapel Hill: University of North Carolina Press, 1977), p. 72.

[17] Nathan O. Hatch and Mark A. Noll, eds., *The Bible in America: Essays in Cultural History* (New York: Oxford University Press, 1982).

[18] *McGuffey's Fifth Eclectic Reader*, 1879 ed. (New York: New American Library, 1962).

[19] The view that Jesus will set up a literal millennial kingdom is called premillennial (since Jesus returns before the millennium). There are also amillennialists who say essentially that details about the last days are not precisely prophesied.

[20] William R. Hutchison, *Errand to the World: American Protestant Thought and Foreign Missions* (Chicago: University of Chicago Press, 1987), p. 45.

[21] Kenneth Scott Latourette, *A History of Christianity* (New York: Harper and Brothers, 1953), p. 1061.

[22] Timothy L. Smith, *Revivalism and Social Reform: American Protestantism on the Eve of the Civil War* (New York: Harper Torchbook, 1957), pp. 20–21; Robert Baird, *Religion in America* (1844) in McLoughlin, ed., *The American Evangelicals*, p. 33.

[23] See David Brion Davis, *The Problem of Slavery in the Age of Revolution, 1770–1823* (Ithaca: Cornell University Press, 1975) for discussion of additional factors.

[24] Cf. Stanley M. Elkins, *Slavery: A Problem in American Institutional and Intellectual Life* (New York: Grosset and Dunlap, 1963), pp. 37–52.

[25] Max Weber, *The Protestant Ethic and the Spirit of Capitalism* (New York: Charles Scribner's Sons, 1958).

• • •

[26] For example, Frederick Douglass makes this point in "Narrative of the Life of Frederick Douglass" (1845) in *New World Metaphysics: Readings on the Religious Meaning of the American Experience*, Giles Gunn, ed. (New York: Oxford University Press, 1981), pp. 192–95.

[27] Donald Mathews, *Religion in the Old South* (Chicago: University of Chicago Press, 1977); Albert J. Raboteau, *Slave Religion: The "Invisible Institution" in the Antebellum South* (New York: Oxford University Press, 1978).

[28] Raboteau, *Slave Religion;* Lawrence W. Levine, *Black Culture and Black Consciousness: Afro-American Folk Thought from Slavery to Freedom* (New York: Oxford University Press, 1977).

[29] Levine, *Black Culture and Black Consciousness*, p. 17.

[30] As Lawrence W. Levine observes in *Black Culture and Black Consciousness*, p. 54: "If mid-twentieth century historians have difficulty perceiving the sacred universe created by slaves as a serious alternative to the societal system created by southern slaveholders, the problem may be the historians and not the slaves."

[31] Jay A. Dolan, *The American Catholic Experience: A History from Colonial Times to the Present* (Garden City, NY: Doubleday and Company, 1985); Debra Campbell, "Catholicism from Independence to World War I," in *Encyclopedia of the American Religious Experience*, Charles H. Lippy and Peter W. Williams, eds., 3 vols. (New York: Charles Scribner's Sons, 1988), 1:357–73.

[32] Timothy L. Smith, "Religion and Ethnicity in America," *American Historical Review* 83 (December 1983): 1155–85.

[33] Lewis O. Saum, *The Popular Mood of Pre-Civil War America* (Westport, CN: Greenwood Press, 1980), pp. xxiii, 27, 56 and passim.

[34] On the importance of the theologians see Kuklick, *Churchmen and Philosophers*.

[35] Ronald L. Numbers, *Prophetess of Health: A Study of Ellen G. White* (New York: Harper and Row, 1976).

[36] Jan Shipps, *Mormonism: The Story of a New Religious Tradition* (Urbana: University of Illinois Press, 1985).

[37] Klaus J. Hanson, *Mormonism and the American Experience* (Chicago: University of Chicago Press, 1981).

[38] Lawrence Foster, *Religion and Sexuality: Three American Communal Experiments of the Nineteenth Century* (New York: Oxford University Press, 1981).

[39] Barbara Welter, "The Cult of True Womanhood, 1820–1860," *American Quarterly* XVIII:2, pt. 1 (Summer 1966):151–74.

[40] Mary Ryan, *The Cradle of the Middle Class: The Family in Oneida County, New York, 1790–1865* (New York: Cambridge University Press, 1981).

• • •

[41] Mathews, *Religion in the Old South*, pp. 101–24.

[42] Nancy A. Hardesty, *Women Called to Witness: Evangelical Feminism in the Nineteenth Century* (Nashville: Abingdon Press, 1984), pp. 94–100.

[43] Wilson, *Public Religion*, p. 11.

[44] "Introduction to Part Three," *The History of American Electoral Behavior*, Joel H. Silbey, Allan G. Bogue, and William H. Flanigan, eds. (Princeton: Princeton University Press, 1978), pp. 253–56.

[45] Daniel Walker Howe, *The Political Culture of the American Whigs* (Chicago: University of Chicago Press, 1979), pp. 17–18, 159–67 and passim.

[46] Robert Kelley, *Cultural Patterns in American Politics: The First Century* (New York: Alfred A. Knopf, 1979). A very detailed and convincing analysis of these typologies for a later period is offered in Philip R. VanderMeer, *The Hoosier Politician: Officeholding and Political Culture in Indiana: 1896–1920* (Urbana: University of Illinois Press, 1985), pp. 96–120.

[47] Howe, *Political Culture*, pp. 54–7.

[48] Howe, *Political Culture*, p. 18.

[49] Alice Felt Tyler, *Freedom's Ferment: Phases of American Social History to 1860* (Minneapolis: The University of Minnesota Press, [c. 1944]), p. 372.

[50] Tyler, *Freedom's Ferment*, pp. 380–81.

[51] Eugene D. Genovese, "James Thornwell and Southern Religion," *Southern Partisan* 7 (Summer 1987):17–21.

Chapter Three

[1] Cf. William R. Hutchison, *Errand to the World: American Protestant Thought and Foreign Missions* (Chicago: University of Chicago Press, 1987), p. 95.

[2] Ferenc M. Szasz, *The Divided Mind of Protestant America, 1880–1930* (University, AL: University of Alabama Press, 1982). I am indebted to Robert T. Handy, "Protestant Theological Tensions and Political Styles in the Progressive Era," p. 43, paper presented at a conference on "Religion and American Politics," Institute for the Study of American Evangelicalism, Wheaton, Illinois, March 1988 for this and other points on this era.

[3] Richard Hofstadter, *The Age of Reform: From Bryan to F.D.R.* (New York: Random House, 1955).

[4] George L. Prentiss, "The National Crisis," *American Theological Review* 1st ser., 4 (October 1862):674–718.

[5] Horace Bushnell, "Our Obligations to the Dead," [sermon preached in 1865] reprinted in William G. McLoughlin, ed., *The American Evangelicals, 1800–1900* (New York: Harper and Row, 1968), pp. 141–57.

• • •

[6] Mark Twain and Charles Dudley Warner, *The Gilded Age*, 2 vols. (New York: Harper and Brothers, 1915 [1873]), 2:215.

[7] Henry Adams, *Democracy* (1880), quoted in C. Vann Woodward, "A Southern Critique for the Gilded Age," *The Burden of Southern History* (New York: Vintage, 1961), p. 125.

[8] Winthrop Hudson, *American Protestantism* (Chicago: University of Chicago Press, 1961), p. 128, the preceding three quotations are all from Hudson, pp. 125–28.

[9] Cf. Martin Marty, *Three Paths to the Secular* (New York: Harper and Row, 1969).

[10] Richard J. Jensen, *The Winning of the Midwest: Social and Political Conflict, 1888–1896* (Chicago: University of Chicago Press, 1971).

[11] Paul Kleppner, *Who Voted: The Dynamics of Electoral Turnout, 1870–1980* (New York: Praeger, 1982), pp. 77–78.

[12] *Congregationalist*, May 13, 1886, p. 162, quoted in Henry F. May, *The Protestant Churches in Industrial America* (New York: Harper and Row, 1949), p. 101.

[13] Francis Wayland, "The Elements of Political Economy," (1804) in McLoughlin, ed., *The American Evangelicals, 1800–1900*, pp. 113–27.

[14] May, *Protestant Churches*, p. 69.

[15] John H. Westerhoff, III, *McGuffey and His Readers: Piety, Morality, and Education in Nineteenth-Century America* (Nashville: Abington, 1978), p. 98, cf. 15 and 94.

[16] Russell H. Conwell, *Acres of Diamonds* (New York: Harper and Brothers, 1915) quoted in *Sources of the American Mind: A Collection of Documents and Texts in American Intellectual History*, Loren Baritz, ed., 2 vols. (New York: John Wiley and Sons, 1966), 2:41.

[17] Earl Latham, ed., *John D. Rockefeller: Robber Baron or Industrial Statesman?* (Boston: D. C. Heath and Co., 1949).

[18] Sydney E. Ahlstrom, "Thomas Hooker—Puritanism and Democratic Citizenship," *Church History* 32 (December 1963), pp. 415–31.

[19] Arthur M. Schlesinger, Jr., "Ideas and Economic Development," in *Paths of American Thought*, Morton White and Arthur M. Schlesinger, Jr., eds. (Boston: Houghton Mifflin, 1963), pp. 105–19; Arthur M. Schlesinger, Jr., *The Cycles of American History* (Boston: Houghton Mifflin, 1986).

[20] Quoted in Nancy A. Hardesty, *Women Called to Witness: Evangelical Feminism in the 19th Century* (Nashville: Abingdon Press, 1984), p. 152.

[21] Hutchison, *Errand to the World*, p. 93.

• • •

[22] Gerald H. Anderson, "American Protestants in Pursuit of Mission: 1886–1986," *International Bulletin of Missionary Research* vol. 12, no. 3 (July 1988), p. 102.

[23] Josiah Strong, *Our Country*, p. 160, quoted in Edwin S. Gaustad, "Our Country: One Century Later," in *Liberal Protestantism: Realities and Possibilities*, Robert S. Michaelsen and Wade Clark Roof, eds. (New York: Pilgrim Press, 1986), p. 96.

[24] Richard Hofstadter, *Social Darwinism in American Thought* (Boston: Beacon Press, 1959 [c. 1955]), p. 180.

[25] Quoted in Winthrop S. Hudson, *Religion in America: An Historical Account of the Development of American Religious Life*, 3d ed. (New York: Charles Scribner's Sons, 1981), p. 320.

[26] Quoted in Grant Wacker, "A Plural World: The Protestant Awakening to World Religions," *Between the Times: The Travail of the Protestant Establishment: 1900–1960*, William R. Hutchinson, ed. (New York: Cambridge University Press, 1989) from *Christianity the World Religion*, (Madras, 1897).

[27] Hofstadter, *The Age of Reform*, p. 320.

[28] Oliver Wendell Holmes, "The Path of the Law, 1897," in *Sources of the American Mind*, ed. Baritz, 2:102.

[29] Morton White, *Social Thought in America: The Revolt Against Formalism* (New York: Viking Press, 1949).

[30] Westerhoff, *McGuffey and His Readers*, p. 19.

[31] Robert W. Lynn, *Protestant Strategies in Education* (New York: Association Press, 1964), p. 57.

[32] Quoted in Stowe Persons, *American Minds: A History of Ideas* (New York: Holt, Rinehart and Winston, 1958), p. 245.

[33] John Dewey, "The Scientific Factor in Reconstruction of Philosophy, 1920," in *Sources of the American Mind*, 2:159.

[34] James Turner, *Without God, Without Creed: The Origins of Unbelief in America* (Baltimore: Johns Hopkins University Press, 1985).

[35] Neal Gillespie, *Charles Darwin and the Problem of Creation* (Chicago: University of Chicago Press, 1979), 152–53.

[36] David C. Lindberg and Ronald L. Numbers, "Beyond War and Peace: A Reappraisal of the Encounter Between Christianity and Science," *Church History* 55 (September 1986):338–54.

[37] David N. Livingstone, *Darwin's Forgotten Defenders: The Encounter Between Evangelical Theology and Evolutionary Thought* (Grand Rapids: Eerdmans and Scottish Academic Press, 1987).

[38] Henry Ward Beecher, *Yale Lectures in Preaching* (New York, 1872), p.

• • •

90, quoted in George M. Marsden, *Fundamentalism and American Culture: The Shaping of Twentieth Century Evangelicalism, 1870–1925* (New York: Oxford University Press, 1980), p. 25.

Chapter Four

[1] Jay A. Dolan, *The American Catholic Experience: A History from Colonial Times to the Present* (Garden City, NY: Doubleday and Company, 1985), pp. 205–6.

[2] Dolan, *American Catholic Experience*, p. 222.

[3] Cf. Dolan, *American Catholic Experience*, pp. 222–29.

[4] Cf. Dolan, *American Catholic Experience*, pp. 229–35.

[5] Dolan, *American Catholic Experience*, pp. 262–63; Rockne McCarthy, "Protestants and the Parochial School," in *Eerdmans' Handbook to Christianity in America*, Mark A. Noll et al, eds. (Grand Rapids: Eerdmans, 1983), pp. 238–39.

[6] Paul D. Garrett, "Eastern Christianity," in *Encyclopedia of the American Religious Experience*, Charles H. Lippy and Peter W. Williams, eds., 3 vols. (New York: Charles Scribner's Sons, 1988), 1:342.

[7] Garrett, "Eastern Christianity," pp. 325–44.

[8] Henry L. Feingold, *Zion in America: The Jewish Experience from Colonial Times to the Present* (New York: Hippocrene Books, 1974), pp. 36–37, 158–78.

[9] Feingold, *Zion in America*, pp. 182–83.

[10] Israel Zangwill, *The Melting Pot* (New York: Macmillan, 1909), p. 37, quoted in Sydney E. Ahlstrom, *A Religious History of the American People* (New Haven: Yale University Press, 1972), p. 3. Cf. Feingold, *Zion in America*, pp. 142–57.

[11] Marcus L. Hansen, "The Problem of the Third Generation Immigrant," *Augustana Historical Society* (Rock Island, IL, 1938) quoted in Will Herberg, *Protestant-Catholic-Jew: An Essay in American Religious Sociology* (Garden City, NY: Doubleday and Company, 1955), p. 218.

[12] Feingold, *Zion in America*, p. 189; Nathan Glazer, *American Judaism* (Chicago: University of Chicago Press, 1957), p. 85. Cf. Winthrop S. Hudson, *Religion in America: An Historical Account of the Development of American Religious Life*, 4th ed. (New York: MacMillan, 1987), p. 312.

[13] Bertram Wyatt-Brown, *Honor and Violence in the Old South* (New York: Oxford University Press, 1986).

[14] W. E. B. DuBois, "Of the Faith of the Fathers," in *Afro-American Religious History: A Documentary Witness*, Milton C. Sernett, ed., (Durham, NC: Duke University Press, 1985), p. 312.

• • •

[15] Lawrence N. Jones, "Black Churches: A New Agenda," in *Afro-American Religious History*, p. 492.

[16] Lawrence W. Levine, *Black Culture and Black Consciousness* (New York: Oxford University Press, 1977), p. 158.

[17] See Donald W. Dayton, *Theological Roots of Pentecostalism* (Grand Rapids: Francis Asbury Press of Zondervan, 1987), for discussion of the doctrinal background.

[18] See Grant Wacker, "Pentecostalism," in *Encyclopedia of the American Religious Experience*, 2:933–45.

[19] Sydney E. Ahlstrom, *A Religious History of the American People*, pp. 1020–26; Stephen Gottschalk, "Christian Science and Harmonialism," in *Encyclopedia of the American Religious Experience*, 2:901–16; Stephen Gottschalk, *The Emergence of Christian Science in American Religious Life* (Berkeley: University of California Press, 1973).

Chapter Five

[1] Cf. John Shelton Reed, *The Enduring South: Subculture Persistence in Mass Society* (Chapel Hill: University of North Carolina, 1986), who suggested this.

[2] Methodist Episcopal Church, South, General Conference, *Journal*, 1894, 34–35, quoted in Kenneth K. Bailey, *South White Protestantism in the Twentieth Century* (Gloucester, MA: Peter Smith, 1968, 1964), p. 35.

[3] W. J. Rorabaugh, *The Alcoholic Republic; an American Tradition* (New York: Oxford University Press, 1979).

[4] Reprinted in *New World Metaphysics: Readings on the Religious Meaning of the American Experience*, Giles Gunn, ed. (New York: Oxford University Press, 1981), p. 296.

[5] C. Allyn Russell, *Voices of American Fundamentalism: Seven Biographical Studies* (Philadelphia: Westminster Press, 1976), pp. 147–48; Robert Bolt, "American Involvement in World War I," in *The Wars of America: Christian Views*, Ronald A. Wells, ed. (Grand Rapids: Eerdmans, 1981), pp. 127–46.

[6] Bolt, "American Involvement in World War I," p. 142.

[7] Quoted in Douglas W. Frank, *Less Than Conquerors: How Evangelicals Entered the Twentieth Century* (Grand Rapids: Eerdmans, 1986), p. 179.

[8] Heywood Broun, *The New York Tribune* (1915), in *Eerdmans's Handbook to Christianity in America*, Mark A. Noll, et. al, eds. (Grand Rapids: Eerdmans, 1983), p. 369.

[9] Quoted in Ray H. Abrams, *Preacher Present Arms* (New York: Round Table Press, 1933), p. 79; William G. McLoughlin, *Billy Sunday was His Real Name* (Chicago: University of Chicago Press, 1955); Frank, *Less Than Conquerors*, pp. 173–95.

• • •

[10] James R. Moore, *The Post-Darwinian Controversies: A Study of the Protestant Struggle to Come to Terms with Darwin in Great Britain and America, 1870–1900* (New York: Cambridge University Press, 1979), p. 73.

[11] William Jennings Bryan, *In His Image* (New York: Fleming H. Revell, 1922), p. 93.

[12] Quoted in Ned B. Stonehouse, *J. Gresham Machen: A Biographical Memoir* (Grand Rapids: Eerdmans, 1954), p. 232.

[13] J. Gesham Machen, *Christianity and Liberalism* (Grand Rapids: Eerdmans, 1923), p. 160.

[14] Richard Hofstadter, *The Age of Reform* (New York: Vintage Books, 1955), p. 23.

[15] Quoted in Henry May, *The Discontent of the Intellectuals: A Problem of the Twenties* (Chicago: Rand McNally, 1963), p. 26.

[16] May, *Discontent of the Intellectuals*, p. 29.

[17] James Hennesey, S.J., "Religion and American Politics: The Twentieth Century, Roman Catholics." Paper presented at a conference on "Religion and American Politics," Institute for the Study of American Evangelicalism, Wheaton, Illinois, March 1988.

[18] Hennesey, "Religion and American Politics."

[19] Wilfred Parsons, S.J., "Are Protestants Americans?" *America* 36 (February 5, 1927):404–6. I am indebted to Deborah Spears for her valuable paper which provides this reference and the basic information for much of this analysis.

[20] Robert Anthony Orsi, *The Madonna of 115th Street: Faith and Community in Italian Harlem, 1880–1950* (New Haven: Yale University Press, 1985).

[21] I am indebted for some of this to Peter W. Williams, "Catholicism since World War I," in *Encyclopedia of the American Religious Experience*, Charles H. Lippy and Peter W. Williams, eds. 3 vols. (New York: Charles Scribner's Sons, 1988), 1:375–90.

[22] Quoted in Jay P. Dolan, *The American Catholic Experience: A History from Colonial Times to the Present* (Garden City, NY: Doubleday and Company, 1985), p. 403.

[23] Walter Lippmann, *A Preface to Morals* (New York: Macmillan, 1929), p. 12.

[24] Quoted in Ronald Steele, *Walter Lippmann and the American Century* (Boston: Atlantic-Little Brown, 1980), p. 262.

[25] Lippman, *Preface to Morals*, pp. 31–32.

[26] Quoted in Steele, *Walter Lippmann and the American Century*, p. 262.

[27] Pitirim A. Sorokin, *The Crisis of our Age* (New York: E. P. Dutton and Company, 1941).

· · ·

[28] William E. Leuchtenburg, *The Perils of Prosperity, 1914–1932* (Chicago: University of Chicago Press, 1958), p. 168.

[29] For all these examples, I am indebted to the fine discussion of William E. Leuchtenburg, *The Perils of Prosperity*, 168–71.

[30] Frank, *Less than Conquerors*, p. 210. I am indebted to Frank's analysis on this point.

[31] Sydney E. Ahlstrom, *A Religious History of the American People* (New Haven: Yale University Press, 1972), p. 905.

[32] Leuchtenburg, *Perils of Prosperity*, p. 142; cf. p. 153 regarding Mencken's suggestion.

[33] Daniel Pawley, "Ernest Hemingway: Tragedy of an Evangelical Family," *Christianity Today*, November 23, 1984, pp. 20–27.

[34] Joseph Wood Krutch, *The Modern Times* (New York: Harcourt, Brace and Company, 1929).

[35] Carl Becker, *The Heavenly City of the Eighteenth-Century Philosophers* (New Haven: Yale University Press, 1932).

[36] Becker, *Heavenly City*, pp. 14–15.

[37] Henry Steele Commager, *The American Mind* (New Haven: Yale University Press, 1950), p. 100.

[38] William James (quoting John Dewey), "What Pragmatism Means," in Perry Miller, *American Thought; Civil War to WWI* (New York: Holt, Rinehart and Winston, 1963 [1954]), p. 172.

[39] John Dewey, *A Common Faith* (New Haven: Yale University Press, 1934).

[40] Sydney E. Ahlstrom, "Theology in America: A Historical Survey," in *The Shaping of American Religion*, James Ward Smith and A. Leland Jameson, eds. 2 vols. (Princeton: Princeton University Press, 1961), 1:287.

[41] H. Richard Niebuhr, *The Church Against the World* (1935), from excerpt in Sydney E. Ahlstrom, eds., *Theology in America: The Major Protestant Voices from Puritanism to Neo-Orthodoxy* (Indianapolis: Bobbs-Merrill, 1967), p. 616.

[42] See Richard Wightman Fox, *Reinhold Niebuhr: A Biography* (New York: Pantheon Books, 1985) on these points.

[43] See, for example, Reinhold Niebuhr, *The Nature and Destiny of Man* New York: Charles Scribner's Sons, 1941); or *The Irony of American History* (New York: Charles Scribner's Sons, 1962).

[44] Hofstadter, *Age of Reform* (New York: Vintage Books, 1955), p. 320.

Chapter Six

[1] Cf. Carl Becker, "What is Still Living in the Political Philosophy of Thomas Jefferson," *American Historical Review* 48:4 (July 1943):705.

• • •

[2] For examples of the serious academic discussion—during and after the war—of preserving Christian civilization, see C. T. McIntire, ed., *God, History, and Historians: Modern Christian Views of History* (New York: Oxford University Press, 1977).

[3] Richard V. Pierard, "World War II," in *The Wars of America: Christian Views*, Ronald A. Wells, ed. (Grand Rapids: Eerdmans, 1981), pp. 147–74; Paul Johnson, *Modern Times: The World from the Twenties to the Eighties* (New York: Harper and Row, 1983), p. 404.

[4] Reinhold Niebuhr, *The Irony of American History* (New York: Charles Scribner's Sons, 1952), p. 172 and passim.

[5] Robert Wuthnow, *The Restructuring of American Religion: Society and Faith Since World War II* (Princeton: Princeton University Press, 1988), pp. 16–17.

[6] Will Herberg, *Protestant-Catholic-Jew: An Essay in American Religious Sociology* (Garden City, NY: Doubleday and Company, 1955), p. 14.

[7] Martin Marty, *The New Shape of American Religion* (New York: Harper and Row, 1958), p. 15.

[8] Marty, *New Shape of American Religion*, pp. 31–40.

[9] William Lee Miller, *Piety along the Potomac: Notes on Politics and Morals in the Fifties* (Boston: Houghton Mifflin Company, 1964).

[10] Quoted in Herberg, *Protestant-Jew-Catholic*, p. 97 with Herberg's added italic.

[11] Norman Vincent Peale, *The Power of Positive Thinking* (New York: Prentice-Hall, 1952), p. 1.

[12] Herberg, *Protestant-Catholic-Jew*, pp. 91–94.

[13] Herberg, *Protestant-Catholic-Jew*, pp. 86–90.

[14] Herberg, *Protestant-Catholic-Jew*, p. 86.

[15] See George M. Marsden, *Reforming Fundamentalism: Fuller Seminary and the New Fundamentalism* (Grand Rapids: Eerdmans, 1987) for more complete discussion of these issues.

[16] Winthrop S. Hudson, *American Protestantism* (Chicago: University of Chicago Press, 1961), p. 174.

[17] See David Edwin Harrell, Jr., *Oral Roberts: An American Life* (Bloomington, IN: Indiana University Press, 1985).

[18] David O. Levine, *The American College and the Culture of Aspiration, 1915–1940* (Ithaca: Cornell University Press, 1986), pp. 146–50.

[19] E.g., Dan A. Oren, *Joining the Club: A History of Jews at Yale* (New Haven: Yale University Press, 1985).

[20] Neal Gabler, *An Empire of Their Own: How the Jews Invented Hollywood* (New York: Crown Publishers, 1988).

• • •

[21] Jacob Neusner, "Judaism in Contemporary America," in *Encyclopedia of the American Religious Experience*, Charles H. Lippy and Peter W. Williams, eds. 3 vols. (New York: Charles Scribner's Sons, 1988), 1:321.

[22] H. Paul Chalfant, Robert E. Beckley, and C. Eddie Palmer, *Religion in Contemporary Society*, 2d ed. (Palo Alto: Mayfield Publishing, 1987), p. 164.

[23] Chalfant, Beckley, and Palmer, *Religion in Contemporary Society*, p. 164–66. Cf. Herberg, *Protestant-Catholic-Jew*, p. 210.

[24] John Dart, "Woody Allen, Theologian," *The Christian Century*, June 22–29, 1977, pp. 585–88.

[25] Wuthnow, *Restructuring of American Religion*, p. 74.

[26] I am indebted to Robert Moats Miller for this quotation in his unpublished essay, "Catholic-Protestant Tensions in Post-World War II America: The Experience of Methodist Bishop G. Bromley Oxnam" (1987).

[27] Quoted from *Presbyterian Tribune*, January 1946, pp. 9–10 in Wuthnow, *Reconstructing of American Religion*, p. 73.

[28] Wuthnow, *Restructuring of American Religion*, p. 73.

[29] Herberg, *Protestant-Catholic-Jew*, pp. 168, 174.

[30] Jay P. Dolan, *American Catholic Experience: A History from Colonial Times to the Present* (Garden City, NY: Doubleday and Company, 1985), pp. 385–86.

[31] Richard Fox, *Reinhold Niebuhr: A Biography* (New York: Pantheon, 1985), p. 276.

[32] John Courtney Murray, S.J., *We Hold These Truths: Catholic Reflections on the American Proposition*, (New York: Sheed and Ward, 1960), pp. 21–22.

[33] Marty, *New Shape of American Religion*, pp. 76 and 79.

[34] See, for example, Sidney E. Mead, *The Lively Experiment: The Shaping of Christianity in America* (New York: Harper and Row, 1963), p. 68.

[35] From *Ebony*, August 1965, p. 7, quoted in James H. Cone, "Black Religious Thought," in *Encyclopedia of the American Religious Experience*, 2:1181. I am indebted to this article for its insights on King.

[36] Stephen B. Oates, *Let the Trumpet Sound: The Life of Martin Luther King, Jr.* (New York: New American Library, 1985 [1982]), pp. 84–85.

[37] Milton C. Sernett, ed., *Afro-American Religious History* (Durham: Duke University Press, 1985), p. 423.

[38] Oates, *Let the Trumpet Sound*, p. 87.

[39] Quoted from Roger Lundin and Mark A. Noll, eds., *Voices from the Heart: Four Centuries of American Piety* (Grand Rapids: Eerdmans, 1987), p. 358. Source: "I Have a Dream." Copyright © 1963 by Martin Luther King, Jr. Reprinted by permission of Joan Daves.

• • •

[40] National Conference of Black Churchmen, " 'Black Power' Statement, July 31, 1966 and 'Black Theology' Statement, June 13, 1969" in *Afro-American Religious History*, pp. 465–88.

Chapter Seven

[1] Cf. Theodore Roszak, *The Making of a Counter Culture: Reflections on the Technocratic Society and its Youthful Opposition* (Garden City, NY: Doubleday and Company, [c. 1969]), p. 8.

[2] Cf. Roszak, *Making of a Counter Culture*.

[3] Cf. Steven M. Tipton, *Getting Saved from the Sixties* (Berkeley: University of California Press, 1982), p. 15 and passim.

[4] Harvey Cox, *The Secular City: Secularization and Urbanization in Theological Perspective*, rev. ed. (New York: Macmillan, 1966 [1965]), p. 4.

[5] Cox, *Secular City*, p. 10.

[6] Cox, *Secular City*, p. 109.

[7] Leonard Sweet, "The 1960s: The Crises of Liberal Christianity and the Public Emergence of Evangelicalism," in *Evangelicalism and Modern America*, George Marsden, ed. (Grand Rapids: Eerdmans, 1984), p. 33.

[8] Cf. Sweet, "The Crisis of Liberal Christianity;" Tipton, *Getting Saved from the Sixties;* Robert N. Bellah et. al, *Habits of the Heart: Individualism and Commitment in American Life* (Berkeley: University of California Press, 1985).

[9] Statement from Stanley Hauerwas to the author.

[10] H. Paul Chalfant, Robert E. Beckley, and C. Eddie Palmer, *Religion in Contemporary Society*, 2d ed. (Palo Alto, CA: Mayfield, 1987), p. 157 lists 52.5 million Catholics, 39 million mainline Protestants, 37 million conservative Protestants (nonmembers of the National Council of Churches), and five and a half million Jews for 1985.

[11] Jay P. Dolan, *American Catholic Experience: A History from Colonial Times to the Present* (Garden City, NY: Doubleday and Company, 1985), p. 424.

[12] I am grateful for the valuable discussions of Jay P. Dolan, *American Catholic Experience*, pp. 425–30, which I follow closely in this section.

[13] Dolan, *American Catholic Experience*, pp. 433–37.

[14] Peter W. Williams, "Catholicism Since World War I," in *Encyclopedia of the American Religious Experience*, Charles H. Lippy and Peter W. Williams, eds. 3 vols. (New York: Charles Scribner's Sons, 1988), 1:384–86.

[15] Dolan, *American Catholic Experience*, p. 442; Williams, "Catholicism since World War I," p. 387.

[16] Margaret Bendroth, "The Search for Women's Role in American Evangelicalism, 1930–1980," in *Evangelicalism and Modern America*, pp. 122–

• • •

34; Rosemary Skinner Keller, "Women and Religion," in *Encyclopedia of the American Religious Experience*, 3:1547–62.

[17] Charles S. Prebish, "Buddhism," 2:669–82; John Y. Fenton, "Hinduism," 2:683–98; C. Carlyle Haaland, "Shinto and Indigenous Chinese Religion," 2:699–709; Newell S. Booth, Jr., "Islam in North America," 2:723–29, in *Encyclopedia of the American Religious Experience*, Charles H. Lippy and Peter W. Williams, eds. 3 vols. (New York: Charles Scribner's Sons, 1988). Exact numbers for these groups are not available. The largest of these is Islam, with perhaps three million adherents in the United States.

[18] Thomas Robbins and Dick Anthony, " 'Cults' in the Late Twentieth Century," in *Encyclopedia of the American Religious Experience*, 2:747–48.

[19] See Charles S. Prebish, "Buddism," in *Encyclopedia of the American Religious Experience*, 2:669–82; John Y. Fenton, "Hinduism," in *Encyclopedia of the American Religious Experience*, 2:683–98; Robert S. Ellwood, "Occult Movements in America," in *Encyclopedia of the American Religious Experience*, 2:699–710; and Thomas Robbins and Dick Anthony, " 'Cults' in the Late Twentieth Century," 2:741–54.

[20] Ellwood, *Alternative Altars: Unconventional and Eastern Spirituality in America* (Chicago, University of Chicago Press, 1979), p. 21.

[21] Ellwood, *Alternative Altars*, p. 34.

[22] Tipton, *Getting Saved from the Sixties*, pp. 1–24.

[23] Bellah, *Habits of the Heart*, pp. 43–48.

[24] Bellah, *Habits of the Heart*, p. 72.

[25] Bellah, *Habits of the Heart*, p. 228; from a 1978 Gallup poll.

[26] Bellah, *Habits of the Heart*, p. 221.

[27] Constant H. Jacquet, ed., "Church Membership Statistics, 1940–1985, for Selected U. S. Denominations," *Yearbook of American and Canadian Churches, 1987* (Nashville: Abingdon Press, 1987), pp. 254–55.

[28] Jacquet, ed., "Church Membership Statistics," pp. 254–55.

[29] See Jerry Falwell, ed., *The Fundamentalist Phenomenon* (Garden City, NY: Doubleday and Company, 1981), p. 18.

[30] The largest Luthern denomination, formed by merger in 1988 and representing over five million members, chose the name the Evangelical Lutheran Church in America. This use of "evangelical" reflected a continental European useage, essentially meaning "Protestant."

[31] Cf. Dean M. Kelley, *Why Conservative Churches are Growing: A Study in Sociology of Religion* (New York: Harper and Row, 1972).

[32] Robert Wuthnow, *The Restructuring of American Religion: Society and Faith*

• • •

since World War II (Princeton: Princeton University Press, 1988), pp. 200–205.

[33] Wuthnow, *Restructuring of American Religion*, p. 156.

[34] William Martin, "Mass Communications," in *Encyclopedia of the American Religious Experience*, 3:1719–23.

[35] I am indebted to Robert Wuthnow, *Restructuring of American Religion*, pp. 314–22 for his valuable insights on these points.

[36] Tim LaHaye, *The Battle for the Mind* (Old Tappen, NJ: Felming H. Revell, 1980).

[37] I am indebted to some of the publications of the Williamsburg Charter Foundation, Washington, D.C., for some of their formulations of similar points.

• • •

Suggestions for Further Reading

Introduction

There are several excellent general surveys of American religious history:

Catherine L. Albanese. *America: Religions and Religion*. Belmont, CA: Wadsworth, 1981.

Sydney E. Ahlstrom. *A Religious History of the American People*. New Haven: Yale University Press, 1972.

Edwin S. Gaustad, ed. *A Documentary History of Religion in America*. 2 vols. Grand Rapids: Eerdmans, 1982.

Edwin S. Gaustad. *Historical Atlas of Religion in America*. rev. ed. San Francisco: Harper and Row, 1976.

Robert T. Handy. *A Christian America: Protestant Hopes and Historical Realities*. rev. ed. New York: Oxford University Press, 1984.

————. *A History of the Churches in the United States and Canada*. New York: Oxford University Press, 1979 [1976].

Nathan O. Hatch and Mark A. Noll. *The Bible in America: Essays in Cultural History*. New York: Oxford University Press, 1982.

Winthrop S. Hudson. *Religion in America: An Historical Account of the Development of American Religious Life*. 4th ed. New York: Charles Scribner's Sons, 1987.

Charles H. Lippy and Peter W. Williams, eds. *Encyclopedia of the American Religious Experience: Studies of Traditions and Movements*. 3 vols. New York: Charles Scribner's Sons, 1988. This encyclopedia serves as an excellent introduction to almost every aspect of America's religious experience. Each article also has a fine bibliography.

Martin E. Marty. *Righteous Empire: The Protestant Experience in America*. New York: Dial, 1970.

R. Laurence Moore. *Religious Outsiders in the Making of America*. New York: Oxford University Press, 1986.

John M. Mulder and John F. Wilson, eds. *Religion in American History*. Englewood Cliffs, NJ: Prentice-Hall, 1978.

Mark A. Noll. *One Nation Under God? Christian Faith and Political Action*. San Francisco: Harper and Row, 1988.

Mark A. Noll, Nathan O. Hatch, and George M. Marsden. *The Search for Christian America*. rev. ed. Colorado Springs: Helmers and Howard, 1989.

• • •

Mark A. Noll et al. *Eerdman's Handbook to Christianity in America*. Grand Rapids: Eerdmans, 1983.

Ronald A. Wells, ed. *The Wars of America: Christian Views*. Grand Rapids: Eerdmans, 1981.

Chapter One

E. Digby Baltzell. *Puritan Boston and Quaker Philadelphia*. New York: Macmillan Publishing Company, 1979.

Sacvan Bercovitch. *The Puritan Origins of the American Self*. New Haven: Yale University Press, 1975.

Patricia U. Bonomi. *Under the Cope of Heaven: Religion, Society and Politics in Colonial America*. New York: Oxford University Press, 1986.

Henry Warner Bowden. *American Indians and Christian Missions: Studies in Cultural Conflict*. Chicago: University of Chicago Press, 1981.

David B. Davis. *The Problem of Slavery in the Age of Revolution, 1770–1823*. Ithaca: Cornell University Press, 1975.

Edwin S. Gaustad. *The Great Awakening in New England*. San Francisco: Harper and Row, 1957.

Nathan O. Hatch. *The Sacred Cause of Liberty: Republican Thought and the Millennium in Revolutionary New England*. New Haven: Yale University Press, 1977.

Rhys Isaac. *The Transformation of Virginia, 1740–1790*. Chapel Hill: University of North Carolina Press, 1982.

Bruce Kuklick. *Churchmen and Philosophers: From Jonathan Edwards to John Dewey*. New Haven: Yale University Press, 1985.

William G. McLoughlin. *Isaac Backus and the American Pietistic Tradition*. Boston: Little, Brown and Company, 1967.

Henry F. May. *The Enlightenment in America*. New York: Oxford University Press, 1976.

Perry Miller. *Errand into the Wilderness*. Cambridge: The Belknap Press of Harvard University Press, 1956.

———. *The New England Mind*. 2 vols. Boston: Beacon Press, 1961 [1939, 1953].

Edmund S. Morgan. *The Gentle Puritan: A Life of Ezra Stiles, 1727–1795*. New York: W. W. Norton and Company, 1983.

———. *The Puritan Dilemma: The Story of John Winthrop*. Boston: Little, Brown and Company, 1958.

Mark A. Noll. *Christians in the American Revolution*. Washington, D.C.: Christian University Press, 1977.

• • •

Rosemary Radford Ruether and Rosemary Skinner Keller, eds. *Women and Religion in America*. Volume 2: *The Colonial and Revolutionary Periods*. San Francisco: Harper and Row, 1983.

Lester B. Scherer. *Slavery and the Churches in Early America, 1619–1819*. Grand Rapids: Eerdmans, 1975.

Harold Simonson. *Jonathan Edwards: Theologian of the Heart*. Grand Rapids: Eerdmans, 1974.

Harry S. Stout. *The New England Soul: Preaching and Religious Culture in Colonial New England*. New York: Oxford University Press, 1986.

Chapter Two

Whitney R. Cross. *The Burned-Over District: The Social and Intellectual History of Enthusiastic Religion in Western New York, 1800–1850*. Ithaca: Cornell University Press, 1950.

Jay A. Dolan. *The American Catholic Experience: A History from Colonial Times to the Present*. Garden City, NY: Doubleday and Company, 1985.

———. *The Immigrant Church: New York's Irish and German Catholics, 1815–1865*. South Bend: University of Notre Dame Press, 1975.

———. *Catholic Revivalism: The American Experience, 1830–1900*. South Bend: University of Notre Dame Press, 1978.

Ann Douglas. *The Feminization of American Culture*. New York: Knopf, 1978.

Lawrence Foster. *Religion and Sexuality: Three American Communal Experiments of the Nineteenth Century*. Urbana: University of Illinois Press, 1984 [1981].

Edwin S. Gaustad, ed. *The Rise of Adventism: A Commentary on the Social and Religious Ferment of Mid-Nineteenth Century America*. San Francisco: Harper and Row, 1974.

Eugene Genovese. *Roll, Jordan, Roll: The World the Slaves Made*. New York: Vintage Books, 1976 [1974].

C. C. Goen. *Broken Churches, Broken Nation*. Macon: Mercer University Press, 1985.

Klaus J. Hanson. *Mormonism and the American Experience*. Chicago: University of Chicago Press, 1981.

Nancy A. Hardesty. *Women Called to Witness: Evangelical Feminism in the Nineteenth Century*. Nashville: Abingdon, 1984.

Nathan O. Hatch. *The Democratization of American Christianity*. New Haven: Yale University Press, 1989.

James H. Hennessey. *American Catholics: A History of Roman Catholic Community in the United States*. New York: Oxford University Press, 1981.

• • •

Samuel S. Hill. *The South and the North in American Religion*. Athens: University of Georgia Press, 1980.

Daniel Walker Howe. *The Political Culture of the American Whigs*. Chicago: University of Chicago Press, 1979.

———. *The Unitarian Consciousness: Harvard Moral Philosophy, 1805–1861*. Cambridge: Harvard University Press, 1970.

Richard T. Hughes and C. Leonard Allen, eds. *Illusions of Innocence: Protestant Primitivism in America, 1630–1875*. Chicago: University of Chicago Press, 1988.

William R. Hutchison. *Errand to the World: American Protestant Thought and Foreign Missions*. Chicago: University of Chicago Press, 1987.

Lawrence W. Levine. *Black Culture and Black Consciousness: Afro-American Folk Thought From Slavery to Freedom*. New York: Oxford University Press, 1977.

William G. McLoughlin, ed. *The American Evangelicals, 1800–1900*. San Francisco: Harper Torchbooks, 1968.

———. *Cherokees and Missionaries, 1789–1839*. New Haven: Yale University Press, 1984.

George M. Marsden. *The Evangelical Mind and the New School Presbyterian Experience*. New Haven: Yale University Press, 1970.

Donald G. Mathews. *Religion in the Old South*. Chicago: University of Chicago Press, 1977.

Perry Miller, ed. *Life of the Mind in America: From the Revolution to the Civil War*. New York: Holt, Rinehart and Winston, 1967.

James H. Moorhead. *American Apocalypse: Yankee Protestants and the Civil War, 1860–1869*. New Haven: Yale University Press, 1978.

Ronald L. Numbers. *Prophetess of Health: A Study of Ellen G. White*. San Francisco: Harper and Row, 1976.

Albert J. Raboteau. *Slave Religion: The "Invisible Institution" in the Antebellum South*. New York: Oxford University Press, 1978.

Russell E. Richey, ed. *Denominationalism*. Nashville: Abingdon, 1977.

Rosemary Radford Ruether and Rosemary Skinner Keller, eds. *Women and Religion in America*. Volume I: *The Nineteenth Century*. San Francisco: Harper and Row, 1981.

Lewis O. Saum. *The Popular Mood in Pre-Civil War America*. Westport, CN: Greenwood Press, 1980.

Jan Shipps. *Mormonism and the American Experience*. Urbana: University of Illinois Press, 1981.

• • •

Katherine K. Sklar. *Catherine Beecher: A Study in American Domesticity.* New Haven: Yale University Press, 1973.

Timothy L. Smith. *Revivalism and Social Reform: American Protestantism on the Eve of the Civil War.* Nashville: Abingdon Press, 1957.

Chapter Three

Sydney E. Ahlstrom, ed. *Theology in America: The Major Protestant Voices from Puritanism to Neo-Orthodoxy.* New York: Bobbs-Merrill, 1967.

Paul A. Carter. *The Spiritual Crisis of the Gilded Age.* DeKalb: Northern Illinois University Press, 1971.

Clifford E. Clark, Jr. *Henry Ward Beecher: Spokesman for a Middle Class America.* Urbana: University of Illinois Press, 1978.

James F. Finlay, Jr. *Dwight L. Moody: American Evangelist, 1837–1899.* Chicago: University of Chicago Press, 1969.

Neal Gillespie. *Charles Darwin and the Problem of Creation.* Chicago: University of Chicago Press, 1979.

Robert T. Handy, ed. *The Social Gospel in America, 1870–1920.* New York: Oxford University Press, 1966.

Nancy A. Hardesty. *Women Called to Witness: Evangelical Feminism in the Nineteenth Century.* Nashville: Abingdon, 1984.

Richard Hofstadter. *Social Darwinism in American Thought.* Boston: Beacon Press, 1955 [1944].

William R. Hutchison. *Errand to the World: American Protestant Thought and Foreign Missions.* Chicago: University of Chicago Press, 1987.

————. *The Modernist Impulse in American Protestantism.* Cambridge: Harvard University Press, 1976.

Bruce Kuklick. *Churchmen and Philosophers: From Jonathan Edwards to John Dewey.* New Haven: Yale University Press, 1985.

Jackson Lears. *No Place of Grace: Antimodernism and the Transformation of American Culture, 1880–1920.* New York: Pantheon Books, c. 1981.

William G. McLoughlin. *Modern Revivalism: Charles Grandison Finney to Billy Graham.* New York: Ronald Press, c. 1959.

George M. Marsden. *Fundamentalism and American Culture: The Shaping of Twentieth-Century Evangelicalism, 1870–1925.* New York: Oxford University Press, 1980.

James R. Moore. *The Post-Darwinian Controversies: A Study of the Protestant Struggles to Come to Terms with Darwin in Great Britain and America, 1870–1900.* New York: Cambridge University Press, 1979.

• • •

R. Laurence Moore. *Religious Outsiders and the Making of Americans*. New York: Oxford University Press, 1986.

Ernest R. Sandeen. *The Roots of Fundamentalism: British and American Millenarianism, 1800–1930*. Grand Rapids: Baker House Books, 1978 [1970].

Ferenc M. Szasz. *The Divided Mind of Protestant America, 1880–1930*. University, AL: University of Alabama Press, 1982.

James Turner. *Without God, Without Creed: The Origins of Unbelief in America*. Baltimore: Johns Hopkins University Press, 1985.

Timothy P. Weber. *Living in the Shadow of the Second Coming: American Premillennialism, 1875–1982*. Chicago: University of Chicago Press, 1987 [1979, 1983].

Chapter Four

Aaron Abell. *American Catholicism and Social Action: A Search for Social Justice, 1865–1950*. Garden City, NY: Hanover House, 1960.

Robert Mapes Anderson. *Vision of the Disinherited: The Making of American Pentecostalism*. New York: Oxford University Press, 1979.

Joseph L. Blau. *Judaism in America*. Chicago: University of Chicago Press, 1976.

Donald W. Dayton. *Theological Roots of Pentecostalism*. Grand Rapids: Francis Aubury Press of Zondervan, 1987.

Jay A. Dolan. *The American Catholic Experience: A History from Colonial Times to the Present*. Garden City, NY: Doubleday and Company, 1985.

———. *Catholic Revivalism: The American Experience, 1830–1900*. South Bend: University of Notre Dame Press, 1978.

Henry L. Feingold. *Zion in America: The Jewish Experience from Colonial Times to the Present*. New York: Hippocrence Books, 1974.

E. Franklin Frazier. *The Negro Church in America*/C. Eric Lincoln. *The Black Church Since Frazier*. New York: Schocken Books, 1973.

Nathan Glazer. *American Judaism*. 2d ed. Chicago: University of Chicago Press, 1972 [1957].

Stephen Gottschalk. *The Emergence of Christian Science in American Religious Life*. Berkeley: University of California Press, 1973.

James J. Hennessey. *American Catholics: A History of the Roman Catholic Community in the United States*. New York: Oxford University Press, 1981.

Lawrence W. Levine. *Black Culture and Black Consciousness*. New York: Oxford University Press, 1977.

Thomas T. McAvoy. *The Great Crisis in American Catholic History, 1895–1900*. New York: H. Regnery Company, 1957.

• • •

Martin E. Marty. *Modern American Religion*. Volume 1: *The Irony of It All, 1893–1919*. Chicago: University of Chicago Press, 1986.

Milton C. Sernett, ed. *Afro-American Religious History: A Documentary Witness*. Durham, NC: Duke University Press, 1985.

Bertram Wyatt-Brown. *Honor and Violence in the Old South*. New York: Oxford University Press, 1986.

Chapter Five

Paul A. Carter. *The Decline and Revival of the Social Gospel: Social and Political Liberalism in American Protestant Churches, 1920–1940*. Ithaca: Cornell University Press, 1954.

Dorothy Day. *The Long Lonliness: An Autobiography*. San Francisco: Harper and Row, 1981 [1952].

Jay P. Dolan. *The American Catholic Experience: A History from Colonial Times to the Present*. Garden City, NY: Doubleday and Company, 1985.

Richard Fox. *Reinhold Niebuhr: A Biography*. New York: Pantheon, 1985.

Douglas W. Frank. *Less Than Conquerors: How Evangelicals Entered the Twentieth Century*. Grand Rapids: Eerdmans, 1986.

James J. Hennessey. *American Catholics: A History of the Roman Catholic Community in the United States*. New York: Oxford University Press, 1981.

Richard Hofstadter. *The Age of Reform*. New York: Vintage Books, 1955.

William E. Hordern. *A Layman's Guide to Protestant Theology*. rev. ed. New York: Macmillan, 1986 [1968].

William R. Hutchison. *The Modernist Impulse in American Protestantism*. Cambridge: Harvard University Press, 1976.

Joseph Wood Krutch. *The Modern Temper: A Study and a Confession*. New York: Harcourt, Brace and Company, c. 1964 [1929].

Lawrence W. Levine. *Defender of the Faith: William Jennings Bryan, The Last Decade, 1915–1925*. New York: Oxford University Press, 1965.

Walter Lippmann. *A Preface to Morals*. New Brunswick, NJ: Transaction Books, c. 1982 [1929].

Robert S. and Helen Lynd. *Middletown: A Study in Contemporary American Culture*. New York: Harcourt, Brace and Company, 1929.

George M. Marsden. *Fundamentalism and American Culture: The Shaping of Twentieth-Century Evangelicalism: 1870–1925*. New York: Oxford University Press, 1980.

Henry May. *The Discontent of the Intellectuals: A Problem of the Twenties*. Chicago: Rand McNally, 1963.

• • •

————. *The End of American Innocence: A Study of the First Years of Our Own Time, 1912–1917*. New York: Knopf, 1959.

H. Richard Niebuhr. *The Kingdom of God in America*. Middletown, CN: Wesleyan University Press, c. 1988.

Robert A. Orsi. *Madonna of 115th Street: Faith and Community in Italian Harlem, 1880–1950*. New Haven: Yale University Press, c. 1985.

Lewis Perry. *Intellectual Life in America: A History*. New York: F. Watts, 1984.

C. Allyn Russell. *Voices of American Fundamentalism: Seven Biographical Studies*. Philadelphia: Westminster, 1976.

Ernest R. Sandeen. *The Roots of Fundamentalism: British and American Millenarianism, 1800–1930*. Grand Rapids: Baker House Books, 1978 [1970].

Anne Firor Scott. *The Southern Lady: From Pedestal to Politics 1830–1930*. Chicago: University of Chicago Press, 1970.

Chapter Six

Robert Bellah. "Civil Religion in America." *Daedalus* 96 (Winter: 1967): 1–21.

Paul A. Carter. *The Decline and Revival of the Social Gospel: Social and Political Liberalism in American Protestant Churches, 1920–1940*. Ithaca: Cornell University Press, 1954.

Jackson W. Carroll, Douglas W. Johnson, and Martin E. Marty. *Religion in America: 1950 to the Present*. San Francisco: Harper and Row, 1978.

Jay P. Dolan. *American Catholic Experience: A History from Colonial Times to the Present*. Garden City, NY: Doubleday and Company, 1985.

David J. Garrow. *Bearing the Cross: Martin Luther King, Jr. and the Southern Christian Leadership Conference*. New York: William Morrow, 1986.

Andrew M. Greeley. *The American Catholic: A Social Portrait*. New York: Basic Books, 1977.

David Edwin Harrell, Jr. *All Things Are Possible: The Healing and Charismatic Revivals in Modern America*. Bloomington: Indiana University Press, 1975.

Will Herberg. *Protestant-Catholic-Jew: An Essay in American Religious Sociology*. Garden City, NY: Doubleday and Company, 1955.

George M. Marsden. *Reforming Fundamentalism: Fuller Seminary and the New Fundamentalism*. Grand Rapids: Eerdmans, 1987.

Martin E. Marty. *The New Shape of American Religion*. San Francisco: Harper and Row, 1958.

Reinhold Niebuhr. *The Irony of American History*. New York: Charles Scribner's Sons, 1962.

• • •

Stephen B. Oates. *Let the Trumpet Sound: The Life of Martin Luther King, Jr.* New York: New American Library, 1985 [1982].

Richard Quebedeaux. *The New Charismatics II.* rev. ed. San Francisco: Harper and Row, 1983.

Rosemary Radford Ruether and Rosemary Skinner Keller, eds. *Women and Religion in America.* Volume 3: *1900–1968.* San Francisco: Harper and Row, 1986.

John F. Wilson. *Public Religion in American Culture.* Philadelphia: Temple University Press, 1979.

Robert Wuthnow. *The Restructuring of American Religion: Society and Faith Since World War II.* Princeton: Princeton University Press, 1988.

Chapter Seven

Nancy Tatom Ammerman. *Bible Believers: Fundamentalists in the Modern World.* New Brunswick: Rutgers University Press, 1987.

Robert Bellah et al. *Habits of the Heart: Individualism and Commitment in American Life.* Berkeley: University of California Press, 1985.

Theodore Caplow. *All Faithful People: Change and Continuity in Middletown's Religion.* Minneapolis: University of Minnesota Press, 1983.

Harvey Cox. *The Secular City: Secularization and Urbanization in Theological Perspective.* rev. ed. New York: Macmillan, 1966 [1965].

Jay P. Dolan. *American Catholic Experience: A History from Colonial Times to the Present.* Garden City, NY: Doubleday and Company, 1985.

Ann Douglas and Steven Tipton, eds. *Religion and America: Spiritual Life in a Secular Age.* Boston: Beacon Press, 1983.

Robert S. Ellwood, Jr. *Alternative Altars.* Chicago: University of Chicago Press, 1979.

James Davison Hunter. *American Evangelicalism: Conservative Religion and the Quandary of Modernity.* New Brunswick, NJ: Rutgers University Press, 1983.

———. *Evangelicalism: The Coming Generation.* Chicago: University of Chicago Press, 1987.

George M. Marsden, ed. *Evangelicalism and Modern America.* Grand Rapids: Eerdmans, 1984.

———. *Reforming Fundamentalism: Fuller Seminary and the New Fundamentalism.* Grand Rapids: Eerdmans, 1987.

Robert S. Michaelsen and Wade Clark Roof, eds. *Liberal Protestantism: Realities and Possibilities.* New York: Pilgram Press, 1986.

Richard John Neuhaus, ed. *Unsecular America.* Grand Rapids: Eerdmans, 1986.

• • •

Richard Quebedeaux. *The New Charismatics II*. rev. ed. San Francisco: Harper and Row, 1983.

Russell E. Richey and Donald G. Jones. *American Civil Religion*. San Francisco: Harper and Row, 1974.

Rosemary Radford Ruether and Rosemary Skinner Keller, eds. *Women and Religion in America*. Volume 3: *1900–1968*. San Francisco: Harper and Row, 1986.

Theodore Roszak. *The Making of a Counter Culture: Reflections on the Technocratic Society and its Youthful Opposition*. Garden City, NY: Doubleday and Company, 1969.

Steven M. Tipton. *Getting Saved from the Sixties*. Berkeley: University of California Press, 1982.

R. Stephen Warner. *New Wine in Old Wineskins: Evangelicals and Liberals in a Small-Town Church*. Berkeley: University of California Press, 1988.

Robert Wuthnow. *The Restructuring of American Religion: Society and Faith Since World War II*. Princeton: Princeton University Press, 1988.

• • •

Acknowledgments and Credits for Illustrations and Photographs

Introduction

p. 3 David Dyar Massey.

Prologue

p. 9 Library of Congress.

Chapter 1

p. 15 Bettmann Archive. **p. 22** Bettmann Archive. **p. 25** Library of Congress. **p. 38** John Carter Brown Library, Brown University.

Chapter 2

p. 52 Samuel L. Waldo and William Jewett portrait of Charles Grandison Finney, Memorial Art Museum, Oberlin College, Gift of Lewis Tappan. **p. 55** Courtesy of New York Historical Society, New York City. **p. 57** Culver Pictures. **p. 62** Library of Congress. **p. 65** Courtesy of The New York Historical Society, New York City. **p. 70** Courtesy Department of Library Services, American Museum of Natural History. **p. 71** Rare Books and Manuscripts Division, The New York Public Library, Astor, Lenox and Tilden Foundations. **p. 81** Utah State Historical Society.

Chapter 3

p. 97 Courtesy of The New York Historical Society, New York City. **p. 103** THE FAR SIDE copyright 1986 Universal Press Syndicate. Reprinted with permission. All rights reserved. **p. 107** Peter Vanderwarker. **p. 111** Bettmann Archive. **p. 114** The Jacob A. Riis Collection. Museum of the City of New York. **p. 119** Courtesy of Gene Kritsky, College of Mount St. Joseph. **p. 125** Courtesy of the Princeton Engineering Anomalies Research Laboratory, Princeton University.

Chapter 4

p. 137 National Catholic News Service. **p. 141** Bettmann Newsphoto. **p. 155** The Salvation Army Archives and Research Center. **p. 163** Monkmeyer Press Photo.

Chapter 5

p. 186 Bettmann Newsphoto. **p. 189** Bettmann Archive. **p. 192** Bettmann Newsphoto. **p. 192** Bettmann Archive. **p. 196** Bettmann Newsphoto.

Chapter 6

p. 210 UPI/Bettmann Newsphoto. **p. 223** Museum of the City of New York. **p. 226** National Catholic News Service. **p. 228** UPI/Bettmann Newsphoto.

Chapter 7

p. 245 DOONESBURY, copyright 1987 G.B. Trudeau. Reprinted with permission of Universal Press Syndicate. All rights reserved. **p. 247** Wide World. **p. 252** Courtesy of Episcopal Times, the Episcopal Diocese of Massachusetts. **p. 260** Drawing by Ed Fisher; ©1989 The New Yorker Magazine, Inc. **p. 263** UPI/Bettmann Newsphoto. **p. 264** Paul Conklin/Photo Edit. **p. 266** ©1987, Washington Post Writers Group. Reprinted with permission. **p. 267** UPI/Bettmann Newsphoto. **p. 269** David Dyar Massey. **p. 271 (top)** UPI/Bettmann Newsphoto. **p. 271 (bottom)** ©1987, Washington Post Writers Group. Reprinted with permission. **p. 272** UPI/Bettmann Newsphoto.

Index